PRAISE FOR *STRATEGIC TALENT DEVELOPMENT*

"*Strategic Talent Development* is rich with practical and thought-provoking ideas and is perfectly pitched to the challenges facing businesses today. Caplan persuasively argues that getting the best out of people will increase profits and competitiveness and she shows how to do it in an inspiring and easy-to-follow manner. A particular strength of the book comes from Caplan's clear understanding of how to set the cultural tone and direction from the top, as well as deal with day-to-day people problems and create robust processes to support the business strategy." **Sir Michael Bear, Director, Arup Group Ltd, Lord Mayor of London 2010–2011**

"Why has it been so difficult to define usefully the meaning of 'people' in organizations when they are so obviously key to effective organizations? Despite the wonders of technological advances, it is only people who can wreck or develop an organization. This excellent book shows, through a Four-Point Framework, both thought leadership and good practice in engaging the elusive factor of 'talent': how to spot it, develop it, and keep it so that a learning organization is created. This demands new ways of thinking and behaving by leaders and managers. This book shows a stimulating way forward." **Bob Garratt, Visiting Professor at Cass Business School, London and Stellenbosch Business School, South Africa**

"This new publication by Janice Caplan provides businesses with the essential 'how' information. We all know that something different is needed now to engage our workforce and to benefit from them wanting to apply the 'discretionary extra' that is within their power to do. In these pages, Janice not only helps us understand why we need to move away from outdated command and control hierarchies but also provides a road map, showing us the critical path to success. An inspiring read for the world we live and work in today." **Heather Matheson, Managing Director, HR Insight Ltd**

"*Strategic Talent Development* succeeds in being both a g'
thought-provoking and intelligently linked essays to hel
develop their talent. It is in fact a book that aims to dev

D1343123

members of the work team, whether the team is one that is fluid and changing, a more stable one, or a big global corporation." **Emilio Giordano, Chief Financial Officer, Società Italiana per Condotte d'Acqua S.p.A**

"If the world has changed and is constantly changing, organizations need to build new capabilities not only to be agile to adapt to a turbulent world, but also to transform the ways of managing, leading and organizing people. Janice Caplan's book allows us not only to understand the ways firms are influenced by the outer context; she provides clear answers and models to create the new world organization, in which people, culture, talent and engagement have to be rethought. Strategic Talent Development is a must-read book for academics and practitioners alike. A new gem for those trying to find clear answers for the future of organizations." **Professor Andrés Hatum, PhD, author of *Next Generation Talent Management* and *The New Workforce Challenge***

Strategic Talent Development

Develop and engage all your people for business success

Janice Caplan

KoganPage

LONDON PHILADELPHIA NEW DELHI

First published in Great Britain and the United States in 2010 by Kogan Page Limited entitled *The Value of Talent*
Second edition, published in 2013 entitled *Strategic Talent Development*

2nd Floor, 45 Gee Street
London EC1V 3RS
United Kingdom
www.koganpage.com

1518 Walnut Street, Suite1100
Philadelphia PA 19102
USA

4737/23 Ansari Road
Daryaganj
New Delhi 110002
India

© Janice Caplan, 2013

ISBN: 978 0 7494 6936 8
E-ISBN: 978 0 7494 6937 5

British Library Cataloguing-in-Publication Data

A CIP record for this book is available from the British Library.

Library of Congress Cataloging-in-Publication Data

Caplan, Janice.
   Strategic talent development : develop and engage all your people for business success / Janice Caplan.
     pages cm
   Includes bibliographical references and index.
   ISBN 978-0-7494-6936-8 – ISBN 978-0-7494-6937-5 1. Personnel management. 2. Manpower planning. 3. Organizational culture. 4. Success in business. I. Title.
   HF5549.C289 2013
   658.3'124–dc23
                                 2013015898

Typeset by Amnet
Printed and bound by CPI Group (UK) Ltd, Croydon, CR0 4YY

CONTENTS

ACKNOWLEDGEMENTS

My very special thanks for their support, advice and feedback go to my husband Brian Finch; David Reay, Director, Organization Development, Sony Music Entertainment; and my editor at Kogan Page, Kasia Figiel.

This book benefits greatly from the case studies, observations, ideas and feedback that have been given to me by:

Andrew Dyckhoff, Senior Partner, Merryck & Co, especially for his input on neuroscience, and for sharing many ideas

Carolyn Ponder, Partner, The Scala Group

Mel Mayne, Financial Services and Corporate Governance specialist, The Scala Group

Mounir Guen, Chief Executive Officer, MVision Private Equity Advisors

Jane Sutherland, Founding Partner, MVision Private Equity Advisors

Steve Bates, Chief Executive Officer, BioIndustry Association

Peter Arndt, Interim Senior Executive, Iroquois Consult Ltd

Paul Herrick, EMEA, Human Resources Managing Director, Burson-Marsteller

Celia Berk, Chief Talent Officer, Young & Rubicam Group

Alison Hall, Director of Change, Guardian News & Media

Carolyn Gray, Group HR Director, Guardian Media Group

Garcia Williamson, UK Head of Talent and L and D, KPMG LLP

Toby Peyton-Jones, Director of Human Resources, Siemens Plc & North West Europe

Fiona M Anderson, Founder, The Creative Coach, formerly Editor Coaching, BBC College of Journalism, BBC

Jenny Arwas MBE, HR Director, BT Group Functions, BT

PREFACE

Strategic Talent Development addresses the new world of global competition and rapid change through an approach that develops and engages everyone in the success of the enterprise.

I first set out my ideas in *The Value of Talent*. My role as CIPD, Vice-President, Learning and Talent Development was significant for the opportunity it gave me to work on research projects with people at the top of the field. The role also brought me into contact with leading organizations and practitioners. Since then, I have worked in different countries on different continents, discussing my ideas at conferences and seminars. I have also had the good fortune to work with many fantastic businesses and outstanding people who have helped me shape my thinking and develop new ideas. My role as a governor of the University of Portsmouth, where I also chair the Human Resources Committee and sit on the Remuneration Committee, has provided yet another perspective on the increasing complexity of managing people and organizations in today's environment. All these experiences have helped me develop my philosophies further and experience them in practice. My colleagues at Scala and at Network-ACE, which is our European network, have been instrumental in helping me, and I am immensely grateful to them.

www.thescalagroup.co.uk

www.thevalueoftalent.co.uk

Introduction

The central theme of this book is that our world has changed and is changing in ways that call for a transformational response from organizations in attitudes and in ways of doing things, especially in ways of leading, managing and organizing people. My purpose is to put forward a response.

The changes are profound. They affect many aspects of the way organizations structure themselves, how people within them interact, and the detail of how they do things in their day-to-day work. Three particular areas of change must be in our minds:

- globalization;
- communications and technology;
- attitudes across society.

These factors have some common characteristics: one is the speed with which change is happening; another is that it can emerge from anywhere; a third that these are not independent factors but interact with each other. This is creating a new world business environment, where products and services that were revolutionary two years ago are rendered obsolete if they don't adapt to market changes fast enough, and where new competitors seem to spring up overnight.

The new world business environment

How do today's changes compare with previous eras and is there a material difference? Of course, the Industrial Revolution, with its steam engines, machine tools and materials technology, transformed the world in a remarkably short time from agrarian societies to those we could recognize today.

These technologies enabled each other, just as now computing, communications, biotechnology and nanotechnology all reinforce and support development in each other. And this earlier revolution was also characterized by fierce competition and demanded a management revolution in its ways of doing things. I argue that today's knowledge revolution is different in the speed and sources of change, and that these differences also demand a new management revolution.

The change that drives business today may not be characterized by physical icons, such as skyscrapers, great ships, ports and airports, industrial complexes and cityscapes. It may not be characterized by mass travel suddenly becoming easy and affordable, or communications being shrunk from weeks to minutes by telegraph wires snaking across the world. Today's change is subtler but just as real, nonetheless. It arises largely from the invention of the transistor just over 60 years ago, rapidly followed by printed circuit boards and computers and then personal computers and mobile phones, the internet and the world wide web.

Let us try to visualize this immense change. Think about that sophisticated but everyday device used by millions of people around the globe, the Apple iPhone, and how we got to it in 2007. It took over 200 years from early experiments with electricity until the transistor was developed in 1948. Then in just the next 40 years or so, all in a rush, we got serious computing, personal computers and hand-held devices. The world wide web arrived at the end of that time. In the ensuing 20 years, commerce over the web exploded from nothing to an estimated $204 billion in the United States alone in 2008. In 1998 Google reported 26 million web pages on its index; by 2000 it had one billion and by 2008 one trillion. It is hard to imagine life without the web, available to us worldwide and now on tiny hand-held devices. The computer data centres that power the web account for nearly 2 per cent of the world's electricity production. Soon web-enabled devices will be found in mundane devices such as refrigerators and cookers.

And it is not just what the smartphone can do but what we can do with a smartphone that is new. Commerce has changed: books, music and TV are distributed online, as are news and opinion. 'Distributors' are being replaced by selling direct from producer to customer. Banking, shopping and logistics are all done online, the latter enabling modern supermarkets to provide extraordinary choice and drive down costs. The web has enabled e-mailing and social networking, as well as open-source problem solving. Industries, such as national mail services, are being deconstructed as new ones grow.

The word 'globalization' is now common currency. While international trade is not new and events in India affected Europe more than 200 years ago (and vice versa), the scale and immediacy are different. Today a call centre servicing Europe or North America can be in India or the Philippines or Kenya and, at the flip of a switch, can be somewhere else. Going back to that iPhone for illustration, it turns out to be an extraordinarily international project. It was designed at Apple headquarters in California (the lead designer being an Englishman) but components from Japan, South Korea, Taiwan, the UK and Germany are assembled in China.

The speed of change has not levelled off and the business implications of the digital revolution, cheap broadband communications and the world wide web have clearly not run their course. The next technologies, built on these ones, may enable us to do things we only dream of today. If and when this electronic revolution begins to slow, perhaps the next big thing could be new biological industries. And new technologies do not just boost economic growth but have profound implications for what we do, how we do it and how we organize ourselves to do it.

Today's globalization is not just about a growing volume of global trade, its distinctive difference is that competitors, suppliers and customers, enabled by communications and technology, can be anywhere in the world. A company based in Scotland can use software hosted on computers in Canada, written for a US company by a contractor in India to sell a book written and published in France (though printed in China) from a warehouse in Ireland to a customer in Australia. The business's advisers and investors are in London but its competitors can be anywhere in the world while its owner can review and control daily progress from her holiday villa in Italy.

Government processes are different too. Laws and regulations that govern business are increasingly negotiated within supranational bodies and coordinated through international organizations, and infractions may be prosecuted through courts in a dozen jurisdictions. A good example might include Apple and Samsung suing each other for patent infringements in courts around the world. Meanwhile Samsung is a major supplier to Apple. Regulators also have an international reach; in 2012 US regulators investigated US, British and European banks for manipulating UK interest rates. The European Commission, meanwhile, has anti-monopoly processes in progress against Microsoft and Google – giant US-based software firms.

The innovation economy

It is being widely commented that developed Western economies are moving beyond the knowledge or information economy to what is sometimes called the innovation economy. According to interviews conducted by the executive search firm Spencer Stuart, more than two-thirds of directors at the leading global companies it advises cite innovation as critical for long-term success (Cohn, Katzenbach and Vlak, 2008). This has been constantly reinforced since, for example by PwC's 15th Global CEO Survey, which finds that 'supporting the capacity to innovate' is at the forefront of priorities for CEOs (PwC, 2012).

Rapid and often unpredictable change demands rapid reaction and an ability to anticipate it with new products and services: with further innovation. Today's business environment requires people who can innovate, work across organizational boundaries and in partnerships, and who are sufficiently far-sighted and fast-reacting to spot trends, create opportunities and rapidly take advantage of these. Success will come from positioning the business so that when the right option becomes clear, the right people with the right skills are able to pursue it rapidly. If you can jump on a bandwagon, you may already be too late.

New ways of working

Individuals will need to continually reappraise their skills, acquire new ones and be flexible and fleet of foot. They need to have an eye on the horizon to spot changes as they emerge; to be able to create opportunities before others do; to be innovative, creative and adaptable and eagerly willing to learn. Moreover, they need to embrace new ways of working, where they collaborate across boundaries, work in virtual teams, and where reporting lines are fluid. New media is also significant for its effect on people's attitudes: they are more used to sharing information, and more open about themselves and their work. This effect will increase, especially as younger people join the workforce.

The economic downturn

Before considering how to achieve this culture of innovation we must bring in the economic circumstances of our age. The aftermath of the 2008 global financial crisis is still being keenly felt and, while its worst effects have, so far, been felt in the United States and Europe, they are still spreading like ripples on a pond and growth is stuttering around the world. Its effects are unlikely to disappear entirely because it is also one aspect of longer-term adjustment in trading patterns. This is creating the need for some managerial balancing acts: we must balance the need to downsize with the need to grow some areas of the business; the need to shed labour while bringing in new recruits with particular talents; the need to react to current pressures and workloads with the need to innovate, look ahead, and prepare for future challenges. We must maintain existing operations while developing new ones and breaking into new markets. The need to control costs while maintaining employee morale, commitment and motivation lies at the heart of these balancing acts. Intuitively, we know that organizations that truly engage and inspire their employees achieve high productivity, and therefore high performance. There is a buzz about them. The research evidence to support this intuition is compelling, and should shape the way leaders and managers think about and support the people who work for them.

Create a new world organization

All this demands a 'new world' organization in response, where:

- People develop their skills and abilities so that the business has the right capabilities available when needed.
- Organizational culture encourages collaboration, innovation, flexibility and rapid response.
- Autocratic and hierarchical styles are replaced by leadership styles that create 'shared values, shared visions and shared understanding'.
- People are engaged around a compelling vision and strategic direction so that their efforts, motivation and commitment are directed to the success of the enterprise.

It has probably always been impossible to simply instruct people to innovate and have a realistic expectation that they will do so. Rather, it is necessary to create the conditions for such innovation and speed of response. This is exemplified by the experience of Xerox Corporation which famously generated many extraordinary ideas at its Palo Alto research facility. 'Established in 1970 in an industrial park next to Stanford, PARC researchers designed a remarkable array of computer technologies, including the Alto personal computer, the Ethernet office network, laser printing and the graphical user interface' (Markoff, 2011). These brilliant and influential developments also illustrate another lesson, because the Xerox Corporation did not exploit a single one of these inventions that have formed the basis of huge industries.

'Years later, Dr Goldman explained Xerox's failure to enter the personal computing market early on as part of a large corporation's unwillingness to take risks' (Markoff, 2011). Creating the right conditions for innovation requires action that extends beyond the laboratory.

Another leadership challenge lies in a change in how we perceive the world. Our expectation of change is creating 'new world organizations' where the need to adapt quickly to new markets and new competitors and to innovate quickly is driving them to be less hierarchical, to have flatter hierarchies and to employ management structures where people's jobs move from team to team and they work across functional and national boundaries and in partnerships with external organizations. This increase in real collaboration represents a permanent shift in attitudes from the adversarial approach of simply buying-in at the lowest possible price.

The changing internal business model

A consequence of these changes is that traditional 'command and control' management systems, where information is passed up through levels of a hierarchy and instructions pass the other way, simply don't work effectively. They are much too slow and they stifle innovation. Moreover, lean, de-layered and interconnected organization structures have made management through close personal supervision and controlling the detail of what and how people do things mostly impossible.

Today 'shared values, shared visions and shared understanding' set the culture and the tone. When people know where the organization is going, how it is going to get there, when values are clear, this sets the boundaries and people know how to act, take decisions and take responsibility, and they know what is expected of them.

This is also a new world of ideas that create competitive advantage or even whole new business streams; and businesses must be sufficiently agile, future-focused and innovative to keep pace with overnight change in technology or ways of doing business if they are to keep ahead of competition. These ideas may arise anywhere within the organization, at any level. Managers need to recognize them, be open to them, and encourage their colleagues to come up with them. They must create the culture that will encourage their people to spot opportunity, and they must ensure they and their people develop the capabilities that will enable them to take advantage of this opportunity.

The smartphone presents a good example of flexibility. It is easily forgotten that the first such integrated touchscreen device that we would recognize as a smartphone today was unveiled by Apple founder Steve Jobs only some six years before this sentence was being written. He did not invent the concept but he reinvented it and made it better. The new product transformed Apple to be the largest company in the world by market capitalization by 2012. Yet, within months of that first announcement competitors were producing their versions and, before 2012, South Korea's Samsung had overtaken Apple's global market share in smartphones. In contrast, the market share of Finland's Nokia, previously the world's dominant maker of mobile phones, had plummeted and its share price had fallen by 90 per cent (*The Economist*, 2012). The ramifications of its being slow to react were serious on a national scale since in 2011 its revenues totalled 20 per cent of the country's GDP. The point here is not Apple: my point is the contrast between Samsung and Nokia.

Economic pressures on leadership

Years of lower growth and the prospect of an uncertain economic climate ahead have affected attitudes, expectations and perceptions, creating some special leadership challenges. For example, slimmed-down structures have created wider spans of control, which demand new skill-sets and give rise to bigger workloads. These same people who perceive themselves as stretched to the limit are then being asked to find energy to learn new skills, develop new ideas and create growth. Managers are being asked, at one and the same time, to cut costs but invest in the development of their people. Many suddenly find that their skills are no longer as highly valued, or perhaps their sphere of influence, or even their pay, has been reduced, affecting their self-regard and their morale; or maybe they have had their hopes and aspirations dashed as plans and investments have been put on hold. Moreover, many people are frightened to take a risk on untried and untested ideas, even though, when everything is changing, pursuit of the new and different is the key to survival. With growth in home markets slow, businesses need to develop new income streams and exploit new markets but to do this requires new capabilities and an entrepreneurial outlook. Where do these come from? How do we develop them? Leading people has never been easy, but in a difficult climate it also becomes more urgent.

Strategic talent development

I have outlined what needs to be done and the leadership challenges that face us in getting there. But there are ways of overcoming these challenges and that is what this book addresses. My proposition is that if we value everyone, not just the few high performers, meet their aspirations and engage them with business success, this translates into improved, long-term business performance.

This approach is as much about behaviours and values as about systems and processes. It is strategic because it means looking ahead and aligning individual development with future organizational needs and with the strategy of the organization. It is inclusive because it recognizes that decisions and actions that will be pivotal to success may occur anywhere in the organization.

Inclusive talent development is more than aiming to harness people's talents and help them be the best they can be, though that is part of it. It is more than having people available to fill key roles, though that too is part of it. It is a way of thinking and doing things that gets to the heart of relationships within the organization. It includes people in the vision and direction of the business so that they input their ideas and actively seek to create opportunities and make them happen. It includes people in decisions that are made about them or that affect them, so that leadership and management are multi-way processes and people have more control over their destinies. It is also about how staff, managers and HR work together to create an innovative, creative, skilled and adaptable workforce that is willing to learn.

About this book

I set out here a practical approach for achieving this new world organization, which I call 'strategic talent development'.

This book moves through three distinct phases. The first is conceptual. Chapter 1 makes the case for strategic talent development through its relationship with employee engagement. We consider the evidence for how this impacts on profitability and its implications on how to lead and manage people. We consider values and how these bind people and create a common identity. This will give us a deep understanding of organizational culture and help generate insights on how to create leadership styles and processes that suit today's world and translate into hard business results.

FIGURE 0.1 The four-point framework shows the steps to develop your talent and engagement strategy

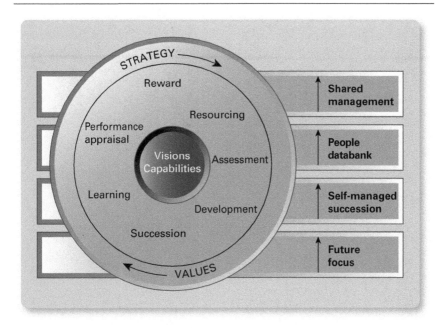

The second phase of the book – Chapters 4 through to 8 – describes the systems and processes needed to assess, develop, deploy and retain people. I present these systems and processes in relation to a four-point talent framework (see Figure 0.1), which guides you through how to put these in place so that they form a coherent and consistent strategy that pulls people in the same direction. I present this four-point framework in Chapter 3, giving an overview of it, and showing how it is business driven and addresses the main leadership challenges of today. I then present the processes that will achieve the business aims of each of the points on the framework.

Finally, phase three – Chapters 9 and 10 – covers the practical actions leaders must take to lead effectively in today's new world, but also to deal with the people problems that economic downturn has brought for many. We consider what leaders must do, and how they might do it, to achieve a highly engaged workforce and a profitable and sustainable future for the business.

The new world organization

In this chapter, I discuss employee engagement as one of the foundation stones of strategic talent development. First, I look at the link between talent management and employee engagement and draw on the research evidence that reveals that high levels of engagement among the workforce lead to improved business performance. I set out the data showing how talent development shares many factors with employee engagement. This provides hard evidence, alongside the conceptual approach, to support the business case for strategic talent development. It will also help to explain the roles of individuals, business leaders, managers and HR in delivering talent development.

Questions of leadership are inextricably linked with both strategic management development and employee engagement and, in this context, there is also evidence of a new leadership model emerging, which devolves leadership in the organization using the guiding principle of 'shared values, shared visions and shared understanding'. I will discuss how this reflects attitudes in modern society, and look at why behaviours and values are so important in the 'new world' organization, and how they underpin this leadership model.

What is employee engagement?

We know that most people are characterized by a desire to do a good job, and intuitively it seems clear that building on this will improve their individual performance, which in turn will improve organizational performance. It is not so much that the concept needs proving; it is more about explaining what is required to achieve it and about proving the correlation with business performance.

This seems a simple idea but it is made up of several elements, which we can group under three headings: people's ability, their motivation and the opportunity (Purcell *et al*, 2003):

Ability refers to personal qualities, skills, and knowledge.

Motivation is itself made up of internal and external elements. Individuals are driven by their own inner motivation but this also needs to be directed.

Opportunity enables ability and motivation to be effective.

Opportunity is critical to this process because success demands effective external management, since individuals will be unable to exercise their abilities and motivation if their work team is badly coordinated or they are poorly managed. Circumstances must also permit people to exercise their abilities and motivation. If there is a breakdown of the opportunity factor – let us say there is a shortage of orders or materials, or a machine breaks down – then even the best machine operators will be prevented from achieving high productivity. However, if the operators have high ability and are well motivated, they are more likely to help the business recover quickly and make up for lost time. It is also reasonable to apply the same model to the overall business simply by aggregating these three factors at the organizational level.

All three factors in this AMO model need to come into play to achieve the benefit of what is commonly referred to as employee engagement. Figure 1.1 illustrates this idea and, for simplicity, it rolls management effectiveness into 'opportunity'.

It is particularly striking how interconnected all this is. Opportunity and effective line management reinforce motivation and ability, while even the desired outcome – 'effectiveness' – will reinforce motivation: success breeds high morale. Which elements of this diagram represent employee engagement? Well, it is hard to tease them apart. Strategic talent development builds on the idea that all these processes within the management of organizations are interconnected and need to be treated as an integrated whole. One bit without the other does not work.

With this model in mind, let's consider how employee engagement is generally defined, and then the evidence of its importance to business performance. Employee engagement has been described as 'a positive attitude held by the employee towards the organization and its values. An engaged employee is aware of business context and works with colleagues to improve performance within the job for the benefit of the organization'

FIGURE 1.1 Employee engagement

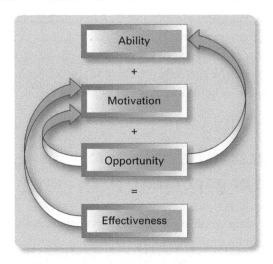

(Robinson, Perryman and Hayday, 2004). It gives rise to the 'degree of discretionary effort employees are willing to apply in their work in the organization' and it recognizes that 'every employee ultimately chooses whether to contribute the minimum levels of performance required (or to sabotage), or to go beyond the minimum required by the post and to offer outstanding effort in their role' (Alimo-Metcalfe and Alban-Metcalfe, 2009).

The engagement index slots people into one of three categories:

- **Engaged** employees work with passion and feel a profound connection to their company. They drive innovation and move the organization forward.

- **Not-engaged** employees are essentially 'checked out'. They are sleepwalking through their workday. They are putting in time, but not enough energy or passion into their work.

- **Actively disengaged** employees aren't just unhappy at work; they're busy acting out their unhappiness. Every day, these workers undermine what their engaged co-workers accomplish.

Why is employee engagement important?

Numerous studies make a persuasive case for how engagement leads to success. No single one has proved this beyond doubt, as proving causality would require comparators where all factors are the same, which is impossible to achieve. However, research data published by leading international recruitment, reward and market research companies such as Towers Watson, Kenexa, Hay, Aon Hewitt and Gallup together make a compelling case that shows companies with high employee engagement levels also experienced a higher operating margin (up to 19 per cent higher), net profit margin, revenue growth and earnings per share (up to 28 per cent higher) than companies with low employee engagement (Towers Perrin, 2005).

The characteristics of employee engagement

The case for creating employee engagement is persuasive but what do you have to do to achieve it? The study 'Unlocking the Black Box' (Purcell *et al*, 2003) adds to our understanding of the AMO model. It concludes that the difference between high- and low-performing organizations is influenced by a combination of managers' proactive and continuous support for the development of their people, and well-designed and effective HR policies for these managers to apply. The policies and practices that make a difference are recruitment and selection; training and development; career opportunity; communications; involvement in decision making; teamworking; appraisal; pay; job security; job challenge/job autonomy; work–life balance. The Black Box study also finds that engaged employees are inspired by a 'big idea'. They describe this as an overall sense of purpose that binds people through a central idea about what is important.

The Gallup Q12 survey also measures employee engagement. The instrument was the result of hundreds of focus groups and interviews which found that there are 12 key expectations that, when satisfied, form the foundation of strong feelings of engagement. So far, 87,000 work units and 1.5 million employees have participated in the Q12 instrument. Comparisons reveal that work units with high Q12 scores exhibit lower employee turnover, higher sales growth, better productivity, better customer loyalty and other manifestations of superior performance.

These studies match my own experience. A few years ago I carried out an assignment with the foreign exchange department of a US bank. The head of the department was convinced that giving more support and attention to his people, and improving teamwork, would impact positively on profits. We set about introducing or revising existing people processes and, importantly, provided coaching for the desk heads and for the head of department himself on how to use these processes, as well as how to apply a range of people-management skills. We tracked profitability over the course of 18 months and saw it rise by 29 per cent during this time.

I have derived the following indicators of an engaged workforce from the studies discussed above and have proven them as practical tools with clients. Engaged employees:

- feel respected and treated fairly in areas such as pay, benefits, job security and opportunity;
- have plenty of opportunity for development, and feel supported;
- know that they are listened to and that their opinions count;
- understand how they contribute to organizational goals and success;
- feel proud of their jobs and their accomplishments;
- know what the future might hold for them;
- enjoy good, productive relationships with their co-workers.

Managers should regularly ask themselves what they are doing to meet these indicators. It cannot be emphasized enough that their delivery demands regular high-quality conversations between individuals and their managers about performance and careers, where individuals are able to contribute their input to decisions, and managers give specific and considered feedback.

Is employee engagement something new or simply a repackaging of previous ideas?

New technology has opened up more sophisticated opportunities to collect and process data. This provides us with the possibility to test assumptions and provide hard data to measure success and identify business improvements. It enables us to go beyond our previous aim of retaining people longer to making people more productive while they are with us, as well as staying longer. So in a sense, employee engagement is a technological measurement process, which provides evidence of what we have to do to drive business success. As the saying goes, 'If you can measure it, then you can manage it.' Yet also, employee engagement has evolved from previous management theories, which emphasize the importance of employee commitment. The distinction is that earlier management theory tended to be one-way – what to do to gain commitment – whereas employee engagement is a two-way interaction between employer and employee.

Collecting data to measure employee engagement is a highly effective management tool

However, there is increasing anecdotal evidence to show that many organizations are just going through the motions when they survey their people, and are being too selective about the results they are taking notice of, underplaying those that contain warning signs that something is amiss. A striking example occurred in a firm that is involved in processes that have significant health and safety implications. They were delighted with their good results in the 'communications' group. However, close examination showed a worrying response against one indicator: 'I am afraid to speak up.' Especially given the nature of the business, this was a major cause for concern and further investigation, which was initially going to be ignored.

There is also evidence that organizations are placing too much emphasis on benchmarking their results with other businesses. It is not the comparison that is important – best of a bad bunch is an expression that comes to mind here – but the need to keep raising performance in your own organization. Such examples are wasting the potential this tool offers.

Get the most out of employee surveys by:

- supplementing questionnaires with one-to-one meetings and focus groups to enable you to get underneath the issues and gain insights and solutions from people on the issues to address and how to do so;
- communicating the results fully and openly: run discussion groups around key issues such as: 'What is causing people to be afraid to speak up?'
- acting on the results and letting people know that you are taking these actions because of what they told you through the survey;
- not ignoring the issues that you find difficult. If you cannot act on something, say so and explain why. Keep it on the agenda.

Strategic talent development: the link between talent management and employee engagement

The attraction of the effects of engagement is obvious; it potentially enables the organization to increase employee effort and productivity and improve teamworking, as well as reduce turnover and absenteeism, without increasing salary costs. It maximizes the value of the organization's investment in people.

Strategic talent development, which includes everyone in the workforce, is intrinsically linked to employee engagement. This is clear because they share many of the same indicators.

Strategic talent development is a process that:

1 delivers capabilities that the organization needs;

2 identifies future capabilities;

3 delivers team capabilities;

4 creates innovation;

5 inspires;

6 seeks out people's ideas;

7 actively communicates.

Let us consider these points in more detail and identify their indicators of success that are also common to employee engagement.

1. Delivers capabilities that the organization needs, when and where it needs them

On the one hand this requires a review of the needs of the organization and its goals in order to identify those needs, but that is not enough – it also demands dialogue with employees to answer their questions about:

- What is expected of me?
- How am I doing?
- How will I be rewarded?
- What does the future hold?
- How will I get there?
- How are we doing as a team?

This process is not just about understanding and matching the individual's capabilities, potential and aspiration to organizational needs but also about broader issues of retaining, motivating and developing staff in order to deliver those capabilities.

These issues relate to employee engagement indicators:

- 'Feeling proud of your job and accomplishments.'
- 'Feeling respected and treated fairly in areas such as pay, benefits, job security and opportunity.'
- 'Having plenty of opportunity for development, and feeling supported.'

2. Identifies future capabilities that the organization will need and develops people to meet them

This requires taking a longer-term view of development than is typical, which tends to be one year ahead, to fit the performance appraisal cycle. It encourages everyone to think about what is evolving, what is changing and what is driving the business so as to identify capability gaps. It encourages managers to think about changing skill-sets and employee expectations. This helps the individual understand what the future might hold for them and identify a career path. It helps the organization prepare people to meet the challenges of its longer-term business strategy.

The process of developing individuals also makes them feel better about themselves and about the organization. They appreciate that they are valued and see their worth to the organization being enhanced, which will improve their sense of engagement. Even if personal development improves an individual's long-term prospects outside the organization, there is still this improved sense of engagement in the short term, which benefits the organization.

These issues relate to employee engagement indicators:

- 'Knowing what the future might hold for them and how they might be supported to get there.'
- 'Having plenty of opportunity for development, and feeling supported.'

3. Delivers not just individual capabilities but those that are part of what the team does as a unit

Strategic talent development provides a process that encourages conversations about performance and careers. It encourages sharing of information and ideas, and emphasizes support and collaboration.

In this way, it is a main contributor to employee engagement, mapping directly to:

- 'Enjoying good, productive relationships with co-workers.'

4. Creates innovation, resilience and flexibility at all levels of the organization

The outcomes from the previous attributes should be directed towards achieving innovation, resilience and flexibility. This is achieved through dialogue around and across the organization about emerging trends on the horizon, about the implications of these, and how to take advantage of them. The business's leaders will stimulate this dialogue by discussing business strategy and performance, and being open to new ideas. This maps directly to factors that lead to high employee engagement:

- 'Knowing your opinions count and are listened to.'
- 'Knowing how you contribute to organizational goals and success.'

5. Inspires people through vision, and clear sense of direction

This again must start at the top. It relates to the Black Box finding of mobilizing people around the 'big idea'.

6. Actively seeks out people's ideas and opinions, listens to these and acts upon them

Employees feel they can voice their ideas and be listened to, with joint sharing of problems and challenges and a commitment to arrive at joint solutions. This connects to point 7.

7. Actively and continuously provides employees with information about the business, its strategies, progress and business results, consulting with employees wherever possible

This involves sharing information at a macro and micro level in the business so that people feel informed, trusted with information, are given bad as well as good news, are consulted about decisions, and given explanations about how and why they were taken. A common failing in organizations is a reluctance to communicate bad news, or failing to communicate when there is no news, leaving people to construct their own version of events – which may be wrong or unsettling. I recall one City firm negotiating a merger, which was common knowledge throughout the organization and the market. Negotiations were protracted and went on far longer than anticipated. The CEO failed to heed advice and to let people know that he had no news, believing it would reflect badly on his negotiating skills. So, there was a long period of no news, during which many of the top performers, especially those who had recently joined the firm through a previous takeover, were headhunted out. Contrast this with the CEO of a manufacturing business who met the economic crisis with an intensive communications programme, giving the detail of the firm's commercial circumstances, making sure the revenue model was completely transparent and understood. He explained the reasoning behind all decisions, and kept people updated on progress, even when there was no news, or bad news. Strikingly, he spoke from the heart, sharing his concerns and anxieties, as well as his hopes. He lost no one, and moreover people remained motivated and engaged and worked hard to turn the business around.

How, what and when you communicate is gaining in importance in the new world organization, where 'command and control', which is based on low trust, is breaking down. Communicating frankly, honestly and extensively builds trust and gains commitment and loyalty. It is a key indicator not just to measure employee engagement, but to embed styles based on 'shared values, shared visions and shared understanding' that are essential to the modern organization.

These issues relate to employee engagement indicators:

- 'Knowing that they are listened to and that their opinions count.'
- 'Understanding how they contribute to organizational goals and success.'
- 'Feeling proud of their jobs and their accomplishments.'
- 'Knowing what the future might hold for them.'

This is not an exhaustive list of engagement indicators. Well-being (how people feel about stress, pressure and work/life balance), Fair deal (how happy they are with their pay and benefits), Giving something back (how much the company puts into the local community and society at large), and My company (pride in the company) are other engagement indicators that are common to key surveys (Best Companies, 2012). These are, however, outside the scope of this book where my concern is with those indicators that get to the heart of collective and individual relationships in the organization with the aim of enabling everyone and the business itself to grow and flourish.

CASE STUDY

KPMG has worked hard to develop a high level of engagement within the organization, and the firm is a regular award winner for its success here. Staff expect managers to tell them how it really is – in good times and bad, and this was the foundation of its Flexible Futures programme, which in 2009 helped KPMG weather the uncertainty of the recession. Following extensive communication on the effects of the recession on the business, staff were consulted on the design and implementation of this programme of voluntarily working reduced hours for a short term. Having set itself a target of 65 per cent sign-up, KPMG were delighted that 85 per cent of staff were willing to sign up for reducing their hours by one day a week, or taking 4–12 weeks off on 30 per cent pay, if business need required it. Sarah Bond, Head of Engagement, said at the time: 'We were open with colleagues about the need to introduce additional flexibility in our staffing arrangements to help prepare for uncertain times. It is a clear indicator that staff at KPMG feel a shared ownership for the organization's fortunes, and I am very sure that we would not have achieved such a positive response without the high level of engagement between staff and management.'

This case study shows how high employee engagement levels build trust and cooperation.

How do we bring talent and engagement policies to life?

For a long time, there has been commonality among the surveys about which factors lead to higher engagement levels, and much of it points to the role of the manager. For example, the Black Box study, referred to earlier, found that front-line managers exercise a strong influence over the level of discretionary effort that an individual directs to their job. Some managers encourage people to be responsible for their own jobs whereas others stifle initiative through controlling or autocratic behaviour. A CMI study found that almost half of workers surveyed (47 per cent) had left a job because of bad management (CMI, 2009). Perhaps even more significantly, the same survey (49 per cent) said they would be prepared to take a pay cut, in order to work with a better manager.

Certainly, a main lever to bring talent and engagement policies to life is the quality of the relationships people have with their top leadership, their manager and with each other. However, there is evidence that 'career development', which used to be the fifth-ranked reason why people left organizations, has now risen to top place, overtaking 'poor relationship with manager' (CRF Institute, 2012). I believe this is to do with our changing perceptions of job security.

Changing perceptions of job security

The theories of motivation first developed in the 1960s by Frederick Herzberg (Herzberg, 1987) and Abraham Maslow continue to be widely used. They both suggest that what Herzberg refers to as 'hygiene' factors, and Maslow as physiological and safety needs, have to be satisfied before people are able to reach a level of 'self-actualization' where they will seek to grow and develop and give of their discretionary effort. Job security comes within these lower-order needs: you need to know you will be able to pay your bills before you are likely to focus concern on feeling fulfilled at work.

A major change of the past 60 years has been that the notion of a job for life has disappeared. The latest statistics in the United States show that 'the median number of years that wage and salary workers had been with their current employer was 4.4 in January 2010' (US Bureau of Labor Statistics, 2012) – somewhat different from the 40 years of service (broken only for army service) that my late father completed with British Home Stores. The boom and bust years, and now the financial crisis, as a result of which unemployment figures have increased globally, have undoubtedly confirmed in people's minds that job security is tenuous. If we assume from the work of Maslow and Herzberg that this basic need remains in all of us, we can deduce that to satisfy our basic need for job security, we must be confident that our skills are up to date so that we remain employable. This gets to the heart of strategic talent development.

What we need to do to raise levels of employee engagement

Both the traditional and emerging consensus points clearly to what organizations need to do to create engaged employees. This can be summed up as:

- Help and support employees to take more responsibility for how they do their jobs.
- Provide developmental opportunities.
- Enable people to see how they contribute to organizational goals.
- Seek out people's views, listen, learn, and keep communicating.

These factors are key attributes of strategic talent development.

It would be disingenuous to ascribe the achievement of employee engagement solely to the behaviour or competence of individual managers, because everyone is affected by the system in which they operate and managers are, of course, affected by the way they themselves are managed. Towers Perrin's research found that while many people are keen to contribute more at work, the culture of their organizations, as well as the behaviour of their managers, discourages them from doing so. Similar conclusions emerge from the Black Box research: 'Organizations that have a strong, shared culture with guiding principles for behaviour embedded into practice over time' were revealed by the research to have been more successful. These findings strongly support one of my central themes that I develop in the next chapter: the importance of aligning visions, values, strategy and behaviour. It also points to the importance of having robust systems.

To recapitulate the key issues:

- Business performance improves when people are engaged with the organization.
- The key drivers of employee engagement are those that involve and empower people, and provide outstanding opportunity for support and development.
- The recurring theme that enables improved engagement is open, honest and supportive dialogue, which includes listening as well as communicating frequently; and that means the bad news as well as the good.

If it is what managers do, combined with strategies, systems and processes, that delivers talent and engagement – in other words, a high-performing organization – it is organizational culture that is the glue to make them stick. This brings us to the leadership role that is instrumental in shaping culture. Employee engagement and leadership are inextricably intertwined.

Leadership models that enhance employee engagement

It is not surprising that a consideration of leadership has led writers to think about failure and to ponder 'destructive' or 'toxic' leadership. Toxic leadership (Whicker, 1996; Lipman-Blumen, 2004) refers to individuals who exhibit a range of behaviours characterized by selfishness that demoralizes those they manage, leads to disengagement and sacrifices employees or whole organizations for ego and self-aggrandizement. Corporate scandals such as Enron and the near collapse of RBS show weaknesses in the 'heroic' or 'great man' leadership models. Malcolm Gladwell of *The New Yorker* illustrates this point with his description of Enron as a 'place where stars did whatever they wanted' (Gladwell, 2002). In his account, business decisions were taken not on the basis of winning customers, or enhancing profitability, but because one of the stars wanted it. Research carried out by Tosi *et al*, which finds no link between organizational success and the perceived charisma of the CEO, supports this critical view (Tosi, Misangyi and Fanelli, 2004). In place of the 'heroic' models, alternatives that include 'being open and considerate of others' and demonstrating 'humility' are being cited as desirable. We also see leadership models that emphasize the distribution of leadership throughout the organization, as well as the importance of 'shared values, shared visions and understanding'.

This new approach to leadership highlights the convergence of two important trends in the 'new world' discussed in the last chapter. First, it seems that people in the new world are less willing to accept the 'command and control' model of management from on high by the 'heroic leader'. It seems to be becoming less common and not to be working very well. The second fact is that the pace and complexity of change in our societies and business environment must stimulate innovation and flexibility at all levels of the organization. These factors make a more devolved leadership style desirable so that companies can cope effectively in these circumstances.

The writer who has done much to promote this view of leadership is Jim Collins. He investigated over 1,400 organizations quoted on the US Stock Exchange, controlling for economic factors and size among other variables. He focused on those who moved their organizations from solidly 'good' performance to 'great' performance and who maintained this position for at least 15 years. He identified two common characteristics: one, the steadfast belief of the chief executive that their company would be the best in the field; and the second, their 'deep personal humility'. The first of these critical factors reflects a strategic approach to business. The latter characteristic reflects a way of managing: it emphasizes the role of the team and identifies the leadership job as enabling that team to perform effectively (Collins, 2001).

What do we mean by leadership?

At the top level of the organization it deals with overall strategy and vision and values, as discussed before. It is a subset of the management process, which is a concept little changed since FW Taylor, the earliest management commentator, developed his theories of scientific management. Taylor described management as being about planning, organizing people and resources, and about control. His emphasis was on efficiency and administration and, in an era when this was achieved through a 'command and control' approach, this was how the manager managed. However, his work did not focus on the 'how' of getting people to do things efficiently, much less on the 'how' of creating an innovative organization. As society has changed, this 'how' has become a much more important consideration, which brings us to leadership.

Our ideas of business leadership grew from the work of behavioural scientists in the 1960s. They introduced the idea that influencing people by virtue of personal attributes and behaviours was important to management success. At first this notion worked within 'command and control' structures, with line managers influencing to gain commitment and enthusiasm. Real, full-blown leadership – 'driving change', 'setting direction', 'interacting with stakeholders' – was the preserve of people at the top. Since the 1960s, rapid change and competitiveness in the business environment, the emergence of the knowledge worker and of the information age and, now, of the innovation age have fomented change and put behaviours centre-stage. These are behaviours related to learning, adaptability, flexibility and teamworking. They are also the different leadership behaviours required at different levels of the organization and for different roles. For example, a professional expert, though not a manager, may be required to lead and direct a significant piece of change, while interacting with and managing others across organizational boundaries – which illustrates that anyone, anywhere, may be required to move in and out of leadership roles at different times.

The distributed leadership model also recognizes that innovation and creativity can come from anywhere in the organization. It allows for individuals anywhere within it to have knowledge and understanding that is a valuable input into decision making. MacBeath argues that 'distributed leadership is premised on trust, implies a mutual acceptance of one another's leadership potential, requires formal leaders to "let go" some of their control and authority, and favours consultation and consensus over command and control'. It is not a zero-sum game, where developing others diminishes the power of those at the top, but 'one where each can mutually reinforce the other' (MacBeath, 2005).

What is the most effective way of leading people?

The importance of 'behaviours' as the means to bring about a culture change was addressed initially through the concept of 'the learning organization'. This is a theory of organizations as 'learning systems' in which success depends on two key skills – learning continuously and giving direction. I believe this idea succeeded, but only to a limited degree; it helped change attitudes and get individuals to recognize the importance of learning. It helped them see learning as something to take control of, as opposed to it being something that is 'done' to them through being sent on a training course. However, this has had little impact on the way people and relationships are managed in the organization. This role has been taken by coaching, which has increasingly gained hold as being the most effective way of managing people and building working relationships. Estimates in the UK, for example, suggest that coaching takes place in around 90 per cent of organizations, with line managers being the main deliverers, and the need to train them in coaching skills being a priority (CIPD, 2009).

Other studies show that a coaching style of management delivers benefits that are manifested in better team relationships, enhanced self-confidence and more general improvements to engagement, flexibility and commitment. A coaching style of management is not about 'being the boss', giving directions, telling people how they should have done it or jumping in with the answer. Rather, a manager's role today is often to enable, encourage and facilitate so that staff have a sense of control over their own work and their own time, so they identify their own options and solutions to problems, so they are involved in decisions and so they learn and develop. A manager may also work with an employee on a more formal coaching basis, perhaps to help that person develop their knowledge or acquire a new skill or responsibility.

It is unsurprising that developing managers' ability to coach is gaining such importance, as 'command and control' styles have a practical drawback: with leaner organizations, managers do not have time to micromanage and, with wider spans of control the new norm, they may have insufficient detailed understanding of the technical aspects of jobs they are managing. Moreover, coaching styles are transferable to different situations and, increasingly, managers must achieve results through people over whom they have no direct authority. In these situations they must influence by using coaching skills rather than command.

The distributed leadership model, whose characteristics are 'shared values, shared visions and shared understanding', is the next step. Using coaching styles as the main delivery mechanism, this leadership model enables decisions and actions important to success to occur anywhere in the organization. It recognizes that innovation requires teamwork and collaboration and that people at all levels must be able to spot trends and adapt to them.

It also takes account of structural pressures that are blurring organizational boundaries and reporting lines.

The way we do things around here

For this strategic talent development approach and distributed leadership to flourish, they must be supported by the organizational culture.

We all know what we mean by culture but most of us have difficulty defining it precisely. It is broadly the shared values and the collection of different behaviours that, taken together, comprise 'the way we do things around here'. These can include rituals and customs such as going for a drink with colleagues on a Friday night, as well as interacting through formal management meetings. It can include the way one is expected to behave on these occasions. It can be built on shared memories and experiences but that does not preclude new colleagues being inducted into the behaviours without having shared those experiences.

Organizational culture can be complex and can vary across the organization. As Schein, an acknowledged expert in corporate culture, points out, 'Wherever a group has enough common experience, a culture begins to form' (Schein, 1999). Culture can reside at all levels in any system: a country has its own culture, as does a whole industry. There may be an organizational culture but, undoubtedly, there will also be a distinct culture for each department, group or team. Culture can also change over time. As it affects the way people do things and make decisions, sometimes changes need to be helped along to ensure the organization has the right culture in the right place. According to Schein, 'There is now abundant evidence that corporate culture makes a difference to corporate performance.' This is a compelling argument for analysing culture and, where appropriate, seeking to manage its development in a particular direction.

Researchers agree that culture is more than 'shared values', yet values are often considered integral to culture. Hofstede used the metaphor of an onion to describe the manifestation of culture at different levels. On the outside layer lie symbols (ie words, gestures and objects), heroes (ie iconic representation of the admired in the culture), rituals (ie collective activities and teachings), and finally values as the core of the culture (Hofstede, 2003). Certainly, values have come to be a shorthand way of describing the culture and I use the term in this way throughout this book. It is such a significant issue that the next chapter will discuss values, what we mean by them and how they affect behaviour.

Key points

- There is strong evidence that employee engagement leads to better individual and organizational performance.

- Employee surveys are valuable tools for engaging people's perceptions and ideas. Use them to truly identify improvements and to understand perceptions. Don't be selective in what you listen to. Benchmarking is over-emphasized. Strive for your own high standards.

- 'Command and control' styles of management run counter to employee expectations and are becoming impractical. A powerful alternative is a coaching style of management where people are supported, challenged and developed rather than told what to do.

- The new leadership model acts through promoting 'shared values, shared visions and shared understanding'.

- Strategic talent development:
  - embodies this leadership approach;
  - guides you to look ahead and align individual development with future organizational needs and business strategy;
  - encourages you to recognize that innovation that will be pivotal to success may occur anywhere in the organization;
  - promotes employee engagement.

Organizational values

Organizational values are the standards that guide the behaviour of individuals within the organization. They give us the opportunity to build an inclusive culture, where people share a common standpoint. This contrasts with 'them and us' ways, where perspectives and interests are markedly different.

More generally, values are the rules that help us make decisions in life (Rokeach, 1968a, 1968b). If there are organizational values to which individuals subscribe or, at least, agree to conform with, they will guide behaviours that the organization desires. Without them, individuals will pursue behaviours in line with their personal value systems, which may lead to behaviours that the organization does not wish to encourage.

Values reflect both current reality and aspiration for a company and make a distinctive statement not just about how the company works but about what it 'thinks' really matters. This distinctive statement reflects the personality of the organization. It is a unique way of pulling the organization together and it also creates differentiation, a critical factor in competitive markets.

In this chapter, I look at values conceptually and practically, giving examples of how some organizations have created individual identities that are clear to all their stakeholders. I consider the relationship between values and ethics. Ethics has risen in people's consciousness, partly because some spectacular failings in banking systems, and in some companies, have made people aware that unethical behaviours, on the part of some, cause hardship for many. It is also commonly thought that the younger generations who are entering the workforce now give a high priority to responsible behaviour and ethics. A strong ethical base will therefore be a lever for attracting and retaining younger people who are in relatively short supply. I am also giving so much space to values because it is the principal driver of the 'shared values, shared visions and shared understanding' process.

Shared values give the enterprise a clear identity. This helps to attract applicants, as people can identify that this is an organization they want to join, and where they will feel comfortable. It helps development, too, through clarifying for people what is expected of them and helps to set performance standards. It also helps in the assessment of performance.

Creating shared values presents the organization with the philosophical problem that values are something an individual holds but might not be shared by a group of people. They are crucial qualities that represent culture and which are shaped by the many influences on us, especially early in our lives, and of course one of the principal influences is national culture.

So, since an organization does not have its own mind, there are four ways in which it can have shared values:

1 Select the organization's values from those that are held by all its members.

2 Only employ people who subscribe to the organization's values.

3 Persuade all members to subscribe to the organization's values.

4 Get all members of the organization to behave as if they subscribe to the organization's values.

Another problem of definition is that we often encounter 'micro-cultures' in different parts of the organization, where different norms and values prevail, depending upon a range of factors including the type of work undertaken and the geographic and physical location. What matters is to have the right culture in the right place: one that suits the work and the way it is done (Harrison and Stokes, 1992; Handy, 1995). The writers who have made this point describe micro-cultures across the organization, but they also describe an overarching organizational culture. This notion of the layering of cultures with one prevailing and overarching culture is important to a pragmatic consideration of how to define values and make them mean something across the organization. The starting point for ensuring that the overarching culture promotes a healthy business is the culture at the top: the board. This is important to the strategic talent development approach, which should be implemented so that it is relevant to and consonant with the values of the organization.

These issues will be addressed during the course of this chapter.

The mathematics of values

What if different values appear to conflict? An example might be a simultaneous belief in 'integrity' but also in 'success'. How do you resolve a situation where a small compromise of integrity will lead to a big gain for success? The clue is in the name: 'value'. These are beliefs and principles to each of which we ascribe a worth, which allows us to create a hierarchy. So it is important to avoid formulations that appear to give the same value to a long list of principles and to try to be more specific, such as 'we will never achieve success at the cost of our integrity'. This tells us clearly that success and integrity are both values but that integrity is more important.

This understanding should also help in the selection of appropriate and meaningful values and in how we express them. Extending the example, we may want a value to be 'customer focused'. Once we consider the relative weighting of values and ask whether that means we would choose the customer's benefit over our own, we realize that 'customer focused' is a subset of 'success'. It is a means to achieving the latter, not an end in itself. That means it should be stated in terms such as 'we achieve success through being customer focused', which makes clear the hierarchy of beliefs. This sort of value is not less important because it is a subset of another value. Companies that say they 'strive for excellence in all they do' or 'strive to innovate' are giving a clear message to their staff, investors and customers about how they achieve success and it does help to guide behaviours.

Values are also frequently conditional, which is particularly relevant at work. For example, the individual usually believes in being loyal to the team or to the organization, but only on condition that this is reciprocated. So being given a poor pay review or being passed over for promotion may be interpreted as breaking the obligation. This is a problem for companies because it is the individual who is in charge of interpreting what breaches the conditionality, while their employer or colleagues may never be aware that the bargain is broken. One of the most relevant problems of this sort arises from perceptions of excessively high levels of reward accorded to bosses; those lower down the organization hierarchy may feel that the requirements for their conditional values of loyalty and honesty have been breached by what they view as bad behaviour higher up.

There is a final problem with values that is useful to have at the back of your mind; if Value A is more important than Value B, and Value B is more important than Value C, does that mean Value A is also more important than Value C? The answer is that we don't know, so it is best to make it clear when communicating values. Continuing the same example as above, suppose another value is that we 'treat people with respect'. For the most part, this is the same thing as behaving with integrity, which is our supreme value. However, if times are hard we may dismiss staff in order to reduce costs, thereby moving this value below our value of 'success'. This tells us that while values are both important and useful, they are also complicated. They may form complex hierarchies, they may be conditional (being sacrificed to economic survival) and open to interpretation. So if staff must be dismissed I will treat them with dignity and give them the best financial package I can afford. But in good times I may have felt that the value of treating people with respect required me to retrain or reallocate people but not to dismiss them. I have reinterpreted the value.

Giving values meaning

Take stock of what you want to achieve by having corporate values. It is likely that as an organizational leader you seek a work environment that encourages behaviour that has positive effects on stakeholders and the community. You are probably aware that an increasing number of customers, employees, regulators and legislators are paying attention to the impact of organizations on society. They will support an organization whose values they identify with: whether because they support its ethical standards or because the brand image suits them sufficiently to buy the products or join as an employee. Values, therefore, reflect what your organization stands for: they encapsulate its personality and link it with its various stakeholders.

It is often hard to describe values briefly, yet being brief makes them far easier to communicate effectively. The solution to this dilemma lies in communicating concise catch phrases but always explaining them in more detail. One of McDonald's published values provides a good example. It is headed 'We are committed to our people', which is brief and has a comforting ring to it but is not very clear; so they go on to elaborate: 'We provide opportunity, nurture talent, develop leaders and reward achievement. We believe that a team of well-trained individuals with diverse backgrounds and experiences, working together in an environment that fosters respect and drives high levels of engagement, is essential to our continued success.' It does not make empty or meaningless promises but does express some specific aims and finishes by making clear that this is a subset of success.

Douglas Macgregor states that organizations that have succeeded in engaging everyone around clearly discernible values do not simply proclaim their values; they immerse their managers as well as their employees in the ideology to an obsessive degree (Macgregor, 1997). New members learn the values of the organization through their initial socialization processes. Many organizations, such as the BBC and the *Guardian* newspaper, have long-held values, and employees are well versed and immersed in them. They act as constant reference points against which people determine policy, interpret challenges and dilemmas, and take decisions.

Guardian Media Group (GMG; www.gmgplc.co.uk) uses its values as a reference point for all employees on a wide range of issues. They act as a focus to pull people together and help to establish a corporate identity and company loyalty; they help people know how to behave; they set boundaries within which people can work – that way you don't need a 'do' and 'don't do' list, or someone to say you can or cannot do something: it is obvious and falls into place.

CASE STUDY

GMG is owned by the Scott Trust Ltd. It has a broad portfolio of businesses and investments. Its core business is Guardian News & Media (GNM), which publishes the *Guardian* and the *Observer* as well as the guardian.co.uk website.

The idea that businesses have obligations to the society in which they operate is often thought of as a relatively new phenomenon even though many businesses, particularly those founded by Quakers in 19th-century Britain, espoused this view. At GMG an awareness of the wider responsibilities of business has always been at the heart of what they do. The *Manchester Guardian* was created to support social reform in the early 19th century, and the ethos of public service has been part of its DNA ever since. The editor CP Scott summed this up in his 1921 leader marking the centenary of the paper, in which he asserted that newspapers have 'a moral as well as material existence'. He listed the essential attributes he believed should form the character of a newspaper. He wrote that the most precious possession was 'honesty, cleanness (integrity), courage, fairness, and a sense of duty to the reader and the community'. The Scott Trust later adopted these values as its own; they continue to inform the way in which GMG runs its business, operating GNM as a commercial enterprise while always seeking to adhere to principles of decency and public service.

Since then, these values have acted as a guiding light and clear reference point in shaping the style and nature of the newspaper and of the group as a place to work. Alison Hall, Director of Change at GNM, says: 'People choose to work here because of the values. You know what is right and what is wrong and what fits with the paper's ethos.

It does not need policing.' This clarity enables people to adapt and act quickly, whether in formulating policy or pursuing a story.

This values-driven approach is illustrated by the response of GNM Editor-in-Chief Alan Rusbridger to a question during a visit to Norway in June 2009 when he revealed that he does not read all the tweets from journalists before they are published: 'I was told that this could not happen in Norway as the editor-in-chief would insist on reading all content', says Rusbridger. 'We are probably ahead of others as we devolve a great deal of responsibility and freedom to our reporters. The idea of journalists publishing directly is not a shocking one for us' (The *Guardian* and the *Observer*, 2008–09).

This last example shows how clear values facilitate trust on the part of the managers and, as a result, leadership is devolved to where and when it matters.

Where organizations do not have the long-held traditions of GNM, identifying values and making them mean the same things to everyone can be problematic, one such problem being that organizations usually, and perhaps inevitably, choose their values from a small set of words or phrases that can equally mean a lot or nothing. At worst, empty phrases give rise to cynicism and discontent, as people find the organization does not live up to its promises. The most common 'value words' used in organizations are: openness, fairness, integrity, honesty, respect, customer focus, team orientation and creativity. Given these difficulties:

How do you identify values and ensure everyone shares their meaning? How can you achieve this while also retaining flexibility for differences across departments, business units and geographical location, where needs may be rather different? How do you ensure that these words are not empty platitudes and really mean something?

GNM again provides some answers to these questions. Carolyn Gray, Group HR Director, receives reports from the HR directors of the individual businesses on various aspects of HR. This includes evidence of how these HR activities are aligned with Scott Trust values. She then presents an overall report to the GNM board, including how effectively values have been upheld. What is striking here is how it remains important to refer continually to values and be conscious of them, even when they have been in place since 1921.

At Standard Chartered Bank, values take the form of five descriptors: courageous, responsive, international, creative, trustworthy. The bank invested considerable time and effort into identifying these values through discussion and workshops and using consultancy support to facilitate discussions. Then, having homed in on just five words that might be expected to be subject to infinite interpretation and confusion, they established a process to make sure that everyone understands and 'lives' them (www.standardchartered.com).

Organizations such as Standard Chartered and global PR firm Burson-Marsteller (Chapters 5, 6, 7) that have embedded their values effectively into their culture generally place considerable emphasis on the importance of conversations. Managers discuss values with their direct reports and within teams. This gives everyone the opportunity to identify what the values, or descriptors, mean to them and what they mean for the team. An effective approach is for each person, or each team, to give particular consideration to how effectively they can incorporate one of the values into their next year's performance. So, for example, 'courageous' might be taken to encourage a little more risk taking in one division or a more individualistic approach in another. Similarly, the descriptor 'international' might just be a statement of organizational fact in one context, but in another it may encourage different functions and business areas to seek out best-practice techniques across the various offices of the business. This enables firms such as Standard Chartered and Burson-Marsteller to establish a 'one company' identity across the world, while allowing for behaviours associated with a value to be different for each part of the business; it also allows for cultural interpretations of the values across the world.

At Standard Chartered, people's performance appraisal review includes how they have upheld their values, as well as whether they have achieved their performance objectives; and evidence is required to substantiate their claims. There are two parts to a performance appraisal rating: achievement of objectives and upholding of values. A low rating for values will pull down someone's bonus award, even if the person has exceeded their objectives (Caplan, 2011).

When an organization embeds its values effectively into the culture, this sets the ethos and the standards. As Mel Mayne, former banker and hedge fund manager, and specialist in ethics and corporate governance, points out: 'It also makes it clear when the standards have not been met so that action can be taken speedily. The fall-out from such breaches is generally likely to be more contained, and the contagion less likely to spread to other parts of the organization.'

The BBC is an example of this. Crisis hit the Corporation in 2012, causing instability and uncertainty within the organization, and leading to a drop in public confidence. When the new Director-General Tony Hall was appointed, Lord Patten, Chairman of the Trust, said the BBC needed 'to take a long, hard look at the way it operates and put in place the changes required to ensure it lives up to the standards that the public expects' (BBC,

2012). The point here is that those standards are clear, and as some commentators remarked, they still hold true in many parts of the Corporation.

To answer our earlier questions, these case studies help us conclude:

- To make values stick, consciously work at embedding them.
- To establish 'shared values', constantly articulate and evaluate behaviour. It is not easy for people to change their values, especially when these are associated with their national culture, but they can change their behaviour – and it is how people behave that brings the values to life. Discussing these behaviours with reference to values will help you put a shared meaning on values, while also allowing for cultural adaptations.
- Check that you actively promote organizational values through your words and your deeds. Facilitate this where necessary.
- Check that organizational values are upheld consistently through all your strategic talent development policies and practices, including performance management.

'Shared values' represent an organization's long-term view of the world; that is, you cannot change them too frequently – you need to make sure you define them properly but then hold your nerve with them and really embed them to reap long-term benefits. Having shared values in an organization does not mean that everyone has to have exactly the same view, but that their views must be mutually supportive and transparent.

A talent and engagement strategy is beneficial in this respect. Drawing up a strategy will engage you in conversations around the business, which lead to insights that do not often emerge when you are caught up in the day-to-day. These conversations are opportunities for reinforcing your values and generating a shared meaning. One aim of a talent and engagement strategy is to join up your people processes and integrate them with business strategy so that your processes transmit consistent messages and influence consistent behaviour. This too is instrumental in creating 'shared values'. As we saw earlier, a role of strategic talent development is to drive the culture and the behaviours that will lead to sustainable success for your business. In an ideal world, the senior management team will actively support this, or indeed your values will already be in place. Where this is not the case, be especially conscious of the behaviours your policies may drive. For example, if you need to drive teamwork or encourage accountability, communicate how a particular initiative will help achieve this. Eventually, as behaviours develop, cultural values will become more evident and will take on a shared meaning.

As Charlie Mayfield, chairman of the John Lewis Partnership, wrote in *The Times*, 'putting emphasis on values is also a recipe for commercial success. Companies that focus most on maximizing profit are often not the most profitable. That's especially true over time' (Mayfield, 2010).

CASE STUDY

Jack Welch, CEO of the US General Electric Company for 20 years, wrote to shareholders about four types of manager (GE Annual Report, 2000):

> ...it's about the four 'types' that represent the way we evaluate and deal with our existing leaders.
>
> Type I: shares our values; makes the numbers – sky's the limit!
>
> Type II: doesn't share the values; doesn't make the numbers – gone.
>
> Type III: shares the values; misses the numbers – typically, another chance, or two.

None of these three are tough calls, but Type IV is the toughest call of all: the manager who doesn't share the values, but delivers the numbers; the 'go to' manager, the hammer, who delivers the bacon but does it on the backs of people, often 'kissing up and kicking down' during the process. This type is the toughest to part with because organizations always want to deliver – it's in the blood – and to let someone go who gets the job done is yet another unnatural act. But we have to remove these Type IVs because they have the power, by themselves, to destroy the open, informal, trust-based culture we need to win today and tomorrow.

We made our leap forward when we began removing our Type IV managers and making it clear to the entire Company why they were asked to leave – not for the usual 'personal reasons' or 'to pursue other opportunities', but for not sharing our values. Until an organization develops the courage to do this, people will never have full confidence that these soft values are truly real. There are undoubtedly a few Type IVs remaining, and they must be found. They must leave the Company, because their behavior weakens the trust that more than 300,000 people have in its leadership.

Organizational success factors

As we have already discussed, clear values that embody what the organization stands for, and that guide the behaviour of its members, is essential in today's organizations where direct supervision and top-down control are becoming increasingly difficult.

Returning to the BBC as an example, their values provide the reference point for establishing the performance standards that make for success in the enterprise.

Lord Reith, the first director-general of the BBC, laid down a definition of the purpose of the BBC to 'inform, educate and entertain'. In the newsroom, for example, this definition is an important reference point giving 'the news-gathering team a clear set of standards to work to, which are set at the highest possible level'. There is 'a regular dialogue with the programme editors about standards to be sure everyone is working to the same ends' (Caplan, 2003).

Walmart is an example of a company that is trying to shift its corporate culture across the world from one based on rules to one based on values. The aim is to ensure that employees will 'feel empowered and have the right values so they can make the right decision. The thing that will decide if Walmart continues to be special as it grows around the world is getting these values across' (*The Economist*, 2011).

Moving to a values-driven culture, and maintaining it once you get there, raises serious challenges. How do you get people to share values across the company, perhaps also across the globe? Before addressing that question, we must consider what can go wrong, so that we can identify the pitfalls to avoid. There is often a disconnection between individual and organizational values, or between what is publicly stated and how people behave. Such disconnections make it difficult for people to know what is acceptable. An example might be a company that has among its stated values to treat everyone with dignity and respect, but whose norms have permitted and perhaps even encouraged a pattern of sexual harassment over a number of years. Do those in the organization know that the behaviour is wrong, but condone it nevertheless?

Business ethics and values

If we talk about values then we should also talk about business ethics. Ethics is a branch of philosophy that deals with what is right and what is wrong behaviour. But it is not just confined to philosophers: we all make ethical decisions every day of our lives. Some of these decisions are on a large scale where we may decide whether to cheat, to steal or to lie. Most of them will fall into more of a grey area where we can convince ourselves either that they are trivial or that we are doing no wrong. Such borderline decisions may be about taking company property, on a small scale, such as pens or paper, accepting entertainment from a supplier that we know is meant to influence a business decision, saying something in a meeting (or remaining silent) with the intention of gaining an advantage over a colleague, or maybe failing to mention a relevant disadvantage of a product we are trying to sell.

There is a clear overlap between business ethics and values but they are not the same thing. Some values will not concern ethics, but all ethics will fall within your set of values. Values that are not ethical issues might include things such as being open with colleagues and sharing information or contributing to the local community or always putting the customer first.

CASE STUDY

A friend of mine was a director of a company trading in an African country. The company sold its services in a number of neighbouring countries where it was often necessary to pay taxes or to have taxes withheld from payments before it was certain how much was due. It turned out that his company had overpaid its taxes in one of those countries and so he was seeking a refund from the authorities. Meeting a senior executive of the revenue authority in a smart city centre hotel he was shocked to be faced with a blatant demand for a bribe in order to secure the release of the monies that were legally due to his business under the nation's tax code.

His decision to refuse was based on an ethical judgement but it was also influenced by the effect it could have on his company's culture. If he paid the bribe then it would have to show in the records of his business and, at the least, his accounting staff would be aware of it. What sort of example would he be setting them? Once they could see that dishonesty was officially countenanced in one context, how could he be sure they would not draw the conclusion that dishonesty was ok in other contexts?

Decisions taken within an organization may be made by individuals or groups, but whoever makes them will be influenced by the culture of the company. Where such decisions have an ethical nature they will also act the other way, affecting the culture of the company too and therefore future decisions. At its simplest, once a decision is made that contravenes your declared company values, this makes it more likely that further decisions of this type will be made. This is the 'slippery slope' argument.

Putting aside the moral issues of right and wrong, there is a clear business case for ethical behaviour. The news media are full of reports of the repercussions of unethical behaviour, ranging from phone hacking through bribery and false reporting of data to money laundering and misrepresentation. The fines levied for law breaking usually dwarf the original benefit and, where the bad behaviour is not actually unlawful, the loss of reputation itself can be enormously costly. Beyond that, there is the hidden cost of people following bad examples from within the organization and feeling that if it or its leaders can behave badly then they themselves have the same right.

Why do individuals behave unethically? One reason is the complexity of the issues leaders deal with, and the difficulty in many instances of determining which is the most ethical alternative. Another is the pressure people are under to perform, such that they start by cutting corners a little and, once done, this marginally questionable behaviour makes it feel easier to cross the next barrier. There are several systemic factors. One is the competition for scarce resources; another the ease with which we slip into unethical acts to gain a competitive advantage in the race for position or power.

Factors related to the dynamics of group and team behaviour can lead to unethical behaviour or failure to act to stop it. One is groupthink,[1] which can occur in a homogeneous group with a strong leader. A second is the presence of idealogues: individuals who view their own extreme positions as 'right' and any opposing positions as 'wrong'. A third is the organization's response to dissent. There are few incentives for 'whistleblowers' or those who try to expose unethical behaviour in organizations. Organizational norms encourage 'going along' and discourage questioning the unethical actions of others. This can quickly compromise ethical standards in any organization.

Values and ethics are not just about having a rulebook that people may or may not look at. The organization must live its values; senior management must set an example, transgressions must be punished, values must be talked about. Constantly examining and re-examining these issues must be part of the regular conversations that occur around the organization. When I worked at Alitalia as a young trainee in HR, safety was, and I feel sure still is, the prime consideration. This wasn't just a written statement, but was reinforced at every opportunity, through formal corporate communication, through informal conversations, and through practices and processes and how these were implemented and controlled. This might seem obvious, but my point is that safety wasn't separated out as a responsibility for just those directly involved but was part of the worldwide fabric of how things were done at Alitalia, and which everyone was conscious of, whatever their role. It permeated everything that was done and what people said and did and how they thought. It was part of the general conversation. There is a common expression that it is not enough to 'talk the talk', you must also 'walk the walk', suggesting talk is cheap but action is what matters. Of course, appropriate actions are the objective, but unless values are discussed and constantly reinforced by repetition they will not be acted upon.

The financial crisis and its aftermath have put ethics centre-stage for the financial services sector of the economy. This is not because financial institutions behave any worse than pharmaceutical companies that sack whistleblowers or industrial companies that pay bribes. It is largely because the crisis has led to questionable practices coming to light but also because the sector has lurched from one highly publicized scandal to another, whether it be selling mortgages to people who couldn't afford them, allegations of fixing Libor rates, allegations of money laundering or sanctions busting. It is also a result of public perceptions of unduly high rewards to some senior staff in the sector, which may have encouraged excessive risk taking. Whether current negative perceptions are right or wrong, fair or unfair, is less significant than the unarguably high profile of the sector. It really is different – there is no other sector of the economy where problems could threaten the savings and livelihoods of the entire population. Certainly, if financial institutions are to regain trust then values-based leadership that takes account of ethical considerations is required. It must also be part of the fabric in the same way that safety was part of the fabric of Alitalia.

Of course, it is not just financial services that need to consider the role they play within wider society. As Lynda Gratton says: 'Companies need to build inner resilience and anchor themselves in communities. Business has a major role to play in contributing to solving the three major global challenges: poverty, youth unemployment and climate change. They need to build alliances with other companies, NGOs and governments and be clear about their role in the world' (Gratton, 2011).

For a number of years, a much-quoted management orthodoxy was that 'great leadership is about creating beliefs in hearts as well as minds'. That sounds superficially good but it is fundamentally wrong. Encouraging unquestioning belief is neither good management nor good leadership. I once heard that the sales people who marketed easy mortgages in the United States had had it hammered into them that they were selling people a better life; and look where that ended up. Rather than the manipulation that this phrase suggests, great leadership is about creating a free and open conversation within a framework of 'shared values, shared visions and shared understanding'. This engages and motivates everyone but it also empowers people to innovate, react quickly and make decisions that are appropriate to the organization's beliefs.

Individual versus shared ethics and values

Individuals possess their own values, which have been determined by a number of influences. There are three qualities that individuals must possess to make ethical decisions. The first is the ability to recognize ethical issues and to reason through the ethical consequences of decisions. The ability to see second- and third-order effects, one of the elements of strategic thinking, is very important. The second is the ability to look at alternative points of view, deciding what is right in a particular set of circumstances. This is similar to the ability to reframe. And the third is the ability to deal with ambiguity and uncertainty: making a decision on the best information available.

Nonetheless, the ethical standards that individuals observe in the organization will have a significant effect on their behaviour. 'People will do what they are rewarded for doing' (National Defense University, nd). The organization has its greatest impact in the standards it establishes for ethical and unethical conduct in its formal reward systems. For example:

> If bonuses are paid for selling mortgages, with no penalty or clawback if the borrower defaults, then it is unsurprising that sales staff may be tempted to accept some risks they know, deep down, they shouldn't.

Informal norms also have a strong influence on behaviour, as do the examples set by the leaders of the organization. Leaders must understand that their actions, more than words alone, will determine the operating values in the organization. In their article entitled 'Why Be Honest If Honesty Doesn't Pay?', Bhide and Stevenson (1990) note that there often are no economic or other incentives to encourage ethical behaviour and discourage unethical behaviour. They contend that it most often is the dishonest individual who gets ahead, and that cases where unethical behaviour was punished are far outweighed by those in which there were either no consequences or unethical behaviour was rewarded. They also point out that people *do* often behave ethically, in spite of the apparent lack of gain. Ethical behaviour must be intrinsically rewarding; and most people behave ethically because it makes them feel better. They often 'choose the harder right instead of the easier wrong' specifically because of their personal values of what is right. This is an important consideration given that surveys consistently find that many of today's under-30s in rich countries want to spend their working day trying to make the world a better place as well as being properly paid, and turn down jobs that do not offer such satisfaction.

How can the leaders of an organization build an ethical climate and embed the organization's values?

There are a number of steps:

- Foremost are the actions of the strategic leadership and the way they deal with ethical issues. The pattern of top leaders' behaviour determines organizational values. Top leaders should regularly review their own actions and communications in the light of the organization's ethical codes and espoused values. They should consciously seek to discuss values.

- A second step is to make explicit ethics policies, through the firm's employment policies, but perhaps additionally by drawing up an organizational ethical code, or by signing up to one. An example of the latter is the Principles of Responsible Investment. This UN-backed initiative, which now has over 1,100 signatories, is a network of international investors who work together to put into practice the six principles that make up the code. Whistleblowing policies are important, especially paying consideration to how these are implemented and the way people who use the policy are treated.

- The next step is to increase awareness of how to apply those ethical codes. Training in how to deal with situations with an ethical dimension, and how to anticipate situations that involve ethical choices, can go a long way towards ethical institutional practices.

- We also need to know what is actually going on in the organization. This requires a culture where full and accurate information is passed upwards through the hierarchy and where individuals are not frightened to convey bad news. However, it also relies upon more senior managers asking probing questions and not using the answers merely as a reason to chastise or punish. When probing questions are used to bully people, it stops the flow of useful information. The information passed upwards helps to inform sound management decisions, but should also support ethical behaviour and allow the strategic leader to know when or where there are potential ethical breaches so that corrective action can be taken. It is a real danger that when unethical behaviour is unnoticed, or unpunished, members will assume that the organization's leadership condones it.

What happens when, as an organization, we fail to live up to our values?

This can happen because we were not serious about them in the first place, which is the negation of everything discussed in this chapter, or because individuals substitute personal and unacceptable values for those of the organization. Typically this occurs when individuals sacrifice integrity for personal gain. In such cases, as long as the organization reinforces its values by disciplining the individuals, or at least stating that they were wrong and that such behaviour will not be tolerated in future, its values are intact. However, if it fails to do this and therefore implicitly adopts the 'new values' or if the breach was so widespread that it had become an organizational value, then there is a problem: if the organization fails to repudiate bad behaviours, its claimed value system is a dead letter.

Sometimes, ethical dilemmas are subtle.

Example: many European businesses operate payment terms of 90 days regardless of the fact that suppliers' terms are often 30 days. This often conflicts with the organization's stated values of trust and integrity. How can you build trust and act with integrity with regard to your contractors and suppliers in these circumstances?

Example: many organizations encourage personal ambition and the single-minded pursuit of personal reward. How does this reconcile with people whose religious upbringing has taught them that there is virtue in charity and abstinence?

Example: it is not unusual for pharmaceutical and cosmetic companies to give less prominence in their advertising and promotion to unflattering studies of the effectiveness of their products than to studies that appear to show favourable results. Or they might avoid carrying out studies that could be unhelpful to those promotions. Does this behaviour cross the line of what is ethical?

Identify practices such as these that might sit uncomfortably with your values. Discuss them openly, and pull actions back into alignment, if you can. Take action with people whose performance is straying from your values, but equally this will help them decide if they do not like the way you are interpreting the organization's values.

Keep values in the consciousness

Recruitment, performance appraisal, development and pay should all reflect and reinforce the organization's values and ethical codes. Increasingly, organizations are expecting people to exhibit how they uphold the firm's values through the performance management process. In some cases, the person's final rating will depend not just on whether they have met their objectives, but on evidence that they have also upheld the firm's values.

Above all, values must be discussed regularly and openly. At leading PR firm Burson-Marsteller, for example, discussions on the firm's values and what they mean to people in different parts of the world can be accessed easily through the firm's internal social media. These discussions keep the firm's values in people's consciousness but also enrich global working, helping people to improve their understanding of each other's cultures and ways of operating.

Key points

- Shared values, shared visions and shared understanding set the boundaries for people to take decisions and know what is expected of them.

- Values must be meaningful and, where they are usually expressed in just a word or phrase, must be expanded upon so that people know what they mean.

- The firm's values must be communicated and discussed regularly and openly to keep them in people's consciousness and ensure that there is a common interpretation of them.

- Make ethics policies explicit, through the firm's employment policies, but additionally by drawing up an ethical code, or by signing up to an existing one.

- Recruitment, performance appraisal, development and pay should all reflect and reinforce the organization's values and ethical codes.

- Values must be lived, not just talked. This applies to everyone, from top to bottom. The organization must act when it fails to live up to them.

- Ethical behaviour is intrinsically rewarding. This will lead to better results.

Note

1 The term 'groupthink' was coined by Irving Janis in 1972.

Strategic framework

Strategic talent development that includes the entire workforce delivers what your business needs to meet the rapid changes in markets, technology, society and techniques that characterize our global business environment. The four-point framework (Figure 3.1) will help you achieve this. Its four points address the challenges of the new world business environment, and guide you through the process of drafting and implementing a people plan that will position your business to survive and prosper through an engaged, flexible and talented workforce. Without an appropriate process, your vision and transformation effort can easily dissolve into a list of confusing, incompatible and time-consuming projects that go in the wrong direction or nowhere at all.

In the Introduction, we considered the broad business environment at the macro level. I now turn to how these changes translate into boardroom concerns. I then show how the four points of the strategic framework address these concerns. I feel it is important to make this direct link between the four points and the strategic needs of the business to emphasize that strategic talent development is business driven. I then give an overview of the four-point framework.

The relevance of the four-point framework to the new world business environment

The starting point, therefore, is to ask what the business needs: or, indeed, what's keeping C-level executives[1] awake at night?

Three of the biggest boardroom challenges that strategic talent development must respond to are: the speed and unpredictability of change, the

FIGURE 3.1 The four-point framework shows the steps to develop your talent and engagement strategy

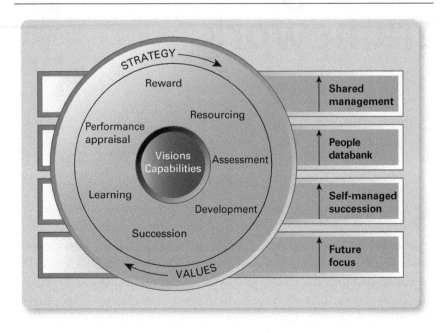

increasingly serious consequences of failing to manage risk effectively, and the constant need to manage the bottom line, especially in light of ever-rising costs. Let's look at these more closely.

The speed and unpredictability of change

Change brings opportunity but it is strikingly the fear of missing opportunity, or of seeing the opportunity but being unable to take advantage of it quickly or smartly enough, that is the prime cause of insomnia for today's C-Suite executives.

Hard evidence to support my own anecdotal evidence comes from IBM's survey of 1,700 CEOs and senior public sector leaders from around the globe (IBM, 2012). This found that 'technology now tops the list of external forces impacting organizations. Above any other external factor – even the economy – CEOs expect technology to drive the most change in their organizations over the next five years' and 'While CEOs are invigorated by the opportunities, they also fear falling behind, given the pace of technology change.' According to this survey, 84 per cent of organizations that outperform their peers 'translate insights into action better than industry peers. 73 per cent more outperformers excel at managing change...'.

PwC's Global CEO Survey in 2012 also supports my view: 'One in four CEOs said they were unable to pursue a market opportunity or have had to cancel or delay a strategic initiative because of talent constraints.' This survey also reports that 'despite weak confidence in global economic growth, CEOs' confidence in their own organization's growth prospects was significantly higher' (PwC, 2012). Clearly, strategic talent development is urgent, as well as important, if organizations are to achieve top-line growth.

In today's technological, connected world, significant change, shaped by leaders' strategic vision and encouraged by the organizational climate, may emerge from a team or an individual anywhere within your organization. The inspiration or insight for a new product or market or way of doing things may come from anyone. The ability to take rapid advantage of it *must* come from everyone.

The first questions we must address, therefore, are: How can we create an environment that empowers people to spot opportunity? How can we engage people so that they will act on the opportunity?

Risk management

This discussion takes us into the risk management arena. What is the risk to the business of pursuing this opportunity? What is the risk of not doing so? Do we have the people who can take this opportunity forward? What impact will it have on others? Will it lead to infighting between different factions and departments? How will those who are currently pre-eminent react to this upstart idea? How will it disrupt an existing market and value network, or displace earlier technology? Who will block this decision? Who will support it?

There are probably other questions but these are the key talent questions to which there are two answers: firstly, businesses must create the cultural conditions for change and strategic innovation; secondly, businesses need a deep, current understanding of the people they employ, of their functional and behavioural capabilities, their experiences and their aspirations.

Brand reputation is another area of risk that is increasingly coming within the scope of a talent and engagement strategy because Web 2.0 technologies form a corporate communications frontier. In the past, companies would identify one or two people who were authorized to speak to the press, to investors and to suppliers. The company's public image could be centrally controlled. Now just about everyone is interfacing with the outside world through Facebook or MySpace or Twitter or LinkedIn or specialist forums or personal blogs. This exploding use of social media is not just changing the way an organization manages its brand. It is changing people's attitudes: they are more used to sharing information, hungrier for it; and it is encouraging people to be more open about themselves and about what they are working on. An old-world response would ban such communication to preserve confidentiality; the new-world response is to ensure that people understand what is commercially confidential so they can use these media without giving away trade secrets. In the old world, information was power, so people kept information to themselves. In the new world, power comes from sharing information.

The bottom line

Another big concern in the C-Suite is, of course, the concern to grow the bottom line. This brings us back to the discussion in Chapter 1, where we looked at studies that show the correlation between high levels of employee engagement and higher productivity, and that therefore provide us with evidence that implementing strategic talent development will directly impact the bottom line.

What does success look like?

The four-point framework will help you address these fears, so that the following are embedded in your culture and become 'how we do things around here'.

Seize opportunity

For an organization to seize opportunity, it requires:

- A workforce with the skills of learning and unlearning so the organization has the agility to move rapidly into new markets, or new products. 'Unlearning' means you not only adopt the new but also stop using the outmoded: these can be difficult habits to break.

- A workforce empowered to spot opportunity from wherever they are in the hierarchy, and from whatever position. This, in turn, demands frequent clear, open and transparent communication within the organization.

FIGURE 3.2 How the four-point talent framework responds to business challenges

- A culture that values everyone's role and contribution, recognizing that all roles are interlinked and does not allow one function to regard itself as superior.
- Everyone to be taking a future-oriented approach so that they recognize an opportunity when they see it.
- An emphasis on innovation, where innovation doesn't just mean small, incremental improvements – these are just part of being a dynamic organization. 'Innovation is about finding new ways of combining things generally. Innovation means offering things in different ways, creating new combinations' (Porter, 2012).

Manage risk

To address the risk related to having appropriate resources of skills and capabilities the organization must:

- Focus on the future so that needs are apparent early.
- Have processes for developing the capabilities it is likely to need in the future.
- Have an understanding of the workforce, of each person's skills and abilities and, importantly, their aspirations. This makes for faster decisions about who can take on new challenges. It also helps engage those who are required to maintain and evolve existing activities (Figure 3.2).
- Employ open communication and trust, to manage reputational risk. These are brought about by clear values that set boundaries, and a culture that brings all employees close to the business strategy. Encourage people to derive the inspiration and ingenuity social media provides that leads to innovation and flexibility.

FIGURE 3.3 How the four-point talent framework relates to employee engagement indicators

Grow the bottom line

To address the bottom line, there are many things to be done, ranging from developing a winning strategy to cutting costs. But, as we have already established, when people feel more engaged with the organization they are more productive and achieve better results. As discussed in Chapter 1, the key indicators that employee engagement shares with strategic talent development are, in summary:

- a positive, future-oriented outlook;
- outstanding development opportunity for everyone;
- effective relationships;
- high levels of two-way communication.

Many businesses – the people at the top of them and within them – have been battered by the economic crisis. Keeping going is taking so much effort that the notion of 'opportunity' seems a mirage in the desert. Strategic talent development is no less relevant in these circumstances, and will help you energize people by focusing them on creating a developing future. Without doubt, it is the focus on the employee engagement indicators, however, that will make a discernible difference by involving people, supporting them, noticing achievement, giving recognition even to little things, and creating a sense of fun and a collegiate atmosphere (Figure 3.3).

FIGURE 3.4   How the four-point framework responds to the new-world environment

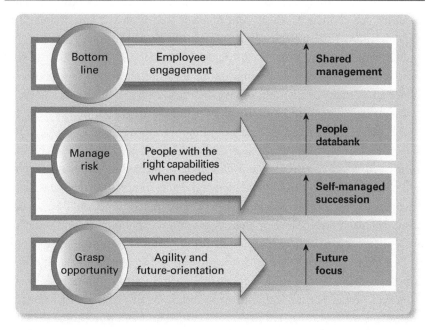

NOTE The diagram helps to give a sense of direction and sequence but reality is complex and there are many linkages and different lines of feedback.

The four-point framework

Let's now take an overview of how to make all this happen (Figure 3.4).

Focus on the future

A business has many strategies that interconnect and integrate with the overall business strategy. The same is true of visions: there is an overall vision for the business, and each function has a vision including, of course, talent development. It is rather like nesting Russian dolls. You are presented with one doll. When you open this, you find another within, another within that, and so on. Each conforms to the overall design but may have different painted features. The different strategies that come within your talent and engagement strategy – for assessing, developing, deploying and engaging people – are connected through an overarching strategic 'focus on the future'.

A focus on the future sets the strategic direction around which people turn strategy into action, and are empowered to spot opportunity in the outside world. It also, through articulated and defined capabilities, creates a common language around success.

Let me illustrate this: FSB is a fund management advisory business. They consider the challenges ahead and identify that with the eurozone still in difficulty, most investment opportunities will be in the Asia-Pacific region and the other rising markets with scalable businesses. They anticipate that their existing clients will become more demanding about the quality of advice and information they receive before deciding whether to invest in new markets. They are likely to be more discerning, too, in assessing the people who run the funds in which they are considering investing. They will probably be looking for longer-term returns than has been the case until now. What capabilities will FSB need to meet these challenges? They will need to develop their knowledge and understanding of the Asia-Pacific region, and of the other rising markets. I class this as 'functional' capability. They will also need to develop their behavioural capability around some key areas: being open to new ideas, and future-oriented thinking, for example to be able to spot the right time to move into different markets, and with which products. Sophisticated client orientation and negotiation skills, for sure, will be needed to deal with new and more discerning customers, for example to surface the client's real needs and help them think these through, or to work out solutions that will be in the interests of all parties. So FSB's functional capability profile will include 'knowledge and understanding of the Asia-Pacific region, and of the other rising markets'. Their behavioural capability profile will include: client orientation, negotiation, being open to new ideas, and future-oriented thinking. These capabilities must be communicated and defined so that they are clearly understood. They then, in effect, become the organization's success factors: 'the skills we must master if we are to achieve success'.

This enables managers to know how to select people for different roles, set expectations for performance, assess performance, give feedback, and support development. It gives individuals a clear understanding of what is expected of them, and enables them to plan their own development and their careers.

Clear success factors that, alongside capabilities, include visions and values that are truly 'lived' in the organization set the boundaries so that people know how to act, how to take responsibility, how to take decisions, and how to develop their roles and themselves. It becomes the default culture, which drives behaviour and performance. It takes the place of 'eyeball' management, or top-down direction, which are no longer possible in the new world organization. It also empowers people at all levels to recognize opportunity that will benefit the business.

The big ideas of a focus on the future are:

- formal processes for engaging people in the business strategy (eg away-days, business plans);

- informal processes that encourage regular dialogue about trends and what's going on in the outside world (eg networking, social media discussion groups);

- visions and values that are truly 'lived' (they are discussed regularly, communicated through social media, and role modelled, especially by managers and those in the C-Suite);

- clear definitions of the functional and behavioural capabilities the business will need to meet its future challenges (as in the example above, functional and behavioural profiles are published, and are also defined through social media, intranets, and self-managed succession initiatives – described below);

- clear definitions of the capabilities around learning and adapting that will ensure your people have the skills to manage change. These are relevant to everyone in the new world environment, and so should be incorporated in your capability profiles.

Self-managed succession

The second point on the framework is self-managed succession. What makes this process self-managed? It places responsibility for managing their performance and their careers squarely on individuals. They are best able to understand their own values and to compare trade-offs in their career choices. This will include issues such as the amount of effort or sacrifice individuals are willing to invest to attain their goals. In the new system they must take responsibility for making sure they get the development they need to carry out their current role and for their next role and for the one after that and also for those future roles. This devolved system is more effective and more efficient for the organization. In order to win commitment, organizations must harness people's aspirations and this approach clearly achieves that goal. It also automatically picks up the high performers and the ambitious who will want to buy-in enthusiastically. For those who are content in their current role and don't want to move on or accept stretch and challenge, there will be a problem because nothing stays still any more and failure to develop will almost inevitably lead to eventual performance management problems. For the great majority in the middle, the organization's role becomes an effort to align the individual's aspirations with the organization's needs. This will involve the HR function providing information to managers from its people planning processes which, in turn, draws on the output of the first step of this four-point framework, 'focus on the future'. HR will also make available a wide range of learning, development, career, performance management and assessment practices that are integrated with the organization's capabilities. This range of practices should be designed so that there is something for everyone, to suit different learning needs and different individual learning styles, and for all business needs. Each activity, including performance appraisal, should be designed so that it can be self-managed. This does not diminish the role or importance of a manager but gives more control, and places greater trust in people, which is wholly appropriate to today's new ways of working.

Self-managed succession also places significant importance on providing people with the tools, processes and insightful feedback that will help them become more self-aware of their interpersonal styles, of how they build and manage relationships and achieve results, and of the impact they have on others.

The big ideas of self-managed succession are:

- Most of your learning, development, assessment and career practices should be directed towards your future-focus capabilities, though some may relate to other, specific needs.

- In developing and selecting new HR processes, do so in a way that will also generate information for your people databank (see below), and will facilitate the important conversations about performance and careers between managers and their people. These thus impact the next two points in the framework.

- Self-managed succession works around several important concepts: giving everyone the opportunity to have a long-term (three-stage) career development plan that aligns their aspirations with business needs; creating dynamic succession through the business: providing stretching and challenging developmental work experiences; providing the tools to develop self-awareness of the impact behaviours have on others: empowerment to self-manage performance and careers.

- Self-managed succession is a tripartite relationship: the organization (HR) provides the tools and processes, managers provide the support and feedback, and individuals take advantage of the opportunities.

People databank

The third step of the framework is the people databank. Why is it a critical step in creating a strategic talent development strategy? Your calculations about entering a new venture or taking on a commitment may change if you cannot put the skills in place to carry it out. Too often, delays occur to implementing business decisions, or reacting to changes or needs, either because there isn't an internal flow of people or because managers are reluctant to release people until they are replaced, and so on. At the beginning of this chapter, I referred to survey data that show that talent constraints are impeding business development. The same survey data also indicate that it is still only a minority of businesses that have truly taken advantage of the possibilities offered by new technology not only to record data about their people, but also to analyse those data against other business data. Most businesses strive to know their clients, to understand their expectations, buying patterns, preferences etc, so why do few truly know their own employees? Many business decisions require knowledge of who can undertake a new role, who can support them, and who can fill the gap they leave. A rebalancing of business priorities is necessary.

Strategic talent development emphasizes the importance of meaningful, informed conversations. To be effective, these must be data driven. Do we have people available to fulfil the next stage of our plan? Do they have the right capabilities? Decisions about pay awards, business development and performance and potential reviews come from formal conversations supported by data on people. The managers' role here is critical to achieving high performance and employee engagement. Business conversations are enhanced by comparisons between people data and employee engagement data on the one hand and financial, sales, customer or supplier data on the other.

Data about the workforce also inform decisions from recruitment, through learning and development, to equality and diversity. It should be capable of interrogation to set key strategies and track the progress of these: How many women do we have in management positions, in different parts of the business? How many people from ethnic minorities are employed and in which areas? How effective is our graduate recruitment? What is the composition of the workforce in our highest-performing branches? Are there any correlations? The possibilities are endless.

The big ideas of a people databank are:

- In designing systems for your self-managed succession initiatives, make sure information about people is captured to form part of your people databank. This goes beyond succession planning, which tends to focus on current roles, or job families, to create a known flow of people who are developing the capabilities required for the future. It is flexible and can cope with jobs not yet defined.

- Understanding people's aspirations is a key piece of data that should be captured in a databank. It will also include current capabilities and those being developed.

- Take full advantage of technology to make different data available to people across the business for different purposes. There are many software programs available, but sometimes an Excel spreadsheet can also be effective.

- Set up the data so that they can be manipulated to produce answers to critical strategic questions, 'at what point do we lose our graduate entrants?' being just one example.

- There are many software and social media programs available that can be used and adapted for different purposes; for example, to help people seek each other out to share ideas, learn together, and work together across boundaries.

Shared management

As well as capturing data about people, self-managed succession processes should also be designed so that they help managers and others carry out their critical roles. This immediately gives rise to two important questions: who are managers; what is their role?

Who are managers?

In the new world organization of fluid structures and flat hierarchies a line manager may have large numbers of people within his or her span of direct control. In such cases, it is impossible for them to give so many people the regular support that we know, from engagement survey data, they need. Moreover, performance appraisal becomes a heavy burden, and managers cannot be expected to make reliable assessments about people's performance and potential. This has given rise to increasing use of 360-degree feedback to supplement top-down appraisal, but that too is fraught with dangers, and is not a sufficiently reliable way of making assessments that affect important decisions. As already discussed, survey data also show the increasing importance of giving people career and development opportunities that will keep them employable, as well as meeting their aspirations. Seventy per cent of learning and development comes from work experiences and only 10 per cent from formal training courses. This requires a level of support for the individual – to give them developmental feedback, open appropriate work experiences, and support them in carrying out and learning from these experiences – that over-stretched line managers do not have time for.

What is the manager's role?

This situation calls for a reformatting of the role of the manager. First, separately define the different people-management responsibilities. Separate these from responsibility and accountability for business results. Secondly, allocate these responsibilities to people who can fulfil them. This might mean creating 'people manager' roles, where someone, preferably more senior to the individual, is responsible for their assessment and development. Or it might mean appointing internal coaches who will support the individual's development. But in some cases, traditional structures will, of course, still apply. Thirdly, it means clearly establishing the role of the HR business partner. People managers, and indeed also line managers, should be skilled at supporting 'steady performers' who will make up the majority. HR business partners should be there with practical support and appropriate systems to help people managers and line managers deal with the ambitious high performers and the poor performers.

This situation also calls for a new approach to performance appraisals. Too often, appraisals are viewed as a chore, and a waste of time. Generally, this is because they aim to achieve too much. Simplify the process so that it provides an overview of individual and collective performance, and plans for the forthcoming year, and is controlled and managed by the individual. The purpose should be to help run the business. The model that is emerging provides for an interim review, halfway through the year, that focuses on short- and long-term career and performance development, and a year-end review that concerns assessment of performance and achievement of goals and feeds into the pay review. What are often called talent roundtables, where peer groups of line and people managers meet to discuss people and their performance and potential next moves, help achieve consistency across the business, and also provide all-round views to make up for the lack of eyeball management. The quality conversations that provide feedback and development support take place regularly, perhaps monthly, fulfilling the remaining aims that are currently crammed into annual performance appraisals.

This fourth point on the framework relates to the new leadership model of 'shared values, shared visions and shared understanding', which is replacing the old command and control systems. 'Command and control systems used by the armed forces were deliberately adopted as the best management model for the emerging corporations of the early twentieth century, as a means of ensuring that the most appropriate command decisions were taken by the general staff (senior management) and that these were effectively transmitted to the ranks (workers) via their officers (middle management)' (Gifford, nd). There are some obvious problems here. Firstly, it means there is an over-reliance on one person, the person at the top, whose judgement and decision making are dependent on information flows, yet the information arriving at the top might be second, third or even fourth hand. Moreover, as Jonathan Gifford points out: 'Although people at the top, at least in theory, see the broad picture, they may be wrong about key aspects of reality "on the ground". Whereas, the people at the sharp end are better informed about the local situation, though not about the broader picture, from which they are deliberately excluded. But if they knew about the bigger picture, this might change their interpretation of their immediate environment' (Gifford, nd).

Although 'command and control' styles of leadership are being broken down by the changing ways of working of the new world organization, and by changes in employee expectations and demands, nonetheless, a core legacy of inappropriate 'command and control' policies remains. These limit the free flow of information; they slow change while authorization is sought; and they create departmental and functional silos, blocking collaboration. All this is inappropriate in an era of rapid change.

The word 'shared' emphasizes the importance of conversations, relationships and networking. It does not require everyone to do things in exactly the same way, but rather for everything they do to be congruent, mutually supportive, and transparent, and it leaves scope for individual interpretation.

The big ideas of shared management processes are:

1 When designing your self-managed succession activities ask: How will this help managers hold insightful conversations about performance, careers, and pay? Make sure you have in place practices that will help this.

2 Clarify and simplify managers' roles based on their critical employee engagement responsibilities: providing insightful feedback,

supporting development and opening developmental work opportunities, assessing performance and differentiating between standards of performance, ensuring people understand the standards they are expected to reach.

3 Provide HR business partner support to managers, especially to help them deal appropriately with high performers and with poor performers.

4 Look especially carefully at performance review systems and redesign these so that they help management run the business. Use related, but different, processes to provide regular feedback and support to people.

Using the four-point framework to achieve a coordinated approach

An ad hoc, uncoordinated approach to people management leads to problems such as:

- Confusing employer brand.
- Low morale because promises made at recruitment are not always kept.
- Difficulty in establishing priorities.
- People's energies and talents are misdirected.
- Poor teamwork and high conflict across different teams in the organization.
- Wrong priorities are pursued because reward is only about increased pay and promotion.
- People confuse tasks, responsibilities and accountabilities.
- Higher than desirable staff turnover.

There is also an impact on the business through a confusing brand promise to customers, lower levels of employee engagement and lower levels of customer satisfaction.

Making connections

A strategic approach adds value by creating insights and connecting activities. Imagine an organization pulled in all directions by half a dozen

FIGURE 3.5 Making connections

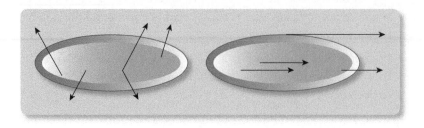

uncoordinated HR initiatives and programmes; then imagine the same organization pushed in one direction by several coordinated programmes – it just seems obvious to me which is more effective (Figure 3.5).

The greatest value of the four-point framework is that it is not just a reminder of key issues to include in your strategy, but is a process that directs your strategy.

What about the 'lone manager?'

I am often asked if change has to be driven from the top. What about managers at other levels who recognize the importance of the approach I set out in this book, but whose top management haven't yet got the message? Can they go it alone? And what about HR, can they go it alone in similar circumstances? My answer is definitely yes, you can do this even with a small team, and perhaps you will become a beacon for the organization. But it must be done with sincerity and commitment, and you will improve results in your area and enhance your own leadership skills and effectiveness. HR too can have a positive impact by identifying one or more people or departments to champion the approach. You need champions even if you are driving this from the top. Champions are likely to be people who are more receptive to the ideas, but who are also more inclined to experiment. Many people want something to be tried and tested before they will embark on it: they will not make good champions. Tap into influential networks in the business to spread the ideas, and be sure to communicate progress against measurable targets. Make sure your champions do this too, and get them networking together. Groups improve on ideas, and spread them faster than individuals. A spin-off benefit is that this approach requires an entrepreneurial, innovative outlook, which is just what you need to encourage in today's business world. Whether you are managing change from the top or as a 'lone manager', it is never quick or easy to achieve. In Chapter

9, we discuss neuroscience findings that prove that change is painful until it becomes habitual. This supports the idea of a connected approach to help the ideas make sense to people. And it shows that, above all, it is important to persevere, because sustained effort will be worthwhile.

Key points

- The four-point talent framework guides you through designing a talent and engagement strategy that helps your business respond to today's challenges.

- The process starts with a focus on the future, which sets the strategic direction, which, in turn, encourages people to think through future challenges and identify the functional and behavioural capabilities that will be needed to achieve them.

- Focus on the future guides you in generating initiatives, which stimulate people to build on trends and new ideas.

- The self-managed succession process offers a wide choice of learning and development interventions that people can self-manage. Guided by 'focus on the future', they will tend to develop the functional and behavioural capabilities it has identified.

- Choose self-managed succession practices that generate information you can capture for your 'people databank'. This will provide data for making better people and business decisions. It must include people's own aspirations, looking as far ahead as possible.

- 'Shared management' recognizes that people management is often no longer a linear process, but must be shared, with an overall 'coordinator' providing the support for performance and development that will help people become high performers, engaged with business success.

Note

1 C-Suite or C-level is a term used to describe the people in the top team, often designated as Chief, eg CEO, COO, CFO. I use it frequently in this book.

A focus on the future

'A focus on the future' must take an extra step beyond conventional corporate planning and beyond three-year strategy exercises. These management processes are useful but are not agile enough to deal with really rapid change. The extra step must encourage people everywhere in the business, and at all levels, to be future-oriented in their outlook, spot trends, and create improvement and opportunity from them.

'A focus on the future' means people should know the behavioural and functional capabilities that they must start developing now to be successful in the future. At the top of this list are the capabilities that will enable you to keep pace with the shift to an innovation-based economy, where success comes not just from what you know, but how you use that knowledge to imagine new ways to get work done, solve problems, and create new knowledge. There are several behavioural capabilities that are universally important to 'new world' organizations: problem solving, handling conflict, building relationships, team-working, adapting, learning, being open to new ideas, and leading through influence. Capabilities related to people management are essential for those in roles where they manage others, and future-oriented thinking is a must for those in the C-Suite.

I believe also that effort must be made to look ahead at the functional capabilities the business will need. The IBM C-Suite Report (IBM, 2012) finds that 'bombarded by change, most organizations simply cannot envision the functional capabilities needed two or three years from now...'. I disagree with this idea. Although this discussion has highlighted ambiguity and uncertainty in the environment, we do not stop trying to envisage the future just because it is uncertain. We still do our best to make predictions about the functional (that is, professional/technical/specialist) capabilities that the

FIGURE 4.1 The four-point framework shows the steps to develop your talent and engagement strategy

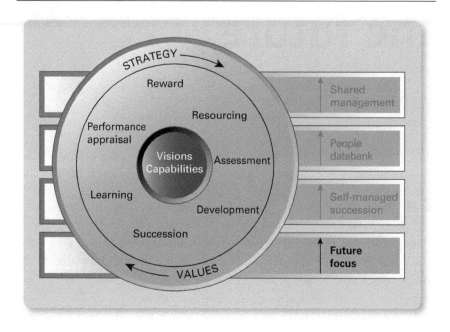

organization is likely to require. The arguments above urge that an appropriate response is to be flexible and able to change direction in a second, entering new markets with new products and adopting new methods and new technologies. But the real world does not always work like that. It often takes time to plan what to do, to develop or hire in skills, design products and arrange for distribution, never mind the time taken to source components and build production lines or entire factories. So a 'focus on the future' must prepare the organization to react quickly, but to plan ahead too.

This first point on the talent framework (Figure 4.1) is created through processes and practices that engage people with the vision and strategic direction. It creates a shared understanding around success factors and what is required to achieve them. It puts the following questions into people's minds, into their actions and into the conversations they have around the organization: Where is the business going? What is the route to get there? What are the trends on the horizon? What are the challenges ahead? How can we take advantage of these? What skills and abilities do we need to meet these? How can we start developing these now? It makes executives in the C-Suite conscious of their role in driving change and organizational transformation.

In this chapter I set out some ideas for achieving this 'focus on the future' from the C-Suite perspective, looking at what leaders must do to create 'a focus on the future', giving examples of practices that have worked well. Finally, I turn to creating a shared understanding of success factors and how to weave these into your strategic talent development processes.

Create a focus on the future from the top

Communicate a clear vision and strategic direction, and live the values

The vision and strategic direction set out what you want to achieve and how you might get there. Without a clear strategic direction people are likely to pursue their own agendas, which can generate conflict, but also lead to them setting easy targets, or setting priorities that are not those the business needs.

In a difficult climate, the lack of a clearly articulated vision and strategic direction gives people the perception that the business's leaders do not know what to do, or are taking the wrong decisions. This leads to loss of trust.

The vision and strategy must, of course, be realistic! I recall the CEO of an international firm, who announced that his strategy was to become the 'world's number one business news and financial information provider'. Staff reacted with scorn. The firm was then ranked third in the world and the distance between them and the top player was vast. The idea of overtaking them was unrealistic.

Andrew Dyckhoff, former CEO and now board-level mentor and coach, believes that the strategic direction should communicate three big ideas, or 'buckets' as Dyckhoff calls them to signify that related and interconnected ideas should be expressed as one concept and 'bucketed' together. Three should be enough to show that the vision is achievable and doable, but not so much as to restrict input and involvement from across the business. It leaves scope for innovation, but pulls everyone in the same direction. It draws on the psychological view that the brain finds it relatively easy to grasp threes. Push that up to four and the brain gets confused about where to look and what to do. The rule of three is especially effective as a communication tool, and so Dyckhoff's approach has the big advantage of aiding the communication of your strategy and encouraging conversations around it.

CASE STUDY

This example illustrates Dyckhoff's approach. The C-Suite executives set the vision for a manufacturing business to become the leading global producer of oil pipe wires within the next five years. They identified three key strategies for achieving this: become a 24/7 operation, adapt the lines to produce an additional shape of wire, and focus on client relationships. This generated discussions, 'think-tanks', workshops, and initiatives of the '*Dragons' Den*' type around the business to flesh out these strategies, make plans and execute them. It focused people's minds and conversations, getting people to think about what they needed to do to meet these goals, and the skills they needed to develop to achieve them.

CASE STUDY

Siemens is a leading global engineering and technology company, providing innovative solutions to help tackle the world's major challenges across the key sectors of energy, infrastructure & cities, industry and healthcare. It employs over 400,000 employees worldwide and had global revenues of €78 billion in 2012.

Siemens has identified four megatrends that must be addressed in the coming years if the world economy is to move towards a more sustainable future: demographic change, urbanization, globalization and climate change. Siemens has for several years now been realigning its business activities around these megatrends, which provide the long-term focus of the company.

Megatrends are long-term processes of transformation with a broad scope and a dramatic impact. They are considered to be powerful factors, which shape future markets. There are three characteristics in which megatrends differ from other trends: they have a much longer time horizon, extending over decades; they have an extensive reach into all areas of politics, society and the economy; and their impact is intense. Megatrends have become a vital component of the strategic direction for Siemens.

Sometimes, a vision might be more of a philosophy: something intangible that sets the tone. Sir Alex Ferguson, the manager of Manchester United football team, has a clear 'vision' of what playing for the club should signify. Ferguson's 'absolute belief in hard work is something that defines the club. Ferguson has long possessed an intuitive understanding of motivation.

By constantly emphasizing the possibility of personal transformation, he has built a club where hard work is not merely centre-stage but embedded within the DNA. As the great man put it: "Every minute spent coasting is a minute wasted"' (Walsh, 2011).

The personal examples of a leader can send very important and powerful messages to the members of an organization, particularly if such actions are ethical and consistent. People in the organization do not only listen to the leader, they also watch what he or she does.

Influence and control, using a 'light touch'

We have already discussed how the old 'command and control' styles and structures do not work effectively any more. Some of it is still required but, in general, management needs to be more 'light touch'. Perhaps 'influence and control' is a more appropriate term. This sets the direction but leaves your people to shape it, and to provide input into how it might be achieved. It influences rather than tells them what to do. It identifies key control factors that help measure performance. Take the example of the museum/academic institution that over the past two years has had three top-level vacancies all of which have been filled through external appointments. This is a world-class institution employing people who are at the top of their respective fields. It seems impossible to think that these roles could not be filled internally. The museum director consults the data (Chapter 7) and finds that the highest staff turnover levels are, in fact, at the middle levels. She notes that career development is not well rated on the employee survey. She decides to use influence from the top to set the tone and direction on this. She asks heads of department to submit succession plans, and fixes meetings with each head to discuss these plans. She asks questions about each of the individuals on the plan, delving into their experience, their skills, their aspirations, and the development opportunity being opened to them. Her questions stimulate thinking and action. She takes advantage of 'corridor conversations' to check how plans are going, but diarizes a formal follow-up meeting for six months' time. She gives no direction, but her interest spawns a whole range of practices, and also changes mindsets. She can consult the data to keep check on progress.

Let's consider this in relation to strategic talent development.

Putting people on the agenda

As we have discussed, the business environment is at a transformational inflection point where people and performance issues have become central to how we meet the challenges of rapid change.

We usually create strategic plans driven by a market analysis, and the organization of people resources to meet that plan is worked out later. Moreover, it is often believed that people management just happens, like refilling the drinks machines. If, on the contrary, we treat our people and their skills (both those they have now and those they can develop) as a strategic resource, then this may completely change our thinking. Instead of approaching strategy by saying, for instance, that we are an aero engine manufacturer with factories and research facilities that can do X, Y and Z, we start from saying that we have, embodied in our people, these capabilities A, B and C. The end result may be to end up at the same place as through the more conventional approach, but it is more likely to open up our thinking to new opportunities and to identify, early on, where we need to develop capabilities.

How do we put 'people' on to the corporate agenda and change the focus to people-management issues? How do we do this in a 'light touch' rather than commanding way? Here is an example that aims to raise people issues to the top of the agenda, driven from the top.

Create a process at the top

Alongside their other business planning inputs, this business gets its unit heads to submit an annual 'strategic people agenda' to the Group CEO and Group HR director. This sets out the people priorities for the unit in areas such as organization design, succession risks, critical talent pools including diversity, building technical and leadership capability, and employee engagement. The business head and HR business partner[1] report on the state of play in these areas, and discuss plans to address gaps or shortcomings, or put forward strategies to meet future business needs. This presents an opportunity for them to be challenged on each aspect by the CEO and HR director, who hold them accountable for achieving their goals, in just the same way as they are held accountable for other business results. They must also make specific commitments regarding the development of talent and show their plans for talent movement. They must demonstrate explicitly how talent moves are aligned with the business strategy. For example, if they propose growth for their business, they are expected to show that they have the talent or can acquire the talent to support that growth. Business heads must show clear links between their agenda and the global business goals.

Top-level conversations such as these set the tone, as well as the agenda. They inspire business heads to go back to their business units and engage their direct reports in similar conversations and then spread practices about talent and performance around the business. A programme such as the one described here can also help create a global, one-company approach, as it focuses on high-level goals and creates a clear, global way of doing things, while leaving scope for local adaptation. The business impact can be significant, as such an approach potentially leads to a consistent brand promise that is clear to all stakeholders, especially customers.

What people at the top pay attention to – including how they allocate budgets and resources – is a big influence over practice and behaviour. The fact that the CEO in this example pays attention to the people agenda, discusses it, and seeks feedback about it is more influential than any policy in any handbook, or any operational report in a bundle of papers.

Make sure your practices transmit consistent messages

Messages must be consistent both to avoid confusion and also to make them more powerful through reinforcement. The best way to guarantee consistency is to mobilize people around a core vision that identifies what the future looks like, and around values that set the tone. This unites and enthuses the team and sets boundaries. Use your values and your visions as a reference point. Refer to them when you are communicating your talent strategy. Also refer to them when making decisions about how to implement initiatives. For example, in the ABC Engineering case study in the next chapter, one of the visions of the organization was to break down the prevalence of people working within their functional divisions, and to encourage better collaboration and teamworking across the firm. We took this as our guide when deciding to create an internal coaching cadre to help implement personal development planning. The idea was for these coaches to work with someone from a different division to support them in drawing up their plans. This started dialogue and cooperation across functions.

Visions and values are work in progress: they must be aspirational and achievable, but they must also be constantly evolving and adapting to the changing environment. For this reason, they must always be in the consciousness, subject to regular dialogue and review, discussed openly, and referenced through different initiatives.

CASE STUDY

KPMG's award-winning 'BraveBanana' initiative is one such example. It is a crowdsourcing tool, which they describe:

> *Clients share a challenge with us, we place it on our network and invite our staff to contribute. We then share their brilliant insights and different ideas with our clients. Everyone joins KPMG with the capacity to be both creative and innovative. We believe in a future where creativity and innovation is the norm. We believe in giving everyone the chance to use their creativity throughout their time at work. We believe in enabling everyone to learn about and engage in client engagements across the firm. BraveBanana influences how the future firm will be shaped.*

Communicate hard, tap into networks, and start conversations

What people are talking about across the organization has a significant impact on behaviour and on results. Create opportunities and processes for people to input into and shape the strategy, discuss and debate what is happening and how to make change go a bit faster. Soliciting views from the ground up and reshaping the approach based on opinion and reaction is a key way to gain ownership of strategic change.

Start conversations that enable the development of new shared meanings of the logic of the changes, and new agreements about how people will work together to accomplish something new. Empower people to interact with the outside world so they scan the horizon and identify future business challenges, and how to work towards these. Create formal and informal networking opportunities so people cross-fertilize their ideas, build on them with others, and think ahead about the skills they will need and how to develop them. Networks seed ideas and turn them into practical applications.

Dialogue helps employees understand the purpose of change, understand their role and have the opportunity to redesign how they work in order to deliver value. Make sure communication is two-way, and always respond. Don't let people's queries, efforts or ideas fall into a black hole. Identify key people, or groups of people, who can champion your change and act as role models and opinion formers. Where significant change is required, give people time to make the change their own. People at the top must remember they have been working on the change for longer than everyone else so they must give others time to catch up emotionally as well as intellectually.

Create formal opportunities to engage people in planning the route and doing some 'blue sky' thinking

Inspired by the popular television series, where people pitch their business ideas in order to secure investment finance from a panel of venture capitalists, initiatives of the *Dragons' Den* type are often used by businesses that want to encourage innovation from their employees. If the idea is accepted, the employee or employees are given a budget and a deadline within which to develop the idea further.

Away-days or retreats are successful for getting people to leave behind their natural focus on the day-to-day and to exchange ideas and make plans. Most commonly, however, they are used to reflect on the previous year, and project its outcomes forward to the next. That does not focus on the future. It simply assumes that the past will continue into that future. It will not. Next year is not far enough into the future. Use these sessions, instead, to engage people in developing the longer-term strategic plan: do not structure them. Think about broad issues. What does five years from now look like, or ten years? What are the trends? What are the big new ideas and the possible sudden shifts to a whole new business model?

Harness social media

Social media technology provides a tool for firms to engage large numbers of employees in developing strategy and decision making, and for brainstorming ideas. Infosys is a large consulting, engineering, and outsourcing firm based in India, with 150,000 employees working from 64 offices and 68 development centres around the world. Using a collective-intelligence portal, they involved some 56,000 employees in a strategy discussion. In today's global enterprises, it is difficult for employees across the enterprise to interact physically. This can lead to a lack of sharing of ideas or expertise across the enterprise, missed business opportunities and duplication of effort. New collaboration platforms such as Microsoft Sharepoint or Salesforce Chatter – a sort of Facebook meets Twitter for companies – make it easy for people to network and work on joint projects within a firm, and for management to see who is doing what with whom, as well as engaging people in dialogue around strategy, or strategic issues (*The Economist*, 2011).

Drive organizational transformation

The points I make throughout this book apply equally to organizational evolution or to creating complete organizational transformation. Most of my examples have been set in the context of evolution, but the following case study, from Guardian News & Media, sets the ideas in the context of transformation.

One of the challenges to an organization taking a new direction is how to motivate and engage those in the legacy part of the business. They are needed to continue that area but probably perceive that it, and their roles, might be losing some of their former glory. To deal successfully with this challenge, it is important to retrain people, involve them in the changes, and give them the opportunity to influence how they are achieved. Communication is critical, and conscious efforts must be made to keep motivating people in these roles, while recruiting and integrating new people with the skills you require. Handling redundancies sensitively and supporting people to make changes are also essential (Chapter 9).

Guardian News & Media – publishers of the *Guardian,* the *Observer* and guardian.co.uk – is currently going through such a transformation. In June 2011, it announced plans to become a digital-first organization, placing open journalism on the web at the heart of its strategy. This means 'moving beyond the newspaper, shifting focus, effort and investment towards digital' (guardian.co.uk, 2011).

Alison Hall is Director of Change at GNM. She has previously managed change there, but this time she says the techniques of previous programmes are no longer viable because of the scale, complexity and type of change. While some people may feel uncertain of their future and fear possible loss of status and opportunity, they are also apprehensive of the heavy financial losses that the newspapers have been making. Yet different parts of the organization experience change in different ways, and at different times. Everything must therefore be more fluid and agile to deal more effectively with such nuances. So you need to keep your ear to the ground and be able to respond quickly. Your strongest communication channels may not be the formal ones. You must also know the informal networks, and how to access them. So much now is viral and social. People use discussion boards, Twitter and other social media more naturally than even in the recent past. These media allow you to tap into the zeitgeist of what's going on now, and how effectively you do that determines how effectively you can keep people engaged.

The internal conversations are changed through formal communication channels, such as the daily editorial meetings, which start by looking at what's happening on the web. Even the GNM head office building at King's Cross plays a part: it was designed to facilitate not just formal meetings but informal 'corridor' conversations. As people move around the building, paths tend to cross so that 'chance meetings' happen frequently. The telephone system is structured to link everyone easily, including people in the United States, who are on the same virtual switchboard. And finally, the CEO makes a point of not remaining fixed in a bounded office but walks around a great deal and has conversations with many different people.

GNM has been working towards a digital future for some time, with a range of initiatives designed to develop skills, products and ways of working towards a new paradigm. It has, for example, been encouraging people to develop versatility in writing skills so that they can write for digital media as well as for print. As the illustration in Chapter 2 showed, they were early adopters of the model of 'open or citizen journalism'. Along with most other newspapers, they publish breaking news first online, and guardian.co.uk, GNM's digital website, does not just replicate the newspapers but carries web-only work from its own staff. There are other initiatives too, such as a series of lunchtime sessions, 'Let's talk digital', which aim to spark interest and enthusiasm for some aspect of digital or social media, for example encouraging adoption of Twitter. As Hall says: 'Once you can light that spark, then you can benefit from people's interest and their self-motivation to become experts. Many of the initiatives follow this process of igniting an initial spark and then enabling people to pursue it for themselves.' One example is 'hack days' where people who come up with a promising idea are given a couple of days to work on it, and then present it to their team or to higher levels of management. GNM is encouraging a 'bottom-up' approach to innovation, giving people the space and freedom to produce and work on ideas and then, if they are successful, move them into the mainstream. These examples illustrate retraining that only partly uses conventional training courses. Most of the development of skills is achieved by creating an environment that provides people with learning opportunity.

GNM has a long tradition of being hugely consultative, open and very democratic: it communicates strategy, holds updates, and discussion sessions and staff briefings; but, as Hall says, you must strike a balance because people want to know that you have a strategic direction, are decisive, have everything under control and know what you are doing. There comes a point where people do not want further discussion and consultation, they want decisions to be made, and to get on with making things happen.

In a significant business transformation, you must recognize power shifts, consider where that power lies within the organization and, where appropriate, redistribute and rebalance it to suit the new ways you want the business to work. In GNM's case, this means getting the right power balance between the editorial and development teams.

For GNM the audience is at the heart of what it does and its particular transformation is changing the conversations around the organization so that people are discussing and building on each other's ideas, such as how to grow, deepen and retain an audience receptive to *Guardian* and *Observer* content. The brand is central too, so they seek to identify ways of developing and delivering content that will strengthen the relationship with the brand to encourage visits and keep people on the website longer.

One of the big cultural changes required of this business transformation is to get people to accept that it is ok to fail. When a daily newspaper goes to print you have just one chance, and have to get it right; but with digital, you can try new ideas and take a risk. The organization has developed mechanisms to allow people to experiment and to encourage them to do so. All proposals are given attention, though they must have a strong rationale to move to trial; then they are assessed at different stages of implementation to identify what needs to be adjusted, developed or abandoned. Error time must be minimized, and, of course, people must not be penalized for trying something that doesn't work. It is easier for strongly argued proposals to float to the top than used to be the case and many different projects are being trialled.

It is not just a pipeline of ideas and initiatives that is under constant review; roles and responsibilities are too, as is the strategy. The top team used to present a five-year plan and sit back. Now this is constantly updated. There are also opportunities for staff to pose questions or make comments on the plan, with or without identifying themselves. This helps improve communication but also allows fresh eyes to critique the plans.

As part of their plans, GNM has set up a digital newsroom in the United States, where guardian.co.uk already had around 11 million unique users reading their content. Part of their strategy is to target further growth there, where they believe there is a demand for the sort of open, internationalist, digital journalism that guardian.co.uk has been pioneering. The opening of another digital newsroom in Sydney further develops their international growth and gives true 24/7 global coverage.

One of the advantages of a digital set-up in a new place is that, whereas the UK is restrained, either consciously or unconsciously, by the legacy of print, this does not apply in the new offices. The people there are able to think in terms of a digital platform all the time, without the constant image of a printed newspaper. The plan is to leverage this relative freedom from preconceptions, to spread new thinking and practices from the United States and also Australia to the UK that will, in time, gradually lessen those legacy restraints and enable the geographically separate locations to work seamlessly. There is already a strong two-way flow of communication across these two offices, sometimes in person but mainly through the use of communications technology. GNM has made it a priority to immerse the people in the new offices in their brand values. A strong brand identity that staff and audience associate with in the UK is one of the group's strengths.

Key lessons

Objectives in the example are to:

- engage people in the transformation;
- maintain existing operations during transformation;
- achieve appropriate cultural changes.

Tools and approaches used include:

- Constant open communication.
- Strike a balance between consultation and leadership.
- Achieve the right power balance for the new order.
- Physical displacement between the new and the old may help but is very specific to this example.
- Encourage people to ask questions, critique plans, input ideas.
- Change the conversation around the business so people are discussing the new plans positively, and building on each other's ideas.
- Encourage people to put forward innovative ideas. This requires appropriate mechanisms to consider every suggestion, encourage risk, support new ideas and efforts, and not penalize failure.

Create a shared understanding of success

So far in this chapter, I have looked at the key things leaders must do to generate a 'focus on the future'. I would now like to turn to process – how you do it. The value of following the four-point framework is that it guides you through the process of creating a talent strategy – that is, connected activities that lead in a coherent direction and conform to our vision for the enterprise. That raises the question: connected through what? In the previous chapter, in explaining the 'focus on the future' concepts, I gave the example of how a financial services business might identify the key functional and behavioural capabilities that people must master if they are to meet the business challenges ahead. It is these capabilities that your activities for selection, development, career and succession planning must connect to. Although this is not very different from current, common practice – where the word 'competencies' is more commonly used – my approach is to use only behavioural capabilities that can be observed, and measured. Often competency profiles include skills, knowledge and sometimes values that are open to differing interpretations and that cannot be observed and measured. With my approach, you can connect a range of assessment and self-assessment tools to the capabilities, and this offers better opportunity for learning and development, and for building understanding of the skills that lead to success. The result is to drive the organization in a coherent direction to develop the capabilities that it will need in the future to carry out its strategies and meet its goals.

There is persuasive evidence that the competency/capability approach works well in practice. The HR Best Practices Report 2012 (CRF Institute, 2012) reveals that:

- 100 per cent of the Best in Class Top Employers provide their staff with access to competencies required for specific jobs;
- 90 per cent of Best in Class Employers have defined competencies for all job levels;
- transparency towards employees regarding competencies required for different job levels has a positive effect on both succession rate as well as turnover.

How to identify future-focused capabilities

The process of identifying these capabilities is as significant as the capabilities themselves, as it is this process that helps put thinking about future challenges into conversations and practices.

It can help to identify capabilities that will be required if people are led through a structured conversation that leads from business planning issues through to their implications for capabilities. In an adaptable, agile business culture, people at all levels are forward-looking and proactive. They anticipate the big business trends and take short-term decisions with the

FIGURE 4.2 Mind the gap

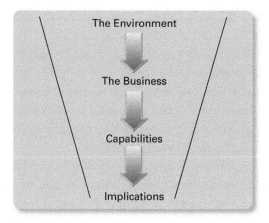

longer term in mind. It is possible to encourage these behaviours by utilizing the normal business planning cycle. This may require a slight shift
in emphasis at the point when people are setting objectives for their next
performance review period, or at the time when workforce or succession
planning is carried out. Conversations at these times and in this context
should look further ahead than the next year, and should stimulate people
to consider what is going on in the outside world. Where will your future
sources of revenue come from? How will you keep close to your customers?
What changes do you perceive in your customers? How will you innovate?
How will you take advantage of new technologies? Follow questions such
as these with questions that relate to capabilities. What will you have to do
differently as a result? What do you need to learn? How can you acquire
that learning? Conversations at these times generate insights and challenge
current thinking, so that constantly reviewing different future scenarios, and
constantly identifying how to do things differently and better, becomes part
of the natural way of thinking for people at all levels.

The points to consider, at this stage, will vary from organization to
organization but suggested questions are set out in the Appendix (Mind the
gap). These, while not exhaustive, are the most likely to be applicable to all
businesses. The aim is to stimulate thinking, but also to collect information
that will enable you to identify the gap between current and future capability requirements (Figure 4.2).

This thinking about future needs and capabilities is a shared responsibility where the front-end manager's manager may be involved and maybe
the divisional director and the HR department.... The point is to accept

that whoever else may be involved, it is the role of each manager and others, especially professional and specialist staff, to be thinking forward, based on what they know of the organization's visions and plans and about the environment. Each must think about the capabilities that will be required within their sphere of influence, working to ensure that these are developed so they are available when needed.

Managers should also give thought to succession issues and identify the capabilities required for roles and then consider who might develop these and how. It may also be wise to identify who has scarce skills or knowledge and how they may pass these on and to whom.

This is not a one-off conversation to help develop the talent strategy but should become a regular process to stimulate people to keep identifying changes on the horizon. The HR director is the ideal person to facilitate this process of conversations, but also consider a business development executive or an external adviser.

CASE STUDY

The following shows the approach taken by the BBC to ensure people keep up with predictable trends.

The BBC's Journalism Group is responsible for all the corporation's news and current affairs output on television, radio and online. Its College of Journalism was formed in 2005 and is responsible for the design and delivery of learning and training to all BBC journalists in the UK and around the world. It teaches every aspect of journalism: craft skills like writing and storytelling; the technical skills required to operate in a digital, multi-platform world; social media and the web; and ethics, values and law. The learning is delivered through a wide range of media, including face-to-face training, one-to-one coaching, a programme of events and an extensive website. All learning interventions are guided by the BBC's five editorial values: Truth and Accuracy; Impartiality; Independence; the Public Interest; and Accountability to audiences.

The BBC has always lived with uncertainty over the licence fee but there are now additional uncertainties, especially the constantly evolving impact of new technologies. As a result, it is difficult to predict what the BBC's television, radio and online news departments will look like in the future. How will they be structured? What demarcation lines, if any, will there be between different media, or different locations? Will the programmes with the biggest following or influence be on television, or online? What will happen if the Corporation's funding is reduced? What external partnerships might the BBC form? It may be hard to answer those questions now, but it is possible to predict that, whatever the answers, the BBC will be required to do more with less; there will be more sharing between the World Service, television and radio and the News website too; there is also likely to be more collaboration with staff increasingly required to work across different media. So, it may not be possible yet to formulate the BBC's long-term strategy, but it is possible to determine the capabilities that will be required in the long term, and given the numbers involved – there are 8,000 people across these departments – a range of training, coaching and online learning initiatives have been put in place to enable people to start developing them. These initiatives also aim to change perceptions about career paths, and what are regarded as the most prestigious assignments, so that people will recognize the value of, say, building up an online following as a way of reaching a big audience.

The BBC's College of Journalism runs coaching programmes in London, internationally and around the BBC centres producing dedicated news and current affairs output across the UK. Coaching programmes, run for freelancers as well as staff, cover writing, presentation and voice. The focus of coaching at BBC Newsgathering has adapted over the years to keep pace with change, and one of the concerns now is to develop a multi-skilled culture, where people are able to switch confidently from presenting on world television to domestic networks, from regional breakfast television to a late night broadcast, or to radio news, or write for online. The skills required for each are different and require considerable preparation and training. The College tries to track each journalist and prepares them for different challenges, and helps them build their skills incrementally.

Identifying functional capabilities for the future

Let us return to the point about whether you can identify functional capabilities that will be needed in future. As you develop the conversations and the thinking that is all about focusing on the future, it is likely that some emerging functional capabilities will be identified, such as illustrated by the BBC example above, where it is obvious that digital skills will be needed. These particular skills take time to develop, so offering people opportunities to start now helps everyone.

Key points

Create a focus on the future through:

- Communicating a clear vision and strategic direction.
- Listen hard, seek ideas from the ground up, and use these to improve on your strategy.

- Employ light-touch control on the key levers of power to achieve your goals and your vision.
- Communicate your critical messages frequently and consistently.
- The issues that the top team pay attention to communicate their importance more than any other communication.
- Use the power of social media and networking inside and outside the organization.
- Use structured conversations to lead from business planning issues through to their implications for capabilities.

The behavioural capabilities identified through these conversations will form the foundation of self-managed succession, which is the topic of the next two chapters.

Note

1 HR Business Partner is the title commonly given to people who provide direct support to people in the business areas.

Self-managed succession: Learning

The behavioural and functional capability models discussed in the last chapter form the basis of self-managed succession (Figure 5.1). The capabilities the business needs will have been identified from internal conversations about trends, about what is happening on the horizon and about the success factors for the business. These capabilities will guide your recruitment and the development of your people across the business, providing a route map for getting to the desired destination.

While the organization must be aware of the critical capabilities it will need and will be encouraging its people to develop them, it will also support people to gain a wider range of capabilities, and to continually renew and refresh these. As Lynda Gratton and others have pointed out, the pace of change will be so rapid that people may have to acquire a new expertise every few years if they want to be part of the lucrative market for scarce talent. She calls this process 'serial mastery' (Gratton, 2011).

Two concepts that people must understand if they are to achieve 'serial mastery', and which must be embedded in your practices, concern learning and self-awareness. I start this chapter by considering these, before turning to the key practices of self-managed succession. The ultimate aim of self-managed succession is to align individual and organization development, and create movement of people, skills and knowledge through the organization. This covers a range of disciplines, including learning, development and career planning. For ease of reference, I split the discussion into two chapters: here I cover the ideas that make strategic talent development inclusive and 'self-managed', as they focus on learning and personal development opportunity. I give examples of innovative electronic practices that are still emerging, but also consider the latest uses of traditional approaches. These

FIGURE 5.1   The four-point framework shows the steps to develop your talent and engagement strategy

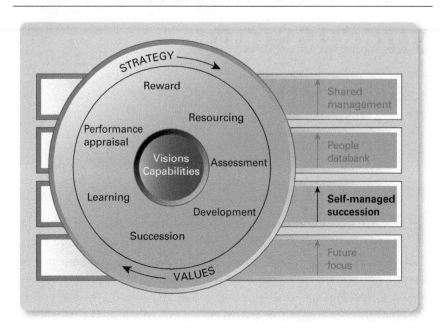

practices address, at least partially, the key issue of how to energize people in today's depressed economic climate. In the next chapter, I look at the practices that create 'succession' through the organization; that is, career development, including long-term development and international mobility.

The importance of learning

Adapting to change requires sophisticated learning ability, to rapidly acquire new, or modify existing, skills, attitudes, knowledge and values. Equally, this might mean the ability to unlearn; that is, to let go of something we currently do, which we may hold dear. How can we best foster this learning agility?

- Although we learn from experience, this doesn't just happen, it requires conscious effort and reflection. Learning at work is, therefore, something that we consciously choose to do.

- There is a difference between 'knowing what', 'knowing why' and 'knowing how'. This suggests a hierarchy, which starts with knowing what you need to learn and why it matters, rising through an understanding of your starting point (that is, how competent you may or may not be), through to being able to apply the new learning. Even at this last 'knowing how' stage, there are several steps. Take learning to drive a car as an example. You pass your test and remove the 'L' plates, but you must make a conscious effort to think about what you are doing for some time, until you suddenly realize that you can do it unconsciously. So it is with many of the things we need to learn at work

- Learner motivation matters: many people are capable of acquiring performance-enhancing skills but do not because they have no interest or incentive.

- Individuals often learn from each other in groups, by asking for advice or guidance, or by sharing ideas. This is commonly how IT skills are learned, but other expertise is acquired in the same way. Indeed, for some 'new economy' jobs the most valued skills are entirely self-directed. The organization's role then becomes one of facilitation – ensuring that there are appropriate learning opportunities and support. We can also see the value of a good 'boss' who supports learning by opening learning opportunities, provides support for reflection and feedback, and gives recognition.

Learning requires motivation, reflection, repetition and recognition

This analysis lends support to several key ideas of strategic talent development, especially those surrounding the importance of motivation to learn, which comes from seeing how it will help you achieve your own, as well as business, goals. Equally important is recognizing that mastering new behavioural skills does not happen overnight. It requires support to reflect on what you have learned and what you will do with this learning, it requires repetition until it becomes habitual, and it requires recognition to reinforce the value of acquiring the skills. (Think of this as the three Rs – reflection, repetition, recognition). I discuss these ideas further in Chapter 9, but it is important to have them in mind when considering other issues in this and the following chapters.

The 70/20/10 formula for learning

This concept is encapsulated in the 70/20/10 formula (Figure 5.2), which describes how learning occurs:

- **70 per cent** from actual and on-the-job experiences, tasks and problem solving – this is the most important aspect of any learning and development plan;

FIGURE 5.2 Formula for learning

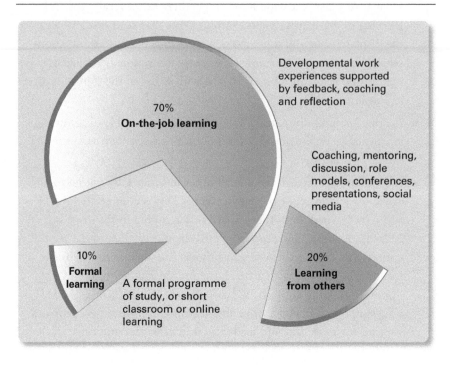

70%
On-the-job learning

Developmental work
experiences supported
by feedback, coaching
and reflection

Coaching, mentoring,
discussion, role
models, conferences,
presentations, social
media

10%
**Formal
learning**   A formal programme
of study, or short
classroom or online
learning

20%
**Learning
from others**

- **20 per cent** from learning from others, for example through feedback and from observing and working with role models, or from coaching and mentoring;
- **10 per cent** from formal training.

This formula is based on the philosophy that the most effective way to learn and develop a new skill or behaviour is to apply and practise it on the job and in real work situations. This is particularly good news in straightened times, as it shows that the best development does not need financial commitment.

The 70/20/10 formula of learning was first developed by M McCall, RW Eichinger and MM Lombardo at the Center for Creative Leadership (Lombardo and Eichinger, 2007) and is widely used in organizations to drive practices of continuous learning. It is especially helpful for encouraging people away from an over-reliance on training to a more holistic approach to learning. It also underlines the importance of opening opportunity for stretching and challenging work experiences, which is a key attribute of self-managed succession.

CASE STUDY

KPMG's 'Smart Development' programme is open to all graduates and assistant managers on a self-selection basis. The aim is to invest in people's potential, especially graduate entrants from one to six years in. Using the 70/20/10 formula, the programme uses minimal formal learning. It recognizes that people have different expectations, and empowers them to generate their own opportunities. It gives people exposure to the experiences that will help them learn quickly, including developing networks which turn into long-term relationships, often with people at 'C-Suite' level.

Garcia Williamson, KPMG's UK Head of Talent and Learning and Development, believes that this programme increases engagement, and improves performance and retention. As would be expected, it is the high performers and high-potential people who are the hungriest to take advantage of what is on offer.

The importance of self-awareness and of understanding behaviours

I believe passionately that the more complete your insight into your performance, the more likely that you will understand your strengths and preferences and how to leverage these, and, similarly, your weaknesses and how to compensate for them. Self-awareness is the bedrock for personal development because it permits a comparison of current with desired capabilities and therefore points the way to what needs to be done to achieve those goals. It is how people can become the best they can be.

Self-awareness focuses on the importance of behaviours more than underlying personality. This is for two related reasons: firstly, because the impact we have on others is a result of how we behave, and secondly, because our achievements result from how we behave. For example: suppose I become aware that my tendency to make quick decisions, while a benefit sometimes, can lead others to think I don't care about their opinions. In turn, this perception leads to poor communication within my team and reduced engagement with me and with the organization we all work for. Through understanding my behaviour and the impact it has on others, I work to seek out others' views as much as possible, before making decisions, and find that my relationships with colleagues improve and that we become a more effective team.

Turning to achievements: suppose I am a brilliant marketing manager, but my brilliant ideas are not, on their own, what lead to success. I succeed because, added to those ideas, I can: work hard, communicate my ideas and persuade others of their worth, work with a team so that their work inspires me, and then work with a team to execute those ideas. These are all to do with behaviours. The genius alone in a room who creates a revolutionary change is largely a myth because, with very few exceptions, we need sources of interaction to fuel our ideas and to be able to communicate them and persuade people of their worth.

We can help people become more self-aware of their impact through insightful feedback as well as diagnostic tools and processes that have this purpose. These bring other benefits too. Most are based on a model that categorizes or explains the theory on which the instrument is based. 'A model helps us understand complex issues and provides a framework for planning or reviewing practices, or to direct behaviour or practice' (Sloman, 2011). For example, many give you an understanding not only of yourself, but also of other people and their styles and ways of operating. This helps you understand what others bring to the table and usually leads to greater tolerance and better teamworking as you recognize the value that differences in behaviours bring.

There are many such instruments that are helpful for understanding specific contexts, such as teamworking, selling, negotiating, handling conflict, learning, leadership and so on. They are beneficial for use in training and coaching, or for more informal learning. They are generally fun to use too, though it is important not to use too many, as this just becomes confusing. I recommend integrating one self-awareness model into self-managed succession, without making it compulsory, leaving scope for using others according to circumstance or personal choice. The self-awareness model you use should reference your behavioural capabilities.

Integrated self-managed succession

Returning to the process of developing a talent strategy, the next point on the framework is using a self-managed succession suite of initiatives that integrates with the behavioural frameworks discussed at the end of the last chapter (Figure 5.3). This process offers people a choice of methods for learning, for becoming more self-aware, and for developing their performance and their careers (Figure 5.4). It is likely that you will also have a wider portfolio of learning and development initiatives that target other, more specific needs, but it is the core suite that we consider here.

FIGURE 5.3 This diagram shows the activities that should connect to the organization's behavioural capability frameworks

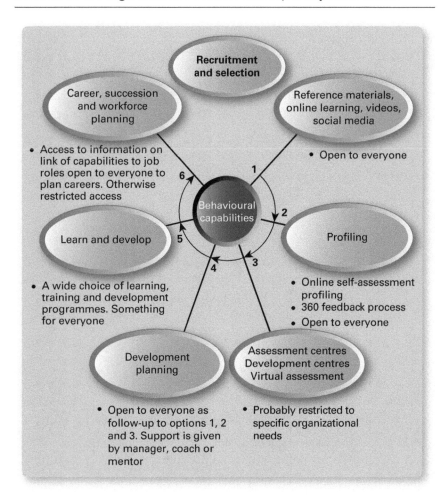

Many of the learning and development initiatives that comprise a core programme will be familiar and well understood, but nonetheless some explanation of them is required, in order to convey new techniques. Most of these new techniques are being driven by technology, which is creating exciting possibilities.

Online profiling

New technology is leading to the emergence of instruments that help people assess their strengths and interests, and help them match those with the

FIGURE 5.4 This diagram shows self-managed succession from the individual's viewpoint. What is available to me? How will it help me?

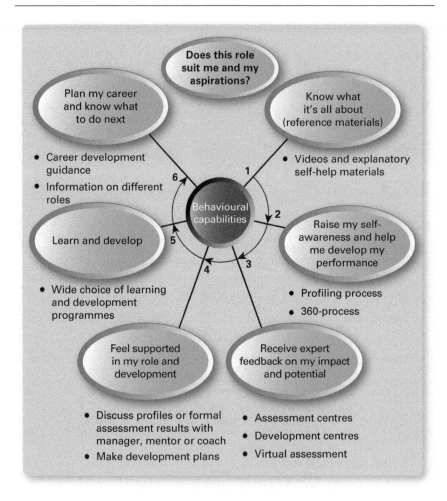

requirements of different jobs in the organization. The practical simplicity of an online tool enables you to include large numbers of people relatively easily and cheaply. In fact, such a tool meets many of the requirements of strategic talent development:

- It is suitable for everyone, and therefore matches our inclusive approach. It helps people gain insights about themselves in relation to organizational success factors, and it helps them plan their development. This is highly motivating.

- It focuses people on key organizational behaviours. This helps them build the skills the business needs.

CASE STUDY

KPMG has an extensive range of learning and development initiatives for different purposes, including diversity and inclusion, aimed specifically at women. They use development centres, 360-degree feedback, coaching and mentoring, structured conversations around performance, and panels or assessment centres for promotion to director or partner level. Promotion to partner level is handled globally, using assessment centre techniques to benchmark skills and abilities. All initiatives are built around and reinforce KPMG's values, brand attributes, and international capability frameworks.

Where capabilities are discussed repeatedly, people get a much better understanding of behaviours and the clusters of characteristics they contain. This leads to better assessment of people, which is helpful for allocation of roles, composition of teams, appointments to new roles, and also to better performance assessment and allocation of reward.

I do not wish to promote any one product, not least because the particular product matters less than how it is used to create an integrated system and offer learning to many. However, we need to understand an integrated system and its benefits through an example, so what follows is based on my experiences of ABC Engineering where we used Iperquest®, a tool that I and my colleagues use extensively. This is an online behavioural assessment process that provides an indication of how a person is likely to behave and communicate in a work role. It is based on a proprietary model of behavioural effectiveness,[1] which comprises 22 capabilities, offering a wide choice that can be matched either to existing competency frameworks, or directly to business challenges to create frameworks that are appropriate for different roles, or different levels in the enterprise.

The capabilities contained within this particular model relate to the mental processes and behaviours that underpin successful performance: how you think, relate to others, do things, manage your emotions and handle change. Because they are fundamental qualities they can be related to how they affect an individual at work and offer causal links between behaviours and performance effectiveness, helping you understand how behaving in a certain way affects the results you achieve. This model has been developed and refined as an assessment process for more than 35 years. The behaviours are instantly recognizable, and therefore understandable as some that we use constantly in our work. They are also, of course, observable and measurable, meeting the requirements discussed in the last chapter.

CASE STUDY   ABC Engineering

ABC Engineering provides a context to illustrate some of the ideas discussed so far in this book. It describes steps taken to identify future capability needs, align these with visions, values and business strategy, and 'listen to the business' to identify business challenges.

We took as our focus for this programme the board's stated values of openness, transparency and fairness. ABC's chief executive felt strongly that these, which were especially relevant to its external stakeholders, had to be applied internally to employees if they, in turn, were to feel committed to them and deliver them externally. He expressed this through his vision, known fondly through the business as the 'Two-dots philosophy': he wanted everyone in the organization to have a dot representing where they were now in career terms, and one on the horizon, representing where they aspired to be. He regularly referred to this philosophy on formal occasions and in casual conversations, giving a clear message about the importance of personal development.

Our first step was to spend a considerable amount of time 'listening to the business' – by talking to people, particularly at executive and senior management levels, to understand where the business stood, what challenges lay ahead and what it needed to deliver. What do five years or ten years ahead look like for our business, and how is this different from now? Until this point, ABC had relied heavily on achieving its goals simply through assembling a high technical capability, but, going forward, the target was to apply these skills to enable the 400 employees to shift up a gear to tackle the next phase of the business's strategic priorities. To do this, different behaviours would be required and would determine success. So, filling this behavioural gap was a priority for our talent programme. These discussions were useful in addressing other issues, such as getting managers comfortable with the concept of development, having a common language and getting people to define the organization culture.

In these conversations, we also sought to find out what current practices worked well, what didn't, and what would help people meet organizational goals and their own aspirations. Managers' concerns often expressed their need to have people who could perform the capabilities they knew would be needed for the future. Individuals expressed the need for more development opportunities and to build better relationships with their managers. They wanted better-quality feedback and help to map and develop their careers.

In addition to interviewing people, we also reviewed performance appraisal forms, aspirational interview forms and employee survey data. Taken together, several problems became evident: managers did not set goals properly, those they set were inconsistent, they had different ideas of what constituted high performance and they were poor at giving feedback.

From this preparatory work we drew up a comprehensive talent strategy. We had a clear vision and a set of organizational values to keep referring to; we had identified the capability gap that we needed to fill to enable the organization to meet its future business challenges; and we had identified the people processes that needed to be discarded, improved or retained. We also had a clear indication that raising the quality of conversations between managers and staff was a priority, and we were able to identify indicators from the employee survey that we could use to measure and track progress.

ABC had a competency framework that had been used for recruitment but for little else. It was poorly understood within the company and inconsistently interpreted. The head of learning and development was keen to have a framework that could serve various different purposes and that the company could use to integrate some of its people processes. We therefore decided to replace this framework entirely with one based on the Iperquest® capabilities that matched the organization's future challenges.

We then set about identifying the key recruitment, learning, training, development, succession and career management practices to link to these capabilities.

We established the following processes aimed at raising self-awareness.

1 Self-assessment against capabilities

This was made available through the firm's intranet and was accompanied by online self-development materials that people could refer to, or work through either on their own, or by contacting one of the internal coaches who had been specifically trained for this purpose.

None of the processes we offered was compulsory, and the prime purpose of these materials was to offer something to those people who opted out of any of the assessment processes, though the materials were also used to help people follow through on their development plans.

2 Online profiling

We launched the online questionnaire that accompanies the Iperquest® behavioural model. It gave people the opportunity to benchmark themselves against the 'capability set' for their grade, or for a future role to which they aspired. They received a profile that identified strengths and development areas, so this tool was both self-diagnostic and an action planner. It also contained guidance to help users discuss their profiles with their manager.

Let's take Gabriella as an example. One aspect of her profile reveals that she takes a detailed approach to drawing up plans and shows that she prefers to gain a thorough understanding before taking a decision. Relating this to her performance, Gabriella realizes that it explains why she is slow to adapt to change, but also why she takes the responsibility of checking thoroughly to ensure change is well implemented. She can use the profile as a guide for self-study, or as part of a coaching process to develop her behaviours, and can draw on supporting materials on the company's intranet for these purposes. The profile also facilitates Gabriella's conversations with her manager, who can use it to give feedback on her performance, discuss development and identify work opportunities that will enable her to deploy her strengths. By focusing on her strengths, Gabriella's profile has given her more confidence to take on bigger challenges, but also indicates how she might develop her behaviours to tackle them. She can check on the company's intranet to see which capabilities are required for different roles in the organization and plan her development accordingly.

At ABC Engineering, we trained a pool of volunteers from across the business as feedback coaches to help individuals understand their profile and how to take it forward. This part of the programme not only gave individuals useful personal skills but we were able to encourage cross-functional working that had an impact on the spirit of collaboration – which was very important as the organization operated under a matrix management structure. The coaches became ambassadors for the processes we introduced and were instrumental in embedding what we had done. The support of the top team also had an enormous impact: making the exercise real. In many companies, such programmes might be introduced with a memo encouraging managers to be coaches and encouraging colleagues to support one another but then nothing happens, and when senior executives hold performance reviews with their staff they never mention these things, just focus on the technical. In this case, through getting active involvement at a senior level, we got them to ask important questions, such as 'How are you getting on as a feedback coach?' and 'What is it doing for you?'

Receiving their profiles raised self-awareness and was the start of the development journey for many people. It also created a shared understanding of standards of performance across the business.

The organization also introduced a range of training and development programmes that related to the capabilities that were being focused on. These included an online campus with materials for either self-study or peer coaching. In some cases existing training programmes were refocused to better reference the capabilities.

The behavioural capability framework and profiling process aligned individual strengths and development to identified business success factors. People were now aware of the importance of behavioural capabilities and especially which ones would be important to meet future challenges. They became more client-oriented and open to new ideas. The next phase of business development demanded an ability to work with outsource partners, so many people had to develop influencing skills when they had no formal authority to direct or impose decisions. Step one in this process made people aware of what was expected. It raised their self-awareness and also interest.

This approach may not sound very different from what is common practice in many organizations but it has several distinguishing features:

- It focused on a behavioural capability model that was observable and measurable. This brought consistency, which helped people build their understanding of what success looked like.

- Self-assessment and assessment tools that integrated with this model gave people the opportunity to become more self-aware and plan their development.

- The capabilities in the model linked to future business challenges for different roles, so as well as focusing people on the future, it enabled career planning.

- It generated data that we captured for our people databank to help workforce planning.

- It provided a better understanding of the behaviours that are valued by the organization and created a shared language around performance standards.

- It facilitated conversations about performance and careers.

- It contained something for everyone, and so was truly inclusive.

There are many possible ways in which a profiling tool such as Iperquest® can be implemented to address your business issues and promote your values. For instance, I have used it as part of a targeted leadership development programme, or focused on training managers to use the process to develop their coaching style of management, or used it for team coaching where it helps people recognize what each brings to the table and how to benefit from each other's strengths and preferences. At ABC, we used the tool to help build a coaching capability in the organization, as well as to spearhead continuous learning and development and emphasize the firm's cultural aim of driving better peer support and collaboration. As the tool includes a reporting facility, it also fed into our databank information about people's strengths and preferences that we could add to information already collected about future career aspirations.

360-degree feedback

Delivery through the internet has made 360-degree feedback systems easy to run and administer. One reason for its growing use is that, with many organizations having more people than ever working in flexible, project, virtual or matrix teams, many managers have wider spans of control and no direct or complete line of sight over the work of their staff. This creates a void where the manager needs more information to form an accurate picture of performance, and the individual needs a way of getting feedback on how they are performing. 360-degree feedback is a way of filling this void. However, it has drawbacks as well as advantages.

The premise behind 360-degree feedback is that people have to work and achieve results together. Therefore, insight into how your behaviour impacts on others should help you develop your performance and improve your results. Moreover, the people who work closely with an employee see that person's behaviour in settings and circumstances which give a more rounded view of their performance.

Problems with 360-degree feedback

However, a number of fairly recent studies indicate that 360-degree feedback programmes may not always match their promise. John Sullivan, Professor of Human Resource Management at San Francisco State University, says, 'There is no data showing that [360-degree feedback] actually improves productivity, increases retention, decreases grievances or is superior to forced ranking and standard performance appraisal systems' (Sullivan, 1998).

Often, failure results from massive gaps between the organization's business objectives and what 360-degree feedback programmes measure. Competencies are so broad that they are not relevant to the average and they do not pick up on specific interpersonal and cultural problems in the organization at a specific time. Assuring context relevance is not easy and calls for a very different type of competency on the part of the HR professionals and others who are helping companies to use 360-degree feedback. Integrating 360 with the business's core capability model partly resolves this problem, however.

A study of the accuracy of those rating colleagues shows that the length of time that they have known the person has the most significant effect on the accuracy of a 360-degree review. Subjects in the group 'known for one to three years' are the most accurate, followed by 'known for less than one year', followed by 'known for three to five years', with the least accurate being 'known for more than five years' (Eichinger and Lombardo, 2004). So the most accurate ratings come from knowing the person long enough to get past first impressions, but not so long as to begin to generalize favourably. The implication is that misplaced loyalty can stand in the way of honest assessment. Moreover, multi-rater assessments regularly generate conflicting opinions. For example, how are employees to react when their manager gives them negative ratings while feedback from their direct reports and peers is satisfactory? This can be a strength of 360 feedback, enabling someone to reflect on why one group or one person views their behaviour more favourably; but it also results in confusion and people are likely to take away the feedback that suits them rather than gain any development benefit.

Other studies found that each rater group has natural biases. For example, supervisor feedback tends to be based on bottom-line results (are tasks completed on time and well?), technical competence and whether an employee's behaviour draws complaints from clients. By contrast, direct reports base their reviews on factors such as trustworthiness, willingness to involve them in decisions and the interest shown in their professional development. Peers who lack perspective on their colleagues' day-to-day performance tend to focus on leadership potential. Their remarks often reflect opinions or whether the participant has the 'right stuff' to motivate and create a compelling vision for others to follow (Mount, Judge and Scullen, 1998). None of these perspectives is wrong and all are valuable insights in creating a 360-degree view of performance. However, it is important that the person being reviewed, and his or her line manager, understand how the filters used by different groups affect their ratings. The use of 360 to aid development is lost if people are sent their results without the opportunity for an individual debrief or coaching session to help them make sense of these different perceptions and turn them into useful insights.

As Vinson (1996) suggests, there is no way to determine whose feedback is accurate. This has implications for the use of 360-degree feedback and shows that it should not be used as a direct input into appraisal ratings or pay awards.

The best of 360

I have known many people who have instantly picked up on 360 feedback to finesse their behaviour and achieve a better impact. However, it is more common for someone to receive the feedback and not know what to do with it. This comes back to my earlier point that there is a difference between 'knowing what' and 'knowing how'. In some cases, I have known 360 be detrimental to people because it is perceived that they didn't act on the feedback. They are then denied promotion, or good performance ratings, when in fact they didn't change because they didn't know how and weren't given appropriate support. Expert coaching helps people truly benefit from 360 feedback, and it is often a false economy to cut back here.

360 is especially useful when it is part of your integrated suite so that it is one of several self-managed options. A common variant on the usual types of 360-degree feedback is where individuals seek feedback from their colleagues using open questions, such as: 'What should I stop, start or continue doing?' This is an excellent way of gaining more insight into your own performance, and being able to give positive feedback and recognition to others. It requires a positive culture, otherwise it risks being used spitefully.

Assessment and development centres

There is a powerful link between development centres and organizational culture. In 2005 we surveyed the use of development centres in 93 UK organizations, employing between 1,000 and 93,000 employees, and compared these findings with organizations from across Europe. Merger and acquisition, culture change, and reorganization emerged as the key drivers of development centre programmes. Others included the need to replace a 'silo' structure or mentality with a more flexible and global approach to career and personal development. In some cases, large investments were made in development centres to support the business strategy or brand development. Several businesses used the programme to convey a top-down message that encouraged everyone to invest in being a good people manager so that this would be part of the DNA of the organization. Another organization used centres to convey that all employees had a 'right' to receive specific, positive and constructive feedback, which they believed was the key to unleashing talent (The Scala Group and ACE Network, 2005). This survey evidence supports the value of development centres, especially now that new technology is making these easier and cheaper to deliver and take part in.

Despite their name, assessment and development centres are not physical buildings but a series of tests, questionnaires, interactions, role-plays, group case studies, interviews or in-tray exercises. Generally, a trained and qualified assessor will match the participant's performance with the established assessment criteria (behavioural capabilities), providing detailed feedback on strengths and on areas for development. There may be just one person assessed at a time, or a group.

The main difference between assessment and development centres is in the name and the purposes for which they are used. Assessment centres assess suitability for specific jobs. A development centre may use similar assessment tools and techniques but is designed to enable people to identify their career aspirations, develop their capabilities and gain insights about themselves. Assessment centres provide extra information to the selection process, and open areas for exploration with the candidate. Development centres facilitate a joint approach in which the organization and participants collaborate to make career and development plans, or prepare for a career move. This is generally highly motivating for people.

The benefits of development centres

I believe that development centres are particularly suited to our times, where we require people to use capabilities that they have not previously had the opportunity to demonstrate. For example, in today's economic climate business growth is more likely to come from new markets than from traditional ones. Breaking into these 'lands of opportunity' demands different, more entrepreneurial skills. It demands cultural sensitivity, and rapid ability to adapt to different cultures. Do we have these skills internally? Who could develop them quickly, or do we need to look outside? Development centres can provide the answers. They can also show who might be ready now for certain roles, or who might need further development. Thus they provide data for your people databank.

Development centres are also valuable for creating a global mindset and way of doing things, and giving greater awareness of diversity issues.

CASE STUDY

I worked on a global programme with Diesel, the clothing brand. To quote Diesel's Group HR Director: 'This is not about identifying high-flyers, but it is about helping the management team and the company to grow as a team... It is also about giving managers a sense of Diesel's corporate identity and values', the 'Diesel planet' as she put it, 'yet without losing cultural and personal individuality', (Paton, 2006).

CASE STUDY

David Reay, currently Director of Organization Development at Sony Music Entertainment, describes development centres he ran for his former FTSE 100 employer in Asia and the Middle East. Reay notes how cultural differences became clear when the assessors, who were the firm's expatriate senior managers, were required to give feedback to the participants. This showed how Western views, for instance, on the communication and influencing competencies valued being assertive, when in fact the local participants valued 'respectful behaviour, and considering team needs, over individual ones'. This opened dialogue and fostered understanding and appreciation of differences.

Involving managers as assessors gives them greater understanding of organizational capabilities, which they then translate into their own performance, and the way they develop others. It has the added benefits of bringing a business relevance to the process and giving it greater visibility, thus enhancing its worth to participants.

Development centres are fantastic learning experiences, giving opportunity to learn by doing, as well as learn from reflection and from expert feedback. The understanding of capabilities gained from the centres is beneficial to both delegates and assessors. Coming back to my earlier point, they can also help you truly understand the skills of your workforce.

Electronic processes

New technology is having a significant impact on the delivery and content of assessment and development centres. For example, an online administration system can take much of the drudgery and cost out of managing the process, coordinating comments and ratings from observers and assessors, and of producing reports. In my own business we can offer individual or group role-plays via webcam, enabling us to link people from anywhere in the world. We can run a three-hour 'day in the life' simulation that integrates with a company's identified capability framework, and that can work alongside the online profiling process discussed above. We can run much of this remotely: there is no need for people to be in the same country, let alone the same room. This makes the process less daunting by removing the need for people watching over you. It also makes the process more realistic. It simulates the global, virtual teamworking that is becoming commonplace. Feedback reports can be produced almost instantly, and the overall cost is a fraction of what it was even a couple of years ago. These technologies are revolutionizing tried and tested techniques, and making them much more accessible. Such programmes invigorate and motivate people. As we have discussed previously, this is a missing ingredient for many in today's tough economic climate. Moreover, they are a highly effective way of focusing people on developing the behaviours that are important to future growth and business success.

Warning

Development centres risk the perception that they carry a hidden agenda and are really a means of weeding out poor performers. On the other hand, participation may also be seen as a mark of status or future career prospects rather than development. Either of these contrasting perceptions can damage performance and risk the loss of key employees if they feel slighted or threatened. It is vital, therefore, to think through how a new programme will be communicated and who will attend. Practically, you probably can't include everyone and so participants must be selected on clear business needs and not because people feel they lose status if they are not chosen. Another danger is that individuals' opinions about their pace of progression may not align with organizational needs, so expectations must be carefully managed.

These problems are avoided if you:

- Use transparent selection processes. For example, invite applications asking people to specify why the centre's aims suit their needs, how they meet the criteria set for participation, how their participation will benefit the business, and what they will do with the learning afterwards.

- Offer support to those rejected and the opportunity to reapply.

- Offer plenty of alternative development opportunities.

- Keep open a particular career route, or next step, to people who fail to get accepted on the programme.

- Avoid pass or fail labels. I recall one centre for people at the top level in the UK subsidiary of a global manufacturer. Its purpose was to identify who could be promoted to the top salary band, which would also open a career path to HQ level. Only one person 'failed', but this person was head of the highest-earning business unit, which regularly achieved the highest customer satisfaction ratings and regularly won the firm's global efficiency awards. He was also respected by his staff who valued the support he gave them, trusted his judgement, and believed that he was fair, consistent and transparent in his dealings. But he did not match the standards of the firm's competencies (which incidentally did not include people management)! Fortunately, this firm gave him the promotion nonetheless, but this example serves as a salutary warning not to use pass or fail, and to think through carefully the other inputs needed for decision making.

Online learning, crowdsourcing and social networking tools

New technologies utilizing 'wikis', social networking and online learning make it easy for people to learn from, and in collaboration with, each other. It enables us to connect people across organizational boundaries and learn from different cultures.

Formal collaborative learning describes a method in which learners at various performance levels work together in small groups towards a common goal. Learners are responsible for each other's learning, as well as their own. Collaborative learning takes place less formally by people sharing ideas, or seeking help from each other. Its proponents claim that the active exchange of ideas within small groups not only increases interest among the participants but also promotes critical thinking. There is persuasive evidence that cooperative teams achieve at higher levels of thought and retain information longer than learners who work quietly as individuals. The shared learning gives learners an opportunity to engage in discussion, take responsibility for their own learning, and thus become critical thinkers. I think we can leverage our innate curiosity and the power of collaboration to create powerful social networks for learning and working at both the community level and online.

CASE STUDY

Burson-Marsteller (B-M) is a leading global public relations and communications firm. It provides clients with counsel and programme development across the spectrum of public relations, public affairs, digital media, advertising, and other communications services. Its clients are global companies, industry associations, professional services firms and other organizations.

B-M has a highly developed and sophisticated use of new media technologies, such as its own internal version of YouTube and its own social networking sites. These enable people to interact with others and learn. For example, people can deepen their understanding of the firm's competencies by looking up anecdotes posted by others, or by accessing videos of the firm's leaders talking about a competency and their experience of using it. People can also view videos of colleagues in different parts of the world discussing the competencies, which give fascinating insights into how people interpret them in different cultural contexts. The social networking sites bring people together from across the world to share experiences, knowledge and understanding. B-M sees new media technologies as offering outstanding possibilities for creating 'one company' – a virtual company.

B-M Source is a discussion forum where people can work together on a project or ask for help on some work. People can also post their profiles on the site and create networks around different topics or problems. These are proving to be an effective way of bringing people together and creating a culture of teamwork and collaboration.

Paul Herrick, EMEA, Human Resources Managing Director at B-M, believes that the success of B-M's social networking and online learning is both a consequence of, as well as a driver of, B-M's culture of reaching out and being responsive to each other.

Coaching and mentoring

Coaching and mentoring have gained in popularity. There are now an estimated 43,000 to 44,000 business coaches operating in 28 countries on all continents (Bresser, 2008–09). Although there is little hard evidence for the direct effect of coaching on individual and business performance, its power to change mindsets, inspire action and help skills development is undoubted, and widely appreciated. The use of mentoring has also increased significantly.

Both coaching and mentoring suit our times. In our de-layered, cost-conscious organizations, people are expected to come to grips with new challenges very rapidly. As people rise through the organization their responsibilities get broader, often covering activities that are outside their own specialism. Moreover, the costs of failure and the pressure to achieve results quickly are high. Additionally, of course, the challenges of managing and leading people today are greater than ever before. In the new world model, therefore, employees are already successful and eager to move to a higher level of functioning but don't know how, and that's where coaching and mentoring help.

Definitions

A defining characteristic of both coaching and mentoring is that they are a one-to-one learning process. The coach or mentor is a collaborative partner who works with the learner to help them achieve goals, solve problems, learn and develop (Caplan, 2003). The coach or mentor may be a more senior executive, an outside consultant or a peer. Generally the relationship involves an encouragement for the learner to discuss issues and identify problems and solutions for themselves, with a minimum of direction. However, the process can cover a wide range of uses and techniques, calling for different skill-sets. It is helpful to differentiate between these uses.

Coaching style

Firstly, let's separate out from the mix a coaching style. This is where the 'coach' employs listening, questioning and feedback skills to help someone identify their own solutions to problems, or to support reflective learning. In supporting reflective learning, the coach asks questions (see Chapter 9) so the learner looks back on an experience and pulls out from it what they have learned, and what they will do again next time, or do differently. This may be a spontaneous conversation or a planned discussion. These are important techniques that managers must master to use with their people, and that are also useful for all kinds of peer interactions, and indeed interactions with clients. I will look at this in more detail in Chapter 9, when I talk about the manager's role, but a coaching style is highly effective for helping people learn, and so is relevant to our discussion here.

The next distinction is between what I term executive coaching, also often known as business, or leadership coaching, and skills coaching.

Executive coaching

This has a clear set of aims and outcomes that are established at the outset. It comprises structured sessions carried out over a predetermined period to guide and support long-lasting change on the part of the learner. The coach is likely to be external, but will certainly be well qualified and experienced in coaching, and able to access a range of tools, methods and advanced coaching techniques. The appeal is that it offers a bespoke solution: it provides individual-centred learning and development at a time, place and duration to suit the learner; it is private and confidential; and the individual can choose their own coach, their own methods and the mode of delivery, such as face-to-face, telephone or even online. This is all in marked contrast to learning in the training room, which has exactly opposite characteristics.

Skills coaching

I use this term to refer to people who are able to use basic coaching techniques, but who also have expertise in a specific topic on which they are able to coach others. This expertise might be IT skills, or selling or negotiating, or it might be interpreting profiles or supporting learning, as in the ABC Engineering example. The coaching techniques required here are the same as those for a coaching style, and the difference between the two is that a coaching style might be spontaneous, and part of day-to-day interactions, whereas skills coaching sessions will serve a specific purpose, and probably be pre-arranged.

I highly recommend the kind of process that I described earlier in the ABC Engineering example, where we trained an internal cadre of skills coaches to help people interpret their Iperquest® profiles, and then provide further support with development planning. This gives people highly beneficial and transferable skills, and it impacts marvellously on the culture, spreading ideas and enhancing collaboration and understanding.

Just-in-time coaching

This is a term I use to describe coaching that is provided just at the point when the person needs the skills and will apply them. The coaching provides a mix of targeted advice and support, with a conceptual understanding of the topic, and the chance to practise the skills before doing it for real. It delivers outstanding results.

In this example, the requirement was to raise the people management capability of all the team leaders in one department of this financial services business. Instead of arranging the usual training course, this firm engaged a coach to work with each team leader individually. The aim was to give people basic coaching skills to equip them for their roles, the main requirements of which were to give performance feedback and support learning. About four and a half hours' coaching was provided to each person, depending on individual needs. The coaching covered appropriate models and techniques, but the individual nature of the sessions meant the learning could be directly related to the people and the issues each person had to handle. So the coach in this instance was part trainer, part coach, part adviser, and part role-model of the coaching skills. It was highly effective. People became confident in handling their new responsibilities, and did so effectively. An important aspect is that the coach covered the same models and techniques with each person, much as you would on a training course, so as to impart a consistent approach across the department.

I have used this method many times for various reasons: to prepare people to handle performance appraisal meetings, or long-term career discussions, or other management issues. I have also used it with people in the C-Suite where it is an effective way of introducing the new leadership approaches I discuss in this book. It is more directive than much executive coaching, as it usually involves technical input and advice. For this reason, it often achieves superior results faster, as what is discussed is put into practice straight away and generally has urgency attached to it. Because it is practised immediately, this also helps the learning stick.

Mentoring

The specific purpose of mentoring is for one person to pass expertise and knowledge to another. This distinguishes it from coaching, which is to help learners identify their own solutions. In practice, these distinctions can be blurred, as coaches sometimes need to give advice or pass on expertise, and mentors must use a coaching style: being a brilliant marketer doesn't

CASE STUDY

The UK BioIndustry Association, the BIA, is the trade association for innovative enterprises involved in UK bioscience. Members include start-up, emerging and more established bioscience companies; pharmaceutical companies; academic, research and philanthropic organizations; and service providers to the bioscience sector. The BIA works to encourage and promote a financially sound and thriving bioscience sector within the UK economy.

The BIA Mentoring Service matches established practitioners with next-generation leaders from across its member firms. Mentors are typically at board level, with over 15 years' industry experience. They must demonstrate an outstanding track record and the motivation to support others' development. Mentees are sometimes new to the industry, recently promoted to senior management, or are taking on new and unfamiliar responsibilities. Both potential mentors and mentees make a formal, written application, completing a pro forma that asks for their goals, interests, availability and particular requirements. They then both attend an orientation workshop so that they understand what constitutes best practice in mentoring, what is expected of them, and make a formal agreement on logistics, such as where and how often to meet. Carolyn Ponder, the facilitator, runs 'speed-dating' exercises to find a good mentoring match. For people unable to attend, or in different geographic locations, she runs a 'matching' service using videoconferencing. In each case, she helps mentees diagnose their needs, so as to obtain the best match. After six to nine months, Ponder makes contact with each mentee and mentor to review progress, check if new agreements are needed, or if goals have changed, and also to help determine if a relationship should continue or has run its course. Many relationships continue, and turn into friendships. Ponder has evidence that people have benefited from the exposure to wider business and leadership skills, which helps their personal development, but which also gives smaller businesses a better chance of succeeding in today's competitive market.

necessarily mean you can pass your skills and expertise on to others. A mentor is generally someone more experienced and qualified than the learner, but 'reverse or upwards mentoring', where the mentor is younger but has some skill or knowledge to pass on, is being successfully used, for instance to bring senior leaders in touch with social networking. Reverse mentoring is also highly effective at giving people at the top a better understanding of how their actions and decisions impact at other levels. It helps build bridges between levels and functions, giving everyone an enhanced understanding of the business. Mentoring is also proven as a valuable career development tool, and business leaders regularly identify mentoring has having been of critical help to them in their careers.

A coaching style of working together, plus the use of mentoring, spreads skills, creates internal networks, encourages collaborative working, emphasizes personal development and responsibility, and also cross-fertilizes ideas around the business, sowing the seeds for innovation. Mentoring is also valuable for bringing together people from different businesses, but who collaborate together in some way. It fosters understanding of the pressures people in different roles are under, and builds relationships.

Other learning methods

Include in your self-managed succession programme as many different learning options as possible so that people can choose those that best suit their needs. Where you can, reference these to your behavioural capabilities.

Other options include: classroom training, job rotation, secondment, shadowing, mentoring, buddying schemes, action learning sets, internal knowledge-sharing events, formal education courses, external conferences, workshops and events.

In this chapter, I have focused on the self-managed part of self-managed succession. In the next chapter, I look at the practices that create 'succession' through the organization.

Key points

- In the new world, people need to keep reinventing themselves throughout their careers. This includes behavioural skills as well as 'hard' skills.

- Most learning comes from the stretch and challenge and new experiences you have in your job. It requires support to help you reflect on your performance, what you learned from it, and how you might apply that learning.

- Provide people with tools that enhance their self-awareness. Open possibilities to them to receive feedback from others.

- Online technologies applied to profiling, learning, and 360-degree feedback enable you to provide learning and development inclusively and affordably. It helps you know your workforce.

- Development centres spread global mindsets and create consistency across cultures, while allowing for individual interpretation of values and behaviours.

- Embrace social media technologies so that people have maximum opportunity to collaborate and learn from each other both inside and outside the organization.

- Coaching and mentoring provide powerful support to learning and development but also spread ideas and create collaboration.

Notes

1 Proprietary model owned by Idea Management S.r.L.

Self-managed succession:
Careers

This chapter continues looking at self-managed succession (Figure 6.1), by turning to the career development practices that create succession through the organization. Most people want a career or a developing future, and this is one of the principal levers of employee engagement (Chapter 1). However, the changes brought about by globalization, technology and attitudes have brought the need for a revolution in the way we think about and manage our careers. It also changes the notion of succession. Identifying a few people to fill a few top jobs is not enough to future-proof your business. Now you must create continual succession of people, knowledge and skills through the business so that you have people ready at all levels with the right skills to address the right opportunities. Skills shortages, and changes in our society and economy, have also created an urgency to address equal opportunity, especially regarding the appointment of women to senior positions. Business needs have changed too, with the ability to work globally and cross-culturally increasing in significance.

This chapter addresses these issues, starting with the changes in how people view careers and make career decisions.

Fewer 'new world' careers will progress along a linear path

Traditionally, career development was seen as moving upwards along a linear path and was equated with promotion. In our new world of flatter hierarchies, fluid, flexible teams and cross-boundary working, career paths

FIGURE 6.1 The four-point framework shows the steps to develop your talent and engagement strategy

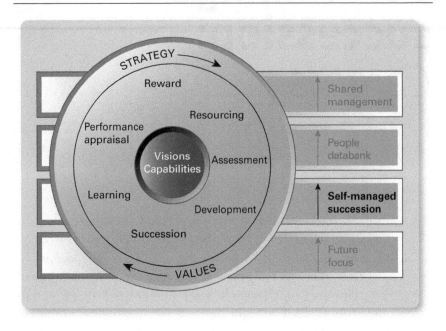

zigzag all over the place and increasing numbers of people are not following traditional career paths, for a whole host of reasons.

Moreover, the underlying skills shortages that first gave rise to the 'War for Talent' are still there, even when they ease in some areas as a result of recession. According to PwC's 15th Global CEO Survey, 'Skills shortages are very real – just 12% of CEOs say they're finding it easier to hire people in their industries – and the constraints are having quantifiable impacts on corporate growth' (PwC, 2012).

Demographic changes mean the workforce is getting older. Better health combined with worse pensions is creating a large pool of workers who years ago would have already retired. As a result of recession, a generation of school leavers and graduates may have been denied the usual training posts, and women returners may have extended their period out of work. The pace of change rapidly makes some skill-sets obsolete and creates others not previously on the radar.

In particular, as organizations have fewer opportunities for career promotion, emphasis has been placed on advancing through sideways rather than upward moves. This has tended to encourage attitudes to career progression that see people taking small career steps. The companies that are prepared to offer rapid advancement have generally been those undergoing rapid growth. However, fast-paced structural change is rendering a risk-averse approach unworkable.

People's expectations are also changing. Since the demise of the 'job for life' mentality, the psychological contract has changed. While small career moves are fine for some, others aren't content to progress slowly; they want development, challenge and opportunity, and they want to be able to see what the future holds for them in the organization. Not everyone is ambitious, but most people recognize that they need to keep pace with change in the environment, and they expect the organization to support this. They also recognize that they must take more responsibility for their own career development and employability (North and Delamare, 2011).

Add to this mix the flux in organizations where some functions are growing and others declining, and it is also clear that career management will involve helping people exit the organization or make career transitions. A McKinsey study found that executives on average experienced five significant transition points in their careers (Baumgarten, Desvaux and Devillard, 2007), while a survey begun in 1979 by the US Bureau of Labor Statistics tracked baby boomers born between 1957 and 1964 and found that they held on average 10.8 jobs from ages 18 to 42 (US Bureau of Labor Statistics, 2012).

Clearly, career management helps both parties: for the individual, it is about employability and achieving aspirations; for the organization, it is a vital part of retaining and engaging people, and developing them for future roles.

First stop: the individual's own aspirations

Amidst all this change, what people mean by a career is less likely to be a simple path of progression through one organization. It also means that individuals show less deference and expect to be treated with consideration and as equals. It follows, therefore, that businesses must adjust their mindsets to suit these sea changes in expectations. We must work from the individual's agenda, and help them develop their career with the business strategy. At the same time, as we implement the strategy, we must plan and build roles around people's own aspirations and the experience they want (CRF, 2012). This will open opportunity to all, improving diversity, and our businesses will benefit from a wider talent pool.

The 'three-stage development plan'

For individuals, career development planning represents an opportunity to think through aspirations and development needs, identify preferred

FIGURE 6.2 Three-stage learning

Within
6–10 years

New role or
challenge within 3–5 years

Stretch and challenge
in current role

learning methods, and plan how and when to follow through on these. A proven approach is to encourage people to draw up a long-term development plan that sets out their aspirations over three career stages relating to three time spans, and matches these with development opportunity (Figure 6.2):

- Stage 1 is the immediate future. This is the period generally covered in performance appraisals. It should focus on what stretch and challenge is available in the current role, unless, of course, the person is new to the role and is still on a learning curve.

- Stage 2 will focus on medium-term development and the next possible role for the person, say within the next three to five years, and will aim to produce the capabilities they will need.

- Stage 3 will address longer-term ambitions, perhaps within the next six to ten years.

Roles in this case may not equate to actual positions but to present and future capabilities. The reports generated by self-assessment tools or development centres can provide reference points around which managers can structure conversations with their employees and help them draw up a development plan.

When you do this it is surprisingly easy. In most cases people aim for something that they can start working towards now and it is probably what the organization needs too. This is especially the case if you have recruitment and goal setting right. Suppose that a project worker at head office aspires to being a project manager next and wants subsequently to have an opportunity to work out on site. The project manager role requires some influencing skills, while a site posting requires development of technical knowledge plus a lot more skill in influencing. Both roles require this person to have more exposure to contractors. Suppose also that the manager has identified that this person needs more confidence in dealing with outsiders and must build better relationships with them in order to do their current job better; so the manager could open up opportunities for additional experience, perhaps supported by some studying or maybe coaching to help build confidence, influencing and relationship-building skills.

This illustrates how it is often possible to open opportunities to people that will meet a short-term organizational need, while also moving them towards longer-term career aspirations. If no current project exists, then, having identified a business and individual need that are aligned, you may start planning one. Importantly, this three-stage process is one that addresses the needs of ambitious, high-potential people, who can be difficult to accommodate within general development programmes. It is also a further way of encouraging a focus on the future and an outwards perspective to identify trends and challenges.

Traditionally, development plans have focused on the next year and the performance appraisal process generally sets the scene for this. When I discuss the three-stage plan there are two common objections: firstly, that managers are focused on the present, considering development that will achieve results here and now; and secondly, that individuals are already over-stretched in their current jobs – there is no time for this kind of development. Let us reframe this thinking. Firstly, it is more disruptive to lose someone to another organization, or if they are disengaged, than it is to release them for a special project or other learning. Secondly, juggling to fit things in, whether it is within someone's own schedule or across a team, is a key way in which the organization becomes agile and flexible. Finally, there is never time, but organizations that never try new things are the ones that fail: somehow, those that succeed can always find a way to do new things.

This longer-term perspective on development planning is flexible and can adapt to individual and business needs. If the business need or the individual's ambition changes, there is little downside to either in pursuing such development. Bearing in mind the 70/20/10 formula for learning and development, the costs are seldom significant because much of the development is delivered through experiences and skills that are never wasted. The business gains from the person's contribution and enhanced level of engagement. It lets people know they are valued and gives an indication of what the future might hold, without making commitments that can't be kept. It also adjusts better to changing expectations, such as in the accountancy firm that found their recently qualified professionals were becoming increasingly demanding, especially about career development and promotion prospects. They were no longer prepared to wait years to see if they would be offered partnership, but needed to know now how to manage their careers, and if this should be within the firm, or externally. This situation is increasingly prevalent and places considerable onus on businesses to provide development opportunity, and to make selection and promotion criteria transparent.

Considering longer-term career aspirations also raises the question of what to do about people who are content to remain in the same job or who do not know what they want to do in the future. Development plans do not have to be about a new or different job but equally might be about what may become different in the current job or what could be done differently. Few jobs remain the same these days. It is helpful to encourage the person who does not know what might interest them next to network more across the organization. This may help them to identify areas of interest but, in any case, is likely to benefit them and their department by broadening their understanding of the organization and their personal links to others within it.

You learn and develop from your work experience

The 'three-stage' way of aligning organization and individual development depends on people accepting that most learning and development comes from actual work experience. Learning is something that happens continuously. Strategic talent development encourages this and creates an environment where experience is passed on and shared and where people coach each other naturally as part of their everyday routine.

Many people will not populate the third stage, or even the second stage of the plan. This is not a problem, since the idea is to encourage opportunity but not to force it. There is no hard evidence for correlation between those pursuing the three-stage plan and those having high potential, though anecdotal evidence suggests that ambitious and high-potential individuals are likely to self-select and establish a three-stage plan. Your feedback and support processes will, however, need to manage the expectations of those whose short-term aspirations may be unrealistic, as well as those who may undervalue themselves. Do not discourage people whose long-term aspirations seem unrealistic: they may not turn out to be so. Moreover, the aim of strategic talent development is to offer development choice and career support. In today's increasingly common, but also difficult, situation where managers have to spearhead growth with some people, while downsizing others, a positive attitude to supporting career development, which may lead outside the organization, as well as within, is very helpful.

Finally, there is the practical consideration of when and how to introduce this process. I recommend a performance appraisal and succession planning cycle, where this process is the focus of the mid-year review, leaving the annual review to focus on performance. Succession planning would, therefore, also take place at mid-year so three-stage planning can feed into it.

Making resources available to help people identify career paths

Let us turn now to the provision of information and support to help people identify career moves. If people are to self-manage their learning and plan their careers they need support. One element of this is information.

The CRF survey suggests a list of resources that are commonly found on a career website or portal:

- interactive career tools;
- information about career development that can be downloaded;
- access to psychometrics;
- career path information;
- link to competency information;
- individual career stories;
- information about career workshops;
- online internal job boards;
- link to performance management and development planning;
- online 'mentor matching'.

The provision of intranet-based resources

For organizations with their own intranets, much of this can be tailored to the organization's needs and provided easily online. The provision will include job boards, and clear information about career opportunities, career paths and the experience required to progress. Include here, also, project work that relates to career paths, and show the capabilities required to achieve current and future business goals, show how these capabilities match requirements against roles at different levels within job families, and show the key experiences that will move people along this career path. Make databases of mentors, or internal coaches, readily accessible.

If you don't have your own intranet then the listing of typical resources is still helpful. There are other ways of providing much of it. A public website can have a secure area accessed by password that can provide these resources; links to external resources can be provided to staff; subscriptions to external organizations that offer some of these resources can be distributed by e-mail. Some elements can be provided easily without use of the internet.

Social networking tools

Social networking tools make it easy for people to learn about jobs and roles and therefore identify future career opportunities. They can also have multiple uses, such as collecting and disseminating data about people through internal CVs, as well as opening learning, as discussed in the previous chapter. Use career story videos where the business's leaders describe their careers, or describe the capabilities required for different roles. Take advantage of these new technologies to disseminate capabilities, values and culture. The possibilities are endless and will change the nature of learning, as well as career development.

Rapid development in social media is producing many off-the-shelf programs, which are cost-effective and simple for all businesses, and now within reach for small firms.

CASE STUDY

KPMG believes strongly that to get engagement from their people, they must give them accountability for development, as well as information about the alternative career paths they could follow, and tools to help their development. A web portal shows all career and learning paths, and alternatives, including moving to different disciplines, breaks in service for maternity, or secondment to a client. The information is put across using a range of techniques including cameo videos, and shows career opportunities as a 'spider's web' rather than a linear trajectory.

Targeted support for career development

The approaches listed above, together with processes such as online profiling, and assessment and development centres that help people understand their aptitudes, will help your people manage their careers, and make career decisions. Nonetheless, there are still many instances when extra support is required, whether this is coaching or mentoring support, or the provision of information, and I recommend the following.

1. Career conversations

Career conversations that explore ways to make work challenging and rewarding, and think about the future, are powerful. The CRF research, referred to earlier, shows that career conversations are more highly valued than any other career tools or processes.

Great starter questions to get people thinking about their careers:

What do you get excited about at work?

Where do you add the most value at work? What have been your greatest achievements so far?

What would you like to do more of?

What would you like to know more about?

When you look inside and outside the organization what issues/topics/ challenges inspire you the most?

Where are you playing it safe?

What does success mean to you?

2. Mentoring

I discussed mentoring in the previous chapter, and so will restrict my comment here to noting that mentoring is highly valued for enhancing career development. Mentoring aims include: building confidence through support, feedback and advice on how to develop; serving as role models; helping the mentee to learn to navigate organizational politics.

CASE STUDY

At KPMG, emerging leaders are sponsored by a partner, and assigned a coach or mentor. Mentors must themselves possess the capabilities required of an emerging leader, as well as understand the value of coaching and mentoring others. Their role is to provide broader career ideas and internal exposure to the emerging leader, as well as be someone 'safe' with whom the emerging leader can discuss their concerns and uncertainties. Many at KPMG, where mentoring is well established, are partners, or have themselves been identified as future partners. KPMG has also now started a joint mentoring programme with some of their largest and longest-standing clients, so as to build networks, relationships and understanding.

3. Internal sponsors and networking

Smart employees want access to different people to achieve a variety of development purposes and smart employers will find ways to encourage this. Much conventional wisdom is looking to managers as coaches to help people build their capabilities. This is an unrealistic expectation, but also limiting. Often the specific knowledge needed to complete a task comes from outside the immediate team. People also coordinate contributions from a network of career supporters. Often the networks you belong to make a significant difference not only to how you see yourself in career terms, but to how others see you too. This does not contradict the importance of coaching skills among managers but supplements it. Indeed, it may be an important aspect of those coaching skills to develop managers' abilities to assist their team in developing wider networks within the organization. Networks also assist in spreading best practice and directing learning, as well as opening up new career opportunities to people.

Career sponsors are emerging as new contributors to career management. Their role goes beyond providing individual feedback and advice. They act as an advocate for the mentee, deliberately using their influence with other senior executives to help obtain the development that has been identified for them. For example, Ibarra, Carter and Silva (2010) have written about the role and successes of formal sponsors in helping women advance their careers in large organizations. Their role in this situation is to level the playing field with aspiring male leaders. According to Ibarra: 'Women are over-mentored and under-sponsored relative to their male peers' (Ibarra and Lineback, 2005).

Unlocking the barriers for equal opportunity

This leads us into the topic of equal opportunity, especially as regards the under-representation of women in management posts, particularly at top levels. This is a difficult topic, which is why we have not moved far in decades, so I will not try to solve it here; but there are some considerations that are especially pertinent to a strategic talent development ethos, which is about inclusive opportunity. These considerations are also relevant to selection more generally.

The risks of bias

The bases for our selection decisions can be broken down into how we determine the selection criteria, and how we match individuals against them.

Organizations are often risk-averse when it comes to job appointments, seeking someone already in a similar sales manager role to fill a sales manager vacancy. It has always been rare to find an ideal candidate who fully meets the requirements of the role but, with changing demographics, it is becoming harder to achieve precise matches; further, such a limited outlook also severely restricts the available candidate pool. The person who has done it before may be jaded or out of date.

The narrow focus that tends to be put on identifying job requirements and drawing up the specification of the ideal candidate disadvantages many who could make up the potential pool. It also puts a further constraint on the mindsets of those making the selection decisions, by reinforcing bias relating to gender, ethnicity and disability. Research carried out by talent analytics company, SHL, based on data from over one million people, measured the leadership potential of employees across 25 countries, concluding that while leadership potential is higher in women, the gender difference in senior positions globally is 76 per cent in favour of men (Jacobs, 2012).

Experiments to determine gender bias in candidates for fictitious CEO jobs show a consistent preference for male candidates – except where several male predecessors have failed and the organization is in crisis. This is partly because perceptions of leadership competencies are based upon male behaviours (such as forcefulness, control, task-oriented) and therefore fail to value female leadership behaviours (such as communication, influence, relationship-orientation). The problem is made worse because 'Women on their way up the corporate ladder get caught in two traps: the assumption that women and men have the same leadership qualities and the belief that they must imitate male leadership in order to succeed' (Vanderbroeck, 2010).

Gender bias affects selection for talent programmes and preparation for leadership roles as much as it does the selection decisions themselves. Eugene Burke, SHL's Chief Science and Talent Analytics Officer, puts forward this viewpoint about the UK, which ranks 19th of the 25 in their research with only 20 per cent of leadership roles held by women. He suggests that 'men are motivated by power and fear of failure such that UK boardrooms are self-perpetuating an unbalanced culture which is likely to naturally disengage women from aspiring to reach a senior position' (Jacobs, 2012). Research by international consultancy Catalyst (Warren, 2009) concludes that many talent management programmes unconsciously reflect and promote traits shown by the organization's mainly male leadership team. Even without competency frameworks, it is the traits that are perceived to have made the male leaders successful that influence decisions, while qualities, characteristics and skills considered atypical, or feminine, were perceived less favourably.

When you add these unconscious traps towards bias to the more conscious notions that equate success with a linear upward career path and working long hours, it is not hard to understand why so few women occupy senior executive or board positions. What does the fact that someone took a career break, or has worked part-time, or took a role that favoured work/life balance tell you about their leadership or technical capability, or their ability to do the job? Indeed, what does it tell you about their motivation to do a demanding job at a different stage in their lives? How many men who get to the top leadership positions can honestly say that they shot up there like a rocket, and didn't have a period where they coasted a bit, or took a role that didn't in reality give increased status and responsibility? These career steps are easier to explain, or indeed fudge, than a clear break or part-time working.

It is not only women, of course, who are affected by this kind of bias. I was part of a selection panel where it was commented about a candidate that he had spent too long in one role, and so was not 'leadership material', as he had not demonstrated the hunger to move upwards. This is a big assumption to make. Better to identify what the person achieved in the role, what his motivation was to stay, and to identify his leadership capabilities and motivations separately.

Statistics show that people with disabilities fare even less well in the job hunt than women. A nationwide advertising campaign in the UK featuring someone with a disability together with the powerful strapline 'See the ability behind the disability' expressed how dismissive attitudes to people with disabilities prevent us from recognizing their talents. Time will tell if the success of the 2012 Paralympic Games in London, which the British public greeted with such enthusiasm, will filter into attitudes in business and raise employment levels and prospects for disabled individuals. I certainly hope it does.

Bias affecting racial minorities is also an issue even when individuals are not consciously discriminating. A study by US academics (Westphal and Stern, 2007) found that ingratiatory behaviours towards the CEO and other directors increase the chances of appointment to the board. However, this applies mainly to white males, and the same behaviours in women and people from ethnic minorities may be seen as a negative attribute. A further study on the career patterns of ethnic minorities shows that people from different racial backgrounds take an upward path when they are roughly in the middle, whereas white males start moving upward earlier in their careers. When people are fast-tracked from an early point, or where success is viewed as a steep upward path, racial minorities are clearly disadvantaged.

These biases restrict the talent pool, hold people back, waste talent, and mean that the business does not always get the best person for the job. Clearly, overcoming them must be an objective of strategic talent development, but what are the remedies?

Firstly, as Clutterbuck (2012) suggests, 'coaches and mentors working with these individuals need to be aware of the need for different strategies and to help the coachee understand the issue from both their perspective and that of the existing majority directors'. Boards need to institute procedures that confront and overcome the unconscious discrimination that occurs from evaluating behaviour differently in people of different gender or racial backgrounds in the context of appointments and succession planning. Appointment committees should regularly assess their procedures through a diversity audit.

However, Clutterbuck also suggests that 'women and minorities aiming for the board may need consciously to establish and work to different strategies than their white male counterparts'. While this is helpful, my own view is that it is organizations that need to change their approach and take a more holistic and radical approach to selection that will not only help women, people from ethnic minorities and those with disabilities, but will lead to a widening of the talent pool, a better fit of candidate to role, and a culture which anyway is more suited to today's new ways of working.

Radical approaches to widen the talent pool and select the best candidate

- Don't focus on job and career route but, instead, identify the capabilities the job requires. Be careful not to confuse style and capabilities. A role might require sophisticated negotiation capability but someone may perform equally well using a persuasive style, or a forceful one.

- Then apply assessment criteria to identify if the applicant has the capabilities to do the job, matches the cultural values of the team and of the wider organization, can cope with the change inherent in the job, and if they might fit with a range of potential future job roles. Be open-minded and focus as much on what someone has learned and achieved, and their motivations, as on what they have done. For many roles, especially top leadership posts, it is particularly insightful to look for patterns of achievement, and the ability to learn quickly and apply the learning effectively. Make sure the capabilities you identify relate to the new world, and do not reinforce the old ways. For the recruitment and selection of managers, in particular, place emphasis on the capability dimensions of change, ambiguity and uncertainty, rather than of order and predictability. Where your business, or the particular role, requires people to move into new markets, or new activities, look for a propensity to experiment, take risk, and cope with and then speedily learn from failure, rather than the fear of failure. Sophisticated influencing skills are rising in importance for leadership roles as the enterprise becomes increasingly matrixed and increasingly virtual.

- Past performance is not necessarily the best predictor of future performance, although it has long been the basis of most recruitment and selection. Some candidates in the recruitment process may not have had the opportunity to demonstrate certain skills or behaviours or, conversely, may have had the experience but have become stale. The first type of candidate may not have relevant experience but, if they have the capabilities, will perform well when they are confronted with the tasks; whereas the second type has indeed done it before but may perform badly when confronted with the same challenge yet again: they may be bored or may apply the same solutions they have applied before, even if they are no longer appropriate. Moreover, people are affected by the system in which they operate, the way they are managed, and other factors. That a particular environment brought out certain behaviours you seek is no guarantee that this will be the case again in a different environment. Try to recognize transferable skills to make effective selection decisions. A sideways move may have led to the acquisition of multidisciplinary skills that might be even more valuable in a leadership role than the skills acquired throughout the upward trajectory.

- Don't make assumptions; for instance, assuming that a woman with children will not be willing to travel, or making assumptions based on length of time in a role. Ask and probe. Be willing to make structural changes to get the best person, for example to working hours. When it is possible to be in touch and respond to e-mails 24 hours a day, 7 days a week, does it matter if someone is on flexible hours, job shares or is working 3 days a week?

- Aim to provide as much insight and information about the job and the organization as possible, and the opportunity to meet key people so that the candidate can self-select, as well as give you more insight into how they would tackle key issues. Give the candidate as much information, exposure and time to consider different options as is reasonable. This is as important a decision for them as it is for you.

A key attribute of strategic talent development is, therefore, to have the mindset to 'take a risk' on someone, either for a sideways move for which they do not have the exact experience, or to give them an accelerated career opportunity. If you are able to focus on potential and on capabilities, this may not be a risk at all. Finally, a reminder to be aware of the dangers of bias, and self-awareness of your own biases so these do not influence the process or the decision.

Adhering to this guidance will go some way to addressing gender imbalances at the top of organizations, and there is a strong business case for doing so. In its assessment of the economic case for promoting more women to senior management and director positions, the European Commission said that this 'would improve company performance, ensure better decision-making and improved governance and ethics' (EU, 2012) Various studies suggest that companies with a higher share of women at top levels deliver strong organizational and financial performance. Studies have also shown that where governance is weak, female directors can exercise strong oversight and have a 'positive value-relevant impact' on the company. A gender-balanced board is more likely to pay attention to managing and controlling risk. According to Baumgarten *et al* (2007), the share prices of companies with diverse management teams were 17 per cent higher between 2005 and 2007 than industry averages, while their operating profits were almost double industry norms. Companies with the most females on their boards had a 53 per cent higher return on equity than competitors with no women at the highest level, research by Catalyst showed (Warren, 2009).

Making some of these changes in attitude and structure will reveal a readily available supply of women ready now for top positions. To summarize, this means changing how you rate success and achievement so that your attitude does not write off for promotion a woman who took a career break, or who slowed her career progression, or took a route that is different from the upward career trajectory usually required. Offering flexible working will advantage most of the workforce, and not just women. Similarly, being sure to assess on capabilities and not value judgements such as 'commitment' will also advantage most businesses. Another common argument often used against promoting women to boards is that 'they have not done it before, or boards need people who are ready now'. All boards benefit from providing induction for new members, even if they have already sat on other boards. Moreover, regular development for boards is advised by almost all corporate governance codes and required for listed companies (Spencer Stuart, 2012).

International development

Much of this book is premised on ideas of globalization and its consequences, so it is unsurprising that career development has an international dimension. As economies have become more integrated and technology has connected people globally, we have all become, in a sense, global workers. We are likely, during the course of any day, to be accessing information that originated on the other side of the world, and we may well be conversing with people on the other side of the globe too, tapping them for ideas, or working collaboratively with them. Distance is no longer such a barrier to doing business, as videoconferencing and virtual meetings facilitate us working together. At the very least, therefore, we all need some 'global' communications skills and cultural sensitivity so we are able to exchange ideas effectively with people with whom we share neither a first language nor a cultural heritage. People for whom English is a first language often mistakenly believe that this enables them to communicate easily with everyone. In fact, it gives false confidence and I have been in meetings where native English speakers have not adapted their language sufficiently to the non-native English speakers, resulting in mutual misunderstanding and difficulty establishing rapport and trust. Learning a foreign language helps provide sensitivity to the nuance of language, as well as to understanding different cultures and backgrounds. Include foreign language learning among your learning and development portfolio. Even a basic understanding can help broaden perspectives and improve communication and collaborative working across cultures.

For many, international working is more than using the internet and other technologies. It is also about face-to-face working, and overseas experience, and reports show that without international exposure, executives aren't in the running for senior-level or even second-tier positions with world-class companies. As horizons have expanded, so too have the ways in which people can gain international exposure and understanding (Spencer Stuart, 2012).

Options for international working

There are four main ways of structuring international experience, which differ according to how much overseas living and travel is involved:

- short-term expatriate assignment: relocation for less than one year;
- long-term expatriate assignment: relocation for a year or longer;
- frequent flyer: run operations remotely from base; frequent visits;
- commuter: work abroad weekdays; return home weekends.

International exposure can be a transforming experience for both the individual and the business. For the individual it demonstrates the flexibility to operate effectively and achieve results in a new environment, as well as the ability to cope with stressful situations. The broad range of possibilities for international working is also beneficial to the organization.

There are three main reasons for long-term expatriation: skills transfer, managerial control and management development. Many businesses going into the younger economies find it hard to recruit local people with the right skills and attitudes, and so expatriates are required, at least to get the business going (Cranfield, 2003).

Long-term expatriate assignments are a costly option, giving rise to problems as well as benefits for both the business and the individual. They may become tied to the new country, not wishing to leave at the end of the assignment, or, becoming used to the expatriate lifestyle, or to the independence and autonomy of this kind of role, not wish to return to base. Businesses often find it hard to reintegrate expatriates back into the head office structure and culture and many leave the organization on their return (Cranfield, 2003). Sometimes this is because there is no retention plan put in place. This matters, because companies are sending people abroad in increasing numbers, and because, having developed those people's capabilities, they don't need to lose so many of them. Many of the processes that will assist retention are described in this chapter and earlier in this book: it is essentially about talent development. If an individual sees their assignment as developing them towards their career goals and can see how they are approaching those goals, they are more likely to remain with the organization upon their return. Some of the things you can do comprise simple HR processes:

- The traveller's manager must keep in touch and have regular conversations with the individual about their performance and their career. Among other issues, these must cover timing, because the individual may be impatient – a feeling that may be exacerbated by the travel.

- The HR department must be in contact with the line manager about career opportunities.

Regardless of your use of the best practices, some good people will be lost, but this can be minimized with the right support and forward planning.

The upside, of course, is that from the candidate's point of view, living and working abroad brings the benefits of understanding another business culture, which is often only possible by being immersed in it, particularly in younger economies such as Russia and China.

However, many of these benefits can equally as well be obtained from short-term assignments, which are less problematic, and less costly. The example below shows how Burson-Marsteller use short-term global assignments as a business tool to benefit clients, as well as a development tool for their people.

CASE STUDY   B-M International mobility

Burson-Marsteller achieves cross-cultural understanding and global identity through a programme of short-term assignments that give participants an opportunity to experience a different culture and ways of doing things. It also develops their understanding of B-M and helps people gain deeper insights into some of B-M's clients, many of whom are global organizations. In fact, participants generally continue working remotely with their home clients and also work with them in the other location. So far, around 40 people have participated in this programme and Paul Herrick (B-M's Human Resources Managing Director) has evidence that participation leads to higher engagement levels and company loyalty. Herrick also believes that this programme helps build relationships and strong networks across the business, and helps retention.

Participants apply for the assignment, making both a business and a personal case for their suitability. They state what they expect to gain from the experience and how they would follow it up. They must be supported and recommended by their country CEO. Performance history is also taken into account. Herrick says it is important for people to apply as this makes it individually driven, and not company driven. People must want this and believe it suits their needs and aspirations.

At first, this programme was offered as part of the career path for client-facing people. As a result of its success, and the benefits it brings, it has now been opened to people in the infrastructure departments, who are seen as equally valuable to the company, and who also benefit from having first-hand global experience. Some applicants are unsuccessful in obtaining a place, but the reasons for rejection are explained to them and they are given guidance to enable them to apply again.

While people are on assignment, they are expected to spread their learning and share experiences with others through B-M's social networking sites. Participants 'tweet' regularly. In fact, it is a requirement for them to do so, so that people can follow their adventures. Herrick believes this is a good way of promoting the programme internally, but it also spreads learning and attitudes.

Most B-M offices are geared up for receiving and inducting people on these assignments. There is a standard plan for induction, and participants are also assigned a mentor, who is a quasi manager. They are also assigned a buddy who is on the same level as them, to help them integrate socially. There is a dual purpose to this programme, which is to develop intercultural and life skills, as well as professional development. The social emphasis fits with B-M's culture, which is highly collegiate and sociable and where people build strong relationships and friendships. People look forward to meeting and working together and this leads to better collaboration and better business results.

The sending office bears the cost but also takes the revenue an assignee generates while on assignment. Herrick says there is a general attitude that it is all ultimately coming from the same profit and loss account, but, in reality, it also requires considerable goodwill, which is generally there. The success of this programme bears testament to the culture at B-M, as Herrick believes that such a programme can only work where relationships are good.

The main aims of this initiative, which is a formally structured learning programme, are to build a sense of community globally across B-M, as well as give outstanding development opportunity. Where people gain experience of working with one of their existing clients in a different location, this gives them a deeper understanding of that client, which is another significant benefit.

Herrick believes that a programme of this kind is preferable to longer-term assignments, which are more costly and give problems of reintegration back into the home office, as well as the difficulties of moving people with families.

Offering a wide range of opportunity for gaining international experience can only benefit both individuals and organizations. Research and experience show that it is no longer appropriate to be prescriptive about international experience; for example, making it a requirement of an upward career path, or a top leadership position. Instead, work with the individual's aspirations and personal circumstances to find more creative ways of giving people international exposure. Moreover, overseas roles and assignments can be equally valuable for the majority who may not reach top positions but whose roles benefit from international and cultural understanding and sensitivity. We often set up artificial, administrative barriers that inhibit career management and development – there are always reasons not to do things – but, when we examine why we have not done it there often seems to be no sound reason. Unlock those barriers and let the productivity and success emerge. Career management should be as individualized as possible because everyone has different aspirations, objectives and constraints. While we will often persuade ourselves that it is too much trouble to set up individual programmes and more convenient to deal with categories of people, in reality it is often not so difficult to individualize, and it is often far more effective.

Key points

- Few career paths move in a linear direction.

- Open development opportunities to people that match their aspirations.

- Give everyone the opportunity, at least annually, of long-term career development planning that aligns their aspirations with the business strategy. Career conversations are highly motivating.

- Open development experiences now that move people along their long-term path. The business will benefit from developing their skills, and from energizing them with new experiences.

- Make the most of new technology to provide career information and support.

- Don't restrict your talent pool. Rethink your selection processes, especially the way you identify job requirements. Reflect new ways of working and equal opportunity. Check for bias in processes and attitudes.

- International communication skills and cultural sensitivity are increasingly important in globalized markets and are beneficial to both individual and business. Short-term assignments can be an effective and less costly option.

Creating a people databank: 07
Succession and workforce planning

Collecting data about people – their needs, preferences, behaviours and experiences – used to involve considerable effort and expense. So much so that businesses understandably directed their efforts and expenditure towards knowing and understanding their customers, rather than their workforce. However, cheaper and more powerful technology has now radically altered this landscape, making it easy to collect and store up-to-date data about the people you employ and to interrogate those data for different purposes. This is the third step in the process of compiling your talent and engagement strategy (Figure 7.1), and by now you should have collected quite a bit of people data from many of the self-managed succession initiatives we discussed in the previous two chapters.

I wish now to look at the three main uses of these data: workforce planning, succession planning and employee metrics. My focus is on the 'soft skills' and processes that make the data and the technology work, and not on the different IT systems themselves.

Strategic talent development emphasizes distributed leadership that empowers people to create opportunity, innovate, and self-manage their performance and their development. The organization supports and facilitates this through sound processes, and the organizational culture is there to guide the manner of implementation. The data provide the evidence that helps top-tier leaders, and HR, exercise light-touch control, and nudge people in the right direction. The data show leaders where attention must be emphasized, and help them judge progress (Chapter 4).

FIGURE 7.1 The four-point framework shows the steps to develop your talent and engagement strategy

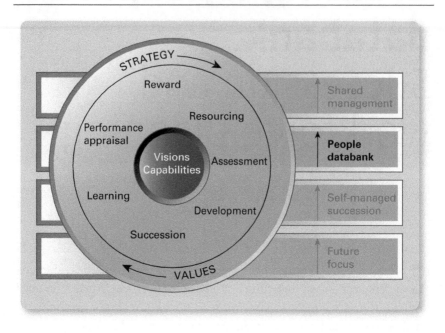

Informing decisions

High-quality, robust data about people also facilitate different business decisions: who speaks fluent Cantonese and has a network of contacts in Hong Kong to help on a particular deal? Who has the technical expertise, leadership and cultural skills, as well as the availability and willingness to set up a new factory in India? Who understands the dynamics of chemical reactions in ultra-low temperatures? Who do we have available to fill our sudden vacancy for a chief engineer? Do we have available candidates to fill this vacancy internally, or should we immediately look at the external market? If we move into this new market, or develop this new product, who is available to manage the project?

These data also facilitate long-term planning. When you understand the skills, potential and aspirations of the current workforce, you can make projections that inform your recruitment, learning and development strategies so that your organization has the right people in the right place at the right time to deliver your business strategy.

The point I emphasize here is the importance of rich data about people that can be cross-referred for different uses.

Workforce planning

There is no consensus over the definition of workforce planning, but I see its aim being to forecast supply and demand so that you can plan your recruitment and your learning and development programmes. Workforce planning is usually more holistic than succession planning and covers the whole workforce.

Workforce planning starts with analysis of the strategic position of the business. The results of this then feed into a forecast of the required demand for people by the business and how it is likely to be supplied. The final stage involves the creation and implementation of a human resources plan, which aims to deliver the right number of the right people for the business. Succession planning is an integral part of workforce planning.

The business challenges are the starting point, and the data warehouse can then present the data you need to help you make decisions and plan.

CASE STUDY

Siemens has a matrix organization with four business sectors – Energy, Infrastructure & Cities, Healthcare and Industry. Over recent years, it has acquired and divested approximately 30–40 businesses globally each year.

At corporate level, Siemens operates on the basis of 'portfolio management' of a set of businesses. The company states that it is driven by working out to which businesses it can be a good parent and which ones can add value to its strategy of being a global integrated technology company. This informs decisions about which businesses to acquire, for example in new growth areas such as wind power technology, and which to dispose of when they no longer add value to the strategy.

This high-level planning takes place in the company's headquarters and is aligned to the sector technology roadmaps, which highlight the capabilities required to exploit future target markets. The time horizon is 5–20 years.

Toby Peyton-Jones, HR Director, Siemens North West Europe, believes that when you acquire a business, it's the same as when you hire an individual. 'You need to see what the most critical capabilities are. Is there a good cultural fit? How can we leverage these capabilities and how can we retain and develop them going forward?'

Siemens' strategic workforce planning works hand in hand with business planning. The business planning process starts at corporate level with an environmental analysis that builds on the megatrends and looks into the market opportunity in each of the relevant sectors and segments (Chapter 4). This informs the development of business strategy in each of the Energy, Infrastructure & Cities, Healthcare and Industry sectors and for each geographical area.

Strategic workforce planning is performed as a dialogue between HR and the management team of a global business unit. The horizon is three to seven years and the focus is on the gap analysis of critical job families that are needed to support the business strategy. Once the gaps have been quantified, this becomes a critical input for the 'global people strategy' for the business unit and geographic hotspots will then execute on this strategy to meet the demand.

Locally, the global people plans become an input to the dialogue between local HR business partners and local business management teams. Here, the review is more tactical with a horizon of one to five years, giving rise to a resource and talent plan that is directly actionable. At its best, this is embedded as part of the local quarterly business review and can be adjusted in the light of business trends and employment data about the market.

In both the global strategic workforce planning and the local resource and talent plans, it is the internal and external data that drive decisions so that recruitment plans, development plans and retention/succession plans are discussed as part of growth, restructuring or wider business development aspirations.

Peyton-Jones believes that we are moving into an era where data will become more and more critical for decision making, and companies that can turn data into information that can be acted upon will have a competitive edge. Siemens moved into data management about its workforce early on and now has an extensive 'data warehouse', which is the backbone for trend analysis and on which other web-based manager and employee self-service tools can be based. One of the first challenges in data management was to create a common language of terms and definitions. How, for example, do you classify job codes or part-time employees or leadership capabilities across so many different businesses and countries?

This workforce planning process informs many aspects of the people strategy, such as compensation and benefit strategy for critical roles, recruitment planning and talent deployment, as well as succession/development strategies. In among all this, retention strategies are often overlooked as organizations focus on recruitment, not realizing, as Peyton-Jones puts it, that we need to re-recruit our own people every day.

Employee engagement is regularly measured through annual surveys, while pulse checks or mood surveys are used to test reactions to, or opinions on, different events. Peyton-Jones views engagement as critical to ensure both performance and retention: 'When you lose people, you don't just lose their technical knowledge, which is probably relatively easy to replace anyway. You lose their meta-knowledge or, in other words, their understanding of your customer supply chain or of "how things work here" and so on.'

Information and data about the talent base are important to Siemens, particularly to meet changes in strategy and direction, such as when they need to redeploy from a business that is retrenching to one that is expanding, or to a new acquisition.

'When we have an opening,' says Peyton-Jones, 'we can interrogate the data and pull off a list of people who have the potential for the role and who have expressed interest in it. This helps create transparency about opportunities in the company by making roles more visible to both possible candidates and recruiting managers. It also accelerates recruitment and selection.'

Peyton-Jones believes strongly in the benefit of extending the talent pool to future and past employees. Siemens has a vibrant alumni network and reaches extensively to universities, as well as to schools, to attract people to its technical and non-technical apprenticeships. Siemens operates a renowned apprenticeship programme.

Peyton-Jones says that data are increasingly owned by the employee who compiles and keeps up to date their own online CV/profile, and who can review their performance data and update the jobs they have done, their development plans, their mentoring relationships and so on.

The data also drive and inform strategy. For example, they might show where there are shortages of women in management, or highlight business units where the leadership is not good, or help to analyse the composition of the workforce where customer surveys show dissatisfaction. Issues such as these are extracted and presented to the management/leadership teams who are steering the business. Just like the finance function, HR is able to come to the table with data that provide insight for critical issues in the development of the business.

This case study shows the value of holding reliable data on people: it helps planning, speeds business decisions, enables you to identify problem areas and make improvements. It gives people in the C-Suite a view of the organization, and a means of control. It also helps ensure that the composition of your workforce matches current and future needs, and achieves diversity.

Succession planning

Succession planning generally has either a tactical or a strategic purpose and sometimes both. The core purpose of tactical strategic planning is to ensure business continuity by identifying replacements for the senior leadership tiers, and other business-critical positions, either in the short or the long term.

The core purpose of strategic succession planning is to make the best use of the possible talent within an organization. The three-stage development process set out in the previous chapter facilitates strategic succession planning, making it a dynamic process – because it is continually updated with new information – that integrates with personal and career development planning. It creates a flow of people who are ready to move into new emerging roles, or vacant ones.

There is, nonetheless, considerable merit to a process that achieves both these purposes. A tactical approach provides a snapshot of the organization at any one time and is helpful for identifying vulnerabilities, taking stock of resources, and also identifying external sources of labour supply. Of course, you might view this as workforce planning, and there is indeed considerable crossover between the two, but it is the processes and the results they achieve that matter.

The way it was

Traditionally, succession planning aimed to:

1 Identify successors for key posts, most often senior leadership posts, so you could plan career moves and development activities for these successors.

2 'Pool' those with similar development needs, such as people with potential for further management and leadership responsibility, or special development for women with leadership potential. Talent pools, in these cases, aimed to help people realize their potential faster. This categorization also concentrated the attention of line management to use the development budget where it would supposedly bring the greatest returns.

3 Identify 'pivotal talent'. These are people believed to make a material difference to your business and whose skills or performance would make you better than your rivals. The aim here was to optimize investment in developing the people who would bring the greatest business return.

These traditional approaches, emphasizing exclusivity and singling out stars, often closed off opportunity to others. Moreover, as we discussed in Chapter 1, it has had a corrosive influence, such as in the example of Enron where it clearly led to poor decision making, among other ills.

Furthermore, succession planning traditionally prepared the organization now for anticipated changes, and methods were generally crafted around this purpose. But what of the 'new world' organization where changes are harder to foresee, and where today's critical skills may be obsolete tomorrow?

The way it is now

The strategic succession planning process, linked to three-stage development planning (Chapter 6), answers this question. It replaces the notion of 'pivotal' talent, which is changing too rapidly to make such a quest worthwhile, and instead encourages people to keep their roles and skills ahead of the challenges on the horizon. It still identifies those who merit accelerated or specially targeted development, and it still develops your future leaders, but it does this in a way that keeps options and opportunity open for everyone.

I will explain my concept through the ABC Engineering case study, introduced in Chapter 5. I now use this story to illustrate the key elements of a succession planning process, but I will also bring in other examples.

The stages of succession planning

Every organization needs to plan for the long term. Succession planning must be relevant to the business and its corporate values. Equally, it must also be relevant to individuals.

At first, we set out to do succession planning at ABC in a traditional way by focusing on people for future leadership posts. However, early on we realized that this wouldn't work with its culture but also because there were some people across all levels – executive, managers, technicians, etc – who had unique experience and scarce skills. ABC is made up of highly qualified specialists who have built their technical skills and understanding over years. Many are leaders in their fields. Developing a traditional leadership pipeline would not address these critical business continuity issues below the top team. We therefore needed to have a more holistic process and match people with critical roles, scarce skills and also with potential to grow and develop other skills. We therefore sought to design a dynamic process that would filter through to everyone and that would also inform the firm's HR and business strategies.

The process we designed achieved three main outcomes:

1 Identification of shortages and vulnerabilities – through taking a snapshot of people able to cover or move into the two top-tier management roles – allowing us to plan recruitment and internal development to overcome them. We also identified pivotal talent; that is, those people who made a significant difference to the business. At ABC, people regarded as 'pivotal' had specialist knowledge and experience vital to the business and not easy to replicate.

2 The opportunity for people to actively pursue a personal development plan that aligned their aspirations with the development needs of the business. For example, G, a qualified engineer, was a project manager. The next development stage she identified on her three-stage development plan was to gain experience on a bigger project, and to work directly with people on one of the sites that ABC controlled. Her third-stage development was to become a site manager. As G was well informed about the business strategy, she knew this would fit perfectly with business needs. This process helped create several talent pipelines to deal with the considerable technical, environmental and leadership challenges the business faced. It also aimed to help people realize their potential. It covered all management, technical and specialist staff.

3 Input into a resourcing strategy and a learning and development strategy. The information we generated provided the main input into these, but also input into the firm's business strategies.

The stages of first-time succession planning:

1 Set the aims of your succession plan.
2 Identify roles, capabilities and organizational requirements.
3 Compile the people databank.
4 Set up talent classifications and run talent roundtables.
5 Analyse the data to identify resourcing and learning and development requirements and business improvements.
6 Review and update the plan regularly.
7 Use the plan to keep track of people and their development.

1. Set the aims of your succession plan

Our remit at ABC was to produce a plan for the firm's Remuneration Committee to show that the business had successors in place to fill top management posts and key roles, and also to ensure business continuity. We added to this the aim of designing a dynamic process that would align individual and organizational development, and therefore serve a purpose beyond the Remuneration Committee.

The first step was to expand on why we needed succession planning and what it should achieve. To do this, we spent a considerable amount of time 'listening to the business' – repeating the process that we had first applied to develop the talent strategy (Chapter 5). These conversations confirmed that future business success would demand sophisticated leadership, project management and relationship-building skills, which would be just as important as highly specialized technical knowledge. These capabilities were already part of the talent management programme.

Wendy Hirsh, a leading authority on the subject, believes that succession planning often enables people to distinguish the main functions of the business, for example service delivery, marketing etc, and identify generic skills patterns, such as project management skills that are required for a range of different posts (Hirsch, 2000). This certainly reflects our experience at ABC where our conversations at this first stage led to us designing a process that, instead of focusing on job functions, would influence the skills development required for the future. These conversations also led to us interpreting the requirement for a flow of people to fill key posts as being a process to include everyone. This aligned well with the chief executive's vision expressed through his 'Two-dots philosophy' as well as with the organization's value of fairness.

Our purpose, therefore, was to create a succession plan that would give us a long-term view, linked to strategic goals. From this, we could extrapolate information for a tactical plan for the Remuneration Committee, and for the immediate HR agenda.

2. Identify roles, capabilities and organizational requirements

Succession planning, at its simplest, involves collecting data on people and roles, matching the two and analysing the gaps.

At ABC, we needed data on present roles, and in relation to the capabilities needed in the future. Much of this information was already available through the talent strategy, and also from the organization chart, the firm's budget, and its business plan. From this we identified:

1　Roles to be covered by the plan (we covered the top two of the three management tiers).
2　Job clusters by capabilities, required experience etc.
3　Functional and situational experience required for each, especially the most senior roles. These two broad categories can be sub-divided:
   – Functional may be scarce and/or critical skills, complex skills requiring long training periods, possible skills required for the future.

- Situational may be multicultural fluency, entrepreneurial skills, leading significant change, international experience etc.

4 Behavioural capabilities. For many roles or job clusters, it was possible to show the key behavioural requirements, such as high-level negotiating skills, or analytical problem solving, or ability to handle conflict.

3. Compile the people databank

Succession processes are underpinned by having detailed, updated information on people and the business. We achieved this by producing for everyone what we called 'Talent Notes'. These extended the three-stage development plan to include summaries of people's behavioural capability profile (see Chapter 5 – this was data collected through the profiling process) and performance data, as well as suggested development needs, career aspirations and career paths. We used these notes as a basis of discussion held by each HR business partner with every manager. We got managers thinking about roles now and in the future and also considering people's development. These discussions helped to make managers more comfortable and confident about talking to their own staff about development.

The value of questions

The questions we asked managers started with current and future business and environmental challenges and the implications of these in terms of skill-sets and capabilities. We then extended the questioning to ask managers to identify successors to their own roles and those of the people in the next management tier. Although we discussed job functions, we focused more on capabilities. Through our line of questioning, managers identified the experience, learning and training that people would require. We also asked them about themselves, their aspirations, future career moves and the experience or learning they needed. We asked who they regarded as possible successors to their boss, and what special skills and experience their boss had that would be hard to replicate.

Importantly, we had encouraged managers to identify successors for roles and for skill-sets from across the organization. We also asked them to identify other parts of the business where their staff could potentially work. This was important to encourage cross-functional career moves and open career paths.

We included in this process not only people currently employed in the organization, but also past employees and external people. Past employees make up a valuable talent pool, combining knowledge of your organization and its culture with the advantages of external perspectives. Increasingly organizations are treasuring their leavers, and using alumni associations to keep in touch, and to keep leavers in touch with the business and with former colleagues.

At ABC, we also captured data on advisers, contractors, suppliers, etc so that our databank included information on how to readily access skills should an employee leave, or should the requirement for those skills increase. This also enabled us to recognize the external advisers who added the most value to the business, so that we could plan how and when to best utilize their talents and how to nurture relationships with them, especially during periods when their services were not required.

The data collected from these conversations were used to populate the databank and to produce draft Talent Notes, which managers could use to guide their forthcoming performance appraisal discussions, which on this occasion were refocused to give greater emphasis to long-term (three-stage) career conversations.

These Talent Notes established vital links between individuals' development plans, their aspirations, their capability strengths, their performance and business needs.

The value of conversations

Conversations around Talent Notes helped managers develop a talent mindset, as they emphasized the importance of:

1 future-focused thinking on the business challenges ahead;
2 providing developmental work experiences;
3 understanding aspirations and aligning these with organizational needs;
4 building on strengths and preferences;
5 facilitating career movement across the business.

A subsequent, highly favourable, review of this process found that managers had especially appreciated their conversations with the HR business partners, which effectively had served as mini-coaching sessions for them, demonstrating skills and a process which they had then repeated with their staff.

Give people control

Having got started, we could then give people responsibility for updating their own Talent Notes and initiating career conversations with their managers, though we emphasized that managers should check in with people about careers. In the next chapter, I suggest incorporating this within the performance review cycle.

The next stage in this process would be to link the Talent Notes to the HR information system, and also to internal social networking. I have already referred to the many systems becoming available to facilitate this so that people compile internal CVs that can be viewed by everyone. It should be possible to add confidential data with restricted access so that this system will replicate the Talent Notes described. This lessens the HR workload and gives control and ownership to the individual. It also makes the process user-friendly and relevant, which makes it more likely that people will follow it. People can of course compile Talent Notes without an online process.

At ABC our succession plan provided a valuable snapshot of organizational health, and at the same time achieved additional benefits, perhaps the two most significant being to put long-term development firmly on the map and to role-model to line managers the skills for holding career conversations.

4. Set up talent classifications and run talent roundtables

Talent considerations are likely to be different for different organizations depending on size and activities. At ABC Engineering, we drew up classifications so that we could track that the people who were ready for the next move, or for stretch and challenge, or who needed more support received the development, experience and promotion they needed. Our approach, especially through the Talent Notes, was essentially to provide the opportunity for individual career development planning at three stages. An advantage of this process is that it naturally takes care of the high performers and those with higher potential and aspiration, by identifying appropriate development, but also because the process gives them feedback and recognition. Moreover, career conversations are highly valued (Chapter 6). At ABC these approaches also took account of people who at different stages, and for different reasons, would be critical to business performance.

CASE STUDY

Paul Herrick at Burson-Marsteller tries to avoid the 'high-potential' term, believing it is often misused. Instead, B-M have identified what is known as 'six for six'; that is, each person has to satisfy each of the six characteristics at their level. The aim is to develop people to be part of a pool of excellence from which the leaders and key roles will be recruited. Examples of these characteristics are: contribution to winning new business; quality of client services; financial and business acumen as demonstrated through depth of understanding of the business and what it is about; outstanding people skills; team player; history of meeting goals; uphold corporate values. As with other professional firms, and in the ABC Engineering example, this is not about succession planning in the sense of identifying people who could perform a particular role, neither is it about identifying leaders; rather it is about providing outstanding development for people so that they develop the skill-sets and capabilities required for the future success of the business, but also to match their own aspirations.

At B-M, towards the beginning of the year, business objectives are cascaded through the organization, so that people are clear about the main performance areas for the following year and set their objectives in line with them. Those who meet the criteria for being in the top pool of talent are then tracked. Herrick and the chief executive check that their performance objectives contain clear, challenging and stretching measures.

While learning and development are especially important for everyone at B-M, particular attention is taken to ensure that people in the top talent pool follow a challenging learning path programme. Line managers are required to discuss learning interventions with the individual to encourage them to reflect on what they have learned and how they can apply the learning. Herrick, and also the person's line manager, identify reading materials for the person, who is also brought into discussions about an element of the firm's business strategy. They are expected to gain a deep understanding of the strategy, its implications and any possible alternatives. They are expected to develop ideas about its implementation, challenging the CEO on aspects of it, being challenged in turn, and championing its implementation. People in the top talent pool have also worked on a joint project around corporate responsibility, which is a major business area on which B-M advises clients.

Note from this example the links created between succession planning, performance appraisal and the role of the line manager, as well as the emphasis on development by experience, especially how this includes exposing someone to the firm's overall business strategy. B-M's method is built around the business need to identify potential around capabilities, rather than job functions.

Nine-Box Grid

The most commonly used system of classifying people is through the Performance and Potential Matrix, or Nine-Box Grid, or a variant of this.

The Nine-Box is a grid on which you plot employees based on their performance ranking and their potential for advancement (Figure 7.2). Based on a method originally developed by McKinsey, this is essentially a convenient way of taking a macro-view of performance and potential

FIGURE 7.2 Nine-Box talent review grid

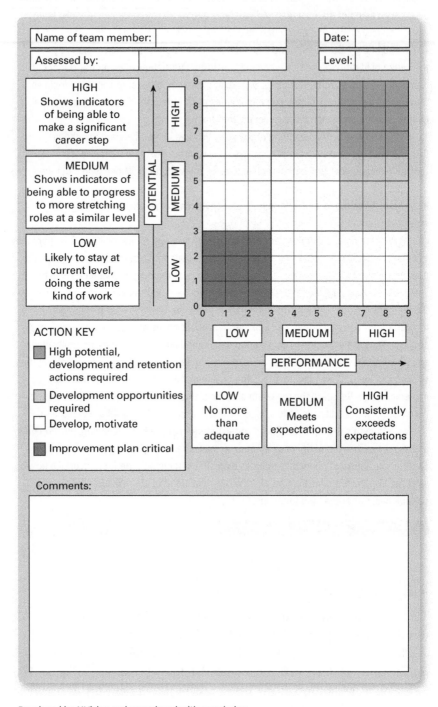

Developed by MVision and reproduced with permission.

CASE STUDY

Bekaert is a global technological and market leader in advanced solutions based on metal transformation and coatings, and the world's largest independent manufacturer of drawn steel wire products. Headquartered in Belgium and employing 27,000 worldwide, Bekaert holds performance reviews twice yearly, using a five-point rating scale that feeds into the talent reviews. The performance review discussion covers the individual's career development aspirations and fields of interest, as well performance, and this is documented.

Bekaert uses the Nine-Box Grid for this review and every manager above a certain Hay classification[1] is assigned to one of the boxes on the matrix. The sponsoring line manager (the person to whom the individual reports) will discuss the level of classification they want to assign someone with their own line manager and with their HR manager. All managers in each unit will then meet together, for one day, to discuss each person in the matrix, their performance levels and their potential. The process is then taken to Executive Committee level, whose focus is on the senior managers and who discuss those capable of filling the top 100 jobs in the organization.

The talent review process brings many benefits. It encourages a team approach to identifying potential and discussing talent, which helps overcome problems of line managers holding on to good people and also means that individuals are not necessarily reliant on one person to sponsor them. It also emphasizes the importance of encouraging and supporting individual development. Once the Executive Committee approves the talent plan, the line manager is required to identify a personal development plan for the individual and is responsible for ensuring that it is carried out, but it is HR's role to facilitate and challenge. Bekaert believes strongly in development through experience.

People know about this process and, through conversations with their line manager, will understand how their performance is perceived in the organization. The classifications are used for workforce planning and control, rather than as a way of labelling people. They are also intended to be fluid, allowing movement in and out of the 'boxes' and the roles on the succession plan, according to business and other changes.

Although this talent review process is globally run for the senior management levels, some of Bekaert's business units extend it to everyone in their unit. The process itself confers strategic and team-building benefits through bringing senior managers together as a team to review the talent flow in and out of the business. When you are confronted, for argument's sake, with all your unit managers in the same left-hand-corner box you realize that you will have future succession problems and that you need to address these. The process focuses senior management on preparing for the next 10–20 years. They do not identify business-critical posts, as all positions in the organization are interconnected and it is difficult to say that one post is more critical than another.

This talent review process links into the business planning cycle, which is a three-year rolling plan that covers both organization and people. It precedes the business plan review, so that plans are made with reference to the people in place and their capabilities.

Bekaert appoints people to senior-level internal vacancies when they know from the talent review process that the person is suitable. There will be an interview but this is generally more about interesting the person in the role than in assessing their suitability. This can lead those who are excluded from consideration to feel frustrated, but this disadvantage is outweighed by the advantage of bringing together experienced people who know both the business and the people well and have them take responsibility for the decision.

Bekaert's process of succession planning and talent reviews is a key process for achieving global consistency, using data and opinion in equal measure. Moreover, its use of assessment and development centres provides additional information for the organization, as well as development support for the individual. An emphasis on development by experience is an important underpinning of the talent review conversations, which seek to ensure that people receive not just the appropriate classification but also the appropriate development and support.

across the organization. The main problem with it is achieving consistency of performance and potential classifications. On the other hand, having discussions around this helps achieve this consistency. Most businesses I deal with find the Nine-Box matrix useful for this reason, but also because it provides an overview and facilitates conversations among managers, and between managers and individuals. The first conversations among managers help them clarify their thinking and articulate standards and development actions, which then equips them to hold better-quality conversations with their people. A further benefit of this tool is that it guides assessment of individuals in a way that helps identify specific actions that ensure the ongoing development of talent across the organization, or a part of the organization.

The use of talent classifications and what you do with them must match organizational needs. Here are some examples.

In large, global organizations, or those comprising different businesses, such as Bekaert, the emphasis is best placed on people who are in mid-career and may rise to be the future business leaders. In these cases, the succession planning model will likely focus on these levels but will encourage a similar, devolved process through the individual businesses.

The bright and ambitious graduates of firms such as Burson-Marsteller cannot all reach the top levels. While these firms can still offer opportunity and career development to those who will not reach director or partner level, many prefer to seek leadership roles elsewhere. This means that career paths need to be well mapped, what is required at each stage must be clearly identified and communicated, and people need to be given appropriate support. This requires identifying leadership potential at an earlier stage than might be the case in, say, a large industrial conglomerate. It is generally preferable in professional services firms to populate the senior levels of the organization mostly from within to provide client continuity.

Some corporations that offer their customers the latest technology and services often have complex organizational structures, and the ability to innovate will be highly prized. As a result, they are likely to be constantly searching for external talent, even at senior levels, and are also likely to search worldwide to find it. In these businesses, talent pools are likely to focus on technical and behavioural capabilities, and provide a strong interface with the external resourcing programme. ABC Engineering is one such example, and the link with external resourcing is discussed in the next section.

Yet another scenario is provided by organizations in retailing and hospitality, for example, that experience high staff turnover. Here succession planning is likely to focus on a small core of people and roles where they wish to build long-term commitment and loyalty.

There are some instances where filling roles externally is more valuable than an internal appointment. One of these concerns organizations going through a major cultural shift, when it might be helpful to import people who have both the desired mindset and the ability to spread it to others.

Another concerns small, entrepreneurial businesses, which generally go through stages of evolution where they outgrow the competencies of the existing employees. In such cases, external hires can help take the business to its next evolutionary stage, though this role might also be filled by external advisers who can be valuable for their broader experience and impartial perspective, as well as for passing on specialist expertise and helping existing people develop the new desired capabilities. In larger businesses, external advisers can bring similar advantages to people in specialist functions, such as HR or marketing, where there are fewer opportunities to develop expertise from within, compared to the front-line business functions.

One of the great dilemmas of talent classifications is whether or not to tell people how they have been classified. The following rules of thumb derive from the key principles of my approach to strategic talent development:

1 Total transparency is essential.

2 Everyone should have opportunity that matches their aspirations, as well as business needs.

3 No assessment should be fixed for all time. People's performance can vary over time, as can the capabilities that are required for different roles and different levels.

4 When everyone perceives plenty of development, they are less likely to be concerned about being judged unready for promotion, or not yet suitable for a leadership programme.

5 Classifications are useful ways of keeping light-touch control over talent and performance and over leadership and management capability too. It also helps identify who needs special development opportunity, and where you might have retention problems.

6 The high-potential tag should be avoided at all costs. It raises expectations that probably cannot be met, and can give people an inflated view of themselves. I have also known it turn the maverick high performer who questions, challenges and pushes for change into a risk-averse person, frightened to rock the boat for fear of losing this status.

Talent review conversations, or 'roundtables'

Perhaps the greatest benefit of talent classifications is that they facilitate talent review conversations such as those described in the Bekaert case study, where peer groups of line managers get together to discuss the performance and potential of the people in their teams. These conversations bring many benefits:

1 They create a talent mindset, making senior management aware of knowing people and developing them in line with the organization's requirements. This raises consciousness that the capabilities of the organization are an aggregation of the people within it.

2 They help achieve consistency in assessing performance and help people develop a common view of what makes for success and high performance.

3 Subjective assessments of people are inevitable and these 'roundtables' enable broader, all-round assessments that give greater fairness and consistency.

4 They bring people to the notice of other parts of the business and result in better development plans.

5 They create a global mindset, reducing the effects of silo working, by creating synergies across boundaries.

6 They throw up business improvements or lead directors and managers to challenge assumptions behind the business strategy.

7 They improve teamwork and understanding among peer levels.

8 They help the business define performance standards so that the value to the organization of steady contributors and high performers is clear. This then enables managers to have better conversations with people about how they are doing and what the future holds for them.

9 They raise employee engagement by giving people answers to their key questions: What is expected of me? How am I doing? What happens next for me? How will I be supported to get there? How will I be rewarded?

10 They emphasize the importance of opening development experiences that align individual aspirations with those of the organization, so this becomes 'how we do things around here'.

11 They provide an overview of performance and potential across the business, which is essential for ensuring that the business has in place adequate attraction and retention strategies. Talent review data and conversations enable the C-Suite and HR to keep a light-touch 'control'.

Talent 'roundtables' achieve a more rounded view of performance and potential than is usual through performance appraisal, or even 360-degree feedback.

The role of the C-Suite

Succession is a major responsibility of those in the C-Suite. Good corporate governance requires that non-executive directors ensure the company has the resources, particularly money and people, sufficient to implement its strategy. Non-executive directors, therefore, have a major interest in the information generated by the succession plan and in ensuring that the business has the people to provide continuity in a crisis and sustainability in the long term. A highly effective process is to set aside time, preferably twice yearly, for the board to review the people who are rising through the organization and aspire to the top roles, or perhaps to other key roles too. This can give rise to detailed and challenging conversations about people, and their development, which also causes the board members to question and discuss different aspects of business strategy and direction, as well as policy and practice.

5. Identify resourcing, learning and development and business improvements

At ABC Engineering, we drew up a succession plan showing people who could cover roles on a contingency basis, as well as who could be ready in the near future and also in the longer term. This resulted in a highlighting of current risks.

However, we produced a parallel plan showing skill-sets and capabilities rather than roles, and who was already able to cover these, or could potentially do so with appropriate development. This gave a more accurate plan to prepare for long-term sustainability, which would depend more on people with the right capabilities than 'filling shoes'.

A major purpose of any succession planning process is to identify organizational vulnerabilities as well as develop resourcing and learning and development plans. A powerful side product is its contribution to business improvements. At ABC Engineering, we drew up a report commenting on the issues that had arisen in the process. These related to the organization overall and each major division or business unit. This was discussed at board level, as part of the corporate governance procedures.

Having a solid appreciation of organizational strengths and vulnerabilities for the immediate and longer term made it easy to create coherent external resourcing and learning and development strategies addressing what we would do about these vulnerabilities. The latter was for everyone: those with high potential, those with scarce skills, valuable steady performers and those with potential skills. In identifying people who were able to cover certain skill needs, or technical areas, especially in the event of a short-term contingency, external suppliers and consultants were also included in the succession plan, as a source of potential cover. By implementing this we were able to mitigate the risk of not having people with the right skills in place, and this piece of the programme closed the loop on aligning individual and organizational requirements.

In global organizations or large conglomerates the succession planning emphasis is likely to be on the top leadership levels to ensure a pipeline of people who can fill future leadership roles. This has become increasingly necessary due to the shortages of leaders worldwide but it also reflects an increasing recognition, shown through studies on employee engagement, that an emphasis on growing your own leaders helps attract and retain people at all levels. However, it must always be kept in mind that the relative importance of certain capabilities might change rapidly in the 'new world' and this must be factored into the analysis, much as we did at ABC by analysing job families and clusters of capabilities.

6. Review and update the plan regularly

The point of having data is to give you a detailed understanding of the people you employ. The point of both workforce and succession planning is to use those data to give you an overview that enables you to exercise control, determine strategies for improvement, and keep check of progress. It goes without saying it must be kept updated.

According to Hirsh, although this devolved model is especially common to large organizations, few successfully sustain it, usually because it is not seen as a high priority and not adequately facilitated by HR. My view is that it must be a major HR responsibility to give an organization-wide perspective to the motivation, development and careers of those who want this.

7. Use the plan to keep track of people and their development

It is, of course, important to keep track and make sure that people are indeed receiving the development and the opportunities agreed for them.

People databank and employee engagement data

In discussing employee engagement in Chapter 2, we considered evidence of the link between engagement and performance. Understanding of current levels of employee engagement within the organization can be matched with data from the people databank to provide a 'datum point' from which to measure change and also to help you to develop your talent strategy, such as in the Siemens example on page 131.

Some organizations are developing highly sophisticated uses of employee engagement data that are being used to make better strategic business decisions. This is generally being achieved by examining the relationship between employee attitudes (and how these are changed by different management policies) on the one hand, and customer attitudes, customer behaviour and business revenue on the other. It addresses questions about whether employees' attitudes to their jobs and company affect customer service and influence customer satisfaction and, in due course, the sales and profitability of the business. For example, if you compare data and find that 35 per cent of the people in your best-performing branches have more than five years' service and believe that someone at work supports their development, then this might suggest that mentoring helps staff retention which, in turn, boosts results. There could be other interpretations but the point is that being able to look at data suggests possible actions that may improve the organization's performance. This can be illustrated with further examples.

Sears, Roebuck & Co has mapped employee engagement data against customer satisfaction with their shopping experience and the likelihood that they would return and would recommend Sears to friends and family. Their research showed that even small improvements in employee attitudes resulted in slightly higher levels of customer satisfaction, which in turn increased customer referrals and produced an increase in revenue growth (Rucci, Kirn and Quinn, 1998).

McDonald's, Royal Bank of Scotland and Standard Chartered are also leaders in the measurement of people and their relationship to business performance. McDonald's has analysed business results against the demographics of its stores and other data and found that, within a predominantly young workforce, customer satisfaction is more than 20 per cent higher in restaurants which employ one or more staff members over the age of 60 than it is in restaurants where none of the staff are over 50. This effect appears to arise through the presence of older workers helping to raise the performance and customer-centredness of all staff, with the result that customer numbers, sales and satisfaction are increased (Cheese, Thomas and Craig, 2008). RBS has focused on establishing the linkage between improvement in people measures, such as engagement and employee satisfaction, and improvement in sales and customer service. They have found that increasing engagement levels will also impact on business output measures. Standard Chartered, similarly, can demonstrate the relationship between levels of engagement and branch profitability. Moreover, Standard Chartered has also reported that in 2007 they found that branches with a statistically significant increase in levels of employee engagement (0.2 or more on a scale of 5) had a 16 per cent higher profit margin growth than branches with decreased levels of employee engagement. This shows the benefit of continually improving engagement levels. Standard Chartered has continued to evolve its external reporting through its Annual Review and its Sustainability Review, which release significantly more data than in the past, and the bank is increasingly candid about the challenges it faces (MacLeod and Clarke, 2009).

Sophisticated use of employee engagement data that show how engaged people are, and what entices them to leave the organization, go much further in aligning people-management decisions with corporate objectives and measuring creation of shareholder value than is possible with the familiar measures such as staff turnover. Perhaps it also moves HR away from a preoccupation about measuring its worth, to focusing on measuring the business. If a new HR policy is designed to have an effect on people that will lead through to a positive impact on business performance, then surely we should not waste time struggling to measure that original effect but should be measuring changes in business performance itself to find whether the policy has worked?

It is clear that employee data from different sources can be used to make real business improvements. For example, a well-known transport company recently had technical problems that were compounded by poor customer service and communication with customers, leading to appallingly bad publicity. Suppose this company had conducted an employee engagement survey: my guess is it would show low engagement in the customer-facing roles, poor internal communications and poor support from line managers, among other issues. Almost certainly, analysis of such data before the calamity occurred would have highlighted serious problems and could have prevented huge financial losses from devastatingly bad publicity. A first step, therefore, in developing a talent strategy is to analyse the data generated by your employee engagement survey and any other data about employee perceptions. Then ask what this tells you about practices that work well and those that don't.

Key points

- Organizations have a variety of needs for succession planning and workforce planning, ranging from assessing vulnerabilities to planning future strategy. What are yours?
- You need robust data about people in order to inform critical business decisions.
- Focus less on jobs that need filling and more on capabilities that will be needed and on providing development to match people's aspirations.

- Use a process such as Talent Notes to facilitate managers' conversations with staff about aspirations and development and to emphasize the importance of development by experience.

- Develop your own leaders because promoting from within leads to higher engagement levels as it demonstrates that individuals are valued.

- Hold regular talent review meetings among groups of managers. This builds their skills and achieves consistency. It opens careers organization-wide. Succession planning will identify people to fill future appointments, but requires a good balance between data and judgement, both of which must come from multiple sources.

- Compare employee data with customer, sales or financial information to identify business improvements: your objective is to improve business performance through your people, not to have bright shiny HR practices.

Note

1 Hay classification refers to a point factor method of job evaluation to determine the relative value of a job. The Hay method measures three factors common to all jobs – know-how, problem solving and accountability – and focuses on internal job relationships and maintaining internal equity. After applying the job evaluation instrument, the resulting points determine where a job is placed in the hierarchy of job classifications, with each job classification assigned to a salary grade within the overall compensation structure.

Performance and pay

T he fourth point of the talent framework is 'shared management' (Figure 8.1). I show this as the last point to emphasize that the responsibility for bringing strategic talent development to life in large part rests with those in management positions. To work effectively, the initiatives that form self-managed succession require management support to have conversations with people about performance and careers, to open developmental work experience, and to link individuals with wider organizational needs. For this latter, managers are helped by having access to a robust and current people databank, as discussed in the last chapter. As we saw in Chapter 1, when managers perform these roles well, this can raise levels of employee engagement to have a significant impact on business performance.

Managers, of course, operate at many different levels of the hierarchy, and it is helpful to our understanding of management roles to make some differentiations. The French term 'management de proximité', which translates as 'nearby management', describes the role of managing (recruiting, engaging, assessing, developing and deploying) the people within one's immediate sphere of responsibility. In contrast, there is the term 'faraway management' to refer to the role of those in the C-Suite and in other management tiers within the wider organization. 'Nearby management' in the new world organization is a shared process, with all protagonists being clear about their responsibilities and accountabilities. C-Suite leaders and other executives are 'nearby managers' to their immediate teams and direct reports, and 'faraway managers' to everyone else.

I look at the different facets of 'nearby management' in this chapter and the next. In this chapter, I look at the performance management process, and consider new approaches to support it. I then turn to reward and consider how to align the messages of your reward programmes with those of

FIGURE 8.1   The four-point framework shows the steps to develop your talent and engagement strategy

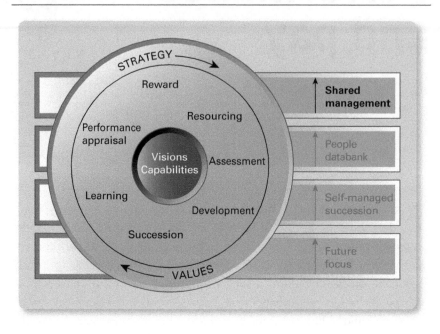

your talent strategy, and look at how pay for performance affects organizational culture and individual motivation. In the next chapter, I look at other aspects of the 'nearby management' role and offer some guidance on how to tackle common problems. I look at faraway management in the last chapter.

I have talked a lot in this book about distributed leadership and the need for light-touch control on the part of management. I place performance management in this chapter to emphasize that it is through this process that managers exercise light-touch control.

Before examining this, it will be helpful to our understanding to look again at the notion of shared management.

Shared management

An effect of the economic downturn is that many employees are in jobs they have grown out of, that do not offer them the stretch and challenge they seek, and are working for businesses that in an earlier age they would have left, and will perhaps leave as soon as the market improves. This gives rise to leadership issues that we will address in the next chapters, but it also impacts on performance management. It reinforces the need for feedback on performance and support for developmental work experience that will invigorate people. To achieve high performance throughout your organization, it is vital to differentiate between high and satisfactory performance. High performers want to be recognized, empowered and challenged; satisfactory performers want feedback to help them raise performance. When managers clearly and consistently recognize standards of performance, this raises performance generally, and makes poor performance more easily recognizable and dealt with.

This all places a significant workload and responsibility on the manager. But whereas in hierarchical organizations employing command and control management line managers had clear responsibilities for their direct reports and closely supervised their work, their role now is more opaque. They often understand less of the detail of what their people do. Moreover, people increasingly work in virtual, global teams, matrix structures, flat hierarchies, or in different project teams. In this new world of lighter touch, direct contact is less frequent.

So there is a conflict between employees' need for feedback and opportunity, on the one hand, and line managers being overloaded with chores, inadequately supported and often displaced from close contact on the other. Can we reconcile this conflict? There is no one answer to fit every situation, but there are three basic rules of thumb:

1 *Everyone must have a clearly designated people manager who has ownership and accountability for their performance, reward and career.* Failure to do this leads to poor motivation, and eventually to the person leaving, or not pulling their weight, because they have not been given sufficient opportunity or support. The people manager's role should be focused on holding a regular dialogue with their people about performance, ensuring they have development support and opportunity, and differentiating between high and satisfactory performance.

2 *Management of people must be a shared process.* The line manager retains ownership and accountability for overall performance for all people within his or her sphere of responsibility. However, the designated people manager manages the input of several people: project or team leaders who are responsible for the business results someone achieves; perhaps a coach who helps someone to achieve a learning goal, and mentors or sponsors who support career

development. This may be achieved through regular meetings to share information about people, roles, performance and aspirations. Communications technology makes this possible, even if we are geographically spread. Such coordination is essential if the organization is to achieve the rapid talent mobility that is needed in our fast-moving world. This model is not entirely new. For instance, it is similar to the model used in the big accountancy practices, law firms and management consultancies where it operates, especially, at trainee level. However, this model is becoming increasingly relevant to most businesses, and at all levels.

3 *HR must support the people manager.* This is through providing backup to deal with poor performers, assistance with development of interpersonal and coaching skills, and backup to deal with high performers and those with high aspirations. On this latter point, HR with its wider view of the organization is best placed to ensure that appropriate, organization-wide opportunities are opened to those who want them, and merit them.

CASE STUDY

The following case study is an example of a firm that has adopted this new model.

MVision Private Equity Advisers is widely recognized as the world's leading independent alternative assets advisory and placement firm. It focuses on private equity, real estate, real assets, infrastructure, credit and direct transactions, in both the developed and emerging markets. MVision operates out of offices in London, New York, Hong Kong and Sydney.

The internal organization covers a range of functional disciplines such as client relationship management, business development, implementation of deals, legal, finance, compliance etc; but many individuals work on several deals (or projects) at any one time. Who do they report to? Who manages them? Who looks after their development; who looks after their well-being; and who does their performance appraisals?

CEO Mounir (Moose) Guen and Founding Partner Jane Sutherland place prime importance on these matters, and have operated a performance appraisal process, comprising both annual and interim reviews, since the firm was established in 2001. For a long time Guen and Sutherland jointly participated in every review discussion with every employee, but the growth of the business, taken together with the high administrative burden of performance appraisal, made this involvement in the detail too time consuming. They needed a new management model.

The new management model separates responsibilities for business results from those for developing and assessing people. The 'functional team leader' (often the chief executive in the example) or project team heads deal with business results, while responsibility for people's assessment and development is incorporated in a new 'development adviser' role. It becomes part of anyone's career development path that, once they are at a certain level (from director level in this example, which roughly equates to middle manager level), they must take on responsibility for the development and assessment of people assigned to them. Fortunately, the management matrix organization structure still retains concepts of seniority, even if there are no structured hierarchies. There are managing directors, directors, vice-presidents, associates and analysts, even if, in a functional sense, it is not clear who reports to whom.

The new 'development advisers' also have project team management responsibilities but those will be separate from the people management role. They may be managing people who are never part of one of their project teams or who are but only intermittently.

These new arrangements have been enthusiastically received by the appointed 'development advisers', though it is too soon, at the time of writing, to see the effect on the firm as a whole, or on business results. The aim, of course, is for people to thrive from the closer attention to their development. A recent review showed that the 'development advisers' valued their roles for the responsibility it gave them. Strikingly, they also valued the skills they were gaining, which they saw as transferable to their client relationships, but also vital for their future careers. It seems clear from this review that the change has given people additional skill-sets that the firm will be able to leverage as it develops.

An interesting light is shed on this new structure by work I was conducting for an international bank at around the same time. I conducted interviews with people in its business areas as part of a development centre programme, based on the bank's existing capability framework. When I asked about their main development needs, they too viewed the ability to lead and manage their team members as critical both to the achievement of business results and to their future career prospects. However, the bank's framework did not recognize 'people management' as a capability needed for promotion or success. It is not the contrast that is striking as much as the fact that powerful advocacy of the importance of these skills and techniques was coming not from HR but from front-line managers. This represents a sea change from attitudes just a few years ago when it was a battle to get this message across.

At MVision, development advisers are expected to hold monthly conversations with their people, which feed through into interim and annual reviews, and into pay decisions. Interim reviews focus on development, while the annual review is primarily concerned with assessing performance and agreeing a performance rating. This rating is one, though not the only, input into the pay award. Consistency and all-round assessment are achieved through talent roundtable discussions, which include both 'development advisers' and senior management.

The appraisal documentation is completed by each individual, who sets out what they have achieved, how they know they were successful and the impact this has had on the business. Other questions, which may vary from one review to another, include 'what did not work out as planned?' or perhaps 'what elements of your job do you like the most/least?' There are two reviewers at each review, one of whom is the individual's 'development adviser'.

The outcome of this new process is to spread detailed people management more widely while still retaining a clear overview at the top. Delegating the process is both a valued development opportunity for many within the organization and develops skills that are valuable to the organization itself. Guen and Sutherland commented that the process also encouraged deeper reflection from each individual, which led to more insightful results.

This shared management model fills the feedback and support vacuum that is becoming increasingly common as management spans of control widen. The above case study shows the model in practice. It also illustrates the following elements, which have a general applicability and which I recommend:

- A different focus to each of the annual and interim reviews. The annual concentrates on performance, the interim on development.
- Using two reviewers at the appraisal meeting.
- Self-appraisal.

I will now turn to consider appraisals in more detail.

Performance appraisal

Performance appraisal is one of the most criticized people-management practices. The criticisms range from 'being too time consuming' and 'something we have to do for HR' (in other words they are of no benefit to me), to having a negative, even destructive impact on the relationship between managers and their team members. A recent US poll of 2,677 people (1,800 employees, 645 HR managers and 232 CEOs) revealed that 98 per cent of staff find annual performance reviews unnecessary (Achievers, 2012). In spite of this, further research (Lawler, 2012) shows that 93 per cent of companies use annual appraisals, and only 6 per cent have considered dropping them. This suggests that they are of benefit to organizations, and we must find ways of making them more meaningful to employees. There is little consensus among commentators, however, about how to achieve this.

My own view is that most performance appraisal systems are a legacy of the top-down 'command-and-control' management systems that no longer suit our more fluid organizational structures. They need a complete overhaul. Another problem is that traditional performance appraisal aims to achieve too much: commonly, it is an annual or sometimes twice-yearly opportunity:

> to engage in a dialogue about each individual's performance and development, as well as the support required from the manager.... Performance appraisals usually review past actions and behaviour and so provide an opportunity to reflect on past performance. But to be successful they should also be used as a basis for making development and improvement plans and reaching agreement about what should be done in the future. (CIPD, 2012)

Often it involves assigning ratings and rankings that input to pay decisions, even though academic theory generally advises against this because it detracts from the important aims of giving feedback to the individual and discussing development. It is generally reckoned that people will not be prepared to admit to failings, or the need for improvement, if their pay increase is at stake. In practice, however, I think this argument applies equally when there is no overt link to pay, as people always connect the two.

The key question to address, therefore, is what do we want the performance appraisal process to achieve? From the point of view of both the organization and the individual, a point in time where you take stock of the past to then plan the immediate future is vital. An annual review helps give a sense of perspective over what has been achieved, and what to do next. This is helpful to the individual so they know how their performance is viewed, how they are contributing, and what they might do next. It also helps effectively run the business, giving data that show who is contributing what, to what, and from where. Data about performance, as well as potential and aspirations, are vital for making pay and promotion decisions, but also for making a host of other business decisions, such as considering who might help you develop new business, or who might be best placed to work on certain key projects, or to develop a client relationship.

It follows, therefore, that an annual review that focuses on these issues is required. Moreover, if we remind ourselves of employee engagement data, it is clear that a time to consider the future and discuss long-term career aspirations is also required. This is especially true if we are to energize people and instil a future-focus and agility in the organization. This points to focusing interim reviews on development and careers.

Performance management process

The following timeline picks up on these ideas, and is a typical process that I find works well. It starts and ends with the business planning cycle.

1 At the annual point of the cycle, performance is formally reviewed. This involves a discussion between individual and reviewer, or indeed two reviewers, and a roundtable discussion between managers, where a person's performance ratings are agreed. Reviewers communicate their ratings back to individuals, and performance goals for the next period are agreed. At this time 80 per cent of the review should be on performance, with 20 per cent to look at the development needs that fall out of this review.

2 At the interim review, the focus switches to 80 per cent on careers and development, following the 'three-stage development plan', and 20 per cent to review performance. This involves a formal career conversation, and probably this time there is just one reviewer, though two may still be appropriate. There is then a roundtable discussion between managers, where someone's career and development are discussed. This should feed into the succession plan.

Assessment of an individual's performance and potential can be made at certain points in time, such as at annual and interim points. However, using points of time to set goals is artificial, as things don't begin and end so neatly. Goal setting should, therefore, be constantly revised, always in line with the strategic priorities of the business.

3 The individual's 'people manager' (or development adviser to apply the term used at MVision in the case study on page 156) meets regularly – preferably monthly – with the individual they are responsible for. I look at these meetings and the responsibilities they involve in the next chapter.

For now, I turn to different elements of the formal performance review process.

Define standards of performance

Clearly articulated standards drive successful business performance. They underpin the firm's business strategy, enable it to attract the right talent, recognize and reward high performance, eliminate underperformance and deliver growth, increased profitability and long-term sustainability. Moreover, there is increasing evidence to show that where companies concentrate on differentiating top performers from those at the bottom, this has the effect of raising levels of achievement among all staff. Nonetheless, this is often an area of weakness (Guest and Conway, 2004).

Ways to achieve a good understanding of standards of performance are the following.

1. Success is about the results you achieve, not what you do

People often describe roles in relation to the tasks that must be performed, such as: 'Maintain a client-calling programme and keep records updated.' This statement does not identify what successful performance looks like. Why are you maintaining the client-calling programme? What will you do with the information? What is the value-add? Failing to express performance through answers to these and similar questions will lead to different levels of effort and, therefore, of success. So one person might interpret this as 'draw up a list of clients in a region, plan to call them say on a quarterly basis to find out if they are seeking new opportunities, and then note this on a spreadsheet'. They might see success as having called 100 people regularly and kept their records up to date, when in fact what is required is to have deeper conversations to find out what the client is engaged with at the present time, what their strategy is, what types of opportunities might interest them, in which markets, etc. This quality of information might then enable the business development team to match the client to a current opportunity. The performance standard is then measured through the quality of the information, not through the number of calls. This, of course, is not only about how to measure results, but this level of clarity also sets expectations and, therefore, directs effort.

CASE STUDY

KPMG uses a balanced scorecard approach for setting objectives for its partner and director population, having identified what is important for the firm's success. Cascading from these, they have key performance indicators for assessing the impact of their emerging leader population (those deemed to have the potential to reach partner). These work around objectives such as how much someone has depth and breadth in their client portfolio, how international their experience is, how much they have worked across skillsets and how they have added exceptional value to clients.

These success factors guide performance and how it will be measured.

2. Behaviours and values contribute to our success

Our behaviours and values often make the biggest difference to the results we achieve. Take this example: T is a reward consultant. He redesigns the client's management incentive bonus plans, and produces a client report. The new scheme is technically robust and well designed, and also suits the goals, activities and culture of the client business. However, T does not explain it properly and his report is not of a good enough quality to go to the client. Someone else picks it up, and re-presents it. It is well received. However, T's failure caused a delay to implementation. How do you rate T's performance? Is he performing below standard because his communication is not good enough, or is he performing to standard because his work is technically good? Much depends on the firm's cultural values, or perhaps the performance characteristics for his role, and whether these emphasize client service and relationships as paramount. These specify the standards and measurement criteria for T's job. If the whole job clearly requires both technical ability and communication and client skills, then T is performing below standard. However, it is important to allow roles to develop around people, so T's job could be redesigned so that he focuses solely on what he is good at. Even then, it is likely that he will need good team-working skills, so there will still be a strong behavioural component to his success. T's lack of communication and client skills might, therefore, not take him to the level of underperformance, but it will probably affect his potential, at least as viewed by his present employer, where it is likely that to achieve promotion, T would need to have mastered the capabilities he lacks. Clearly articulated values, behaviours and performance characteristics help assess T's performance and potential and help T know what development he requires. Indeed, T might realize that his lack of client skills will impede his promotional prospects and he can then decide if this fits his aspirations, or if he needs to move firm.

3. Do targets cover 'soft' objectives?

Soft objectives deliver hard results. In the new world organization, being an effective talent manager must be a required skill for all managers, and should be transferred into a hard objective so as to emphasize accountability for talent development. I also suggest that people should be required to show that they have been continually refreshing and updating their skills, and this too should be taken into account in determining performance ratings. This is especially relevant to our ethos of self-managed succession, where we wish to encourage people to control their own learning and development. It is similar to the notion of continuous professional development, which is imperative to most professions.

CASE STUDY

KPMG views taking on people leadership responsibilities as a key role that someone can play in their career. This experience aids individuals when they are looking at entry into the partnership where stewardship and people leadership are valued qualities. These messages are also embedded in the performance management process. How people manage teams or projects is assessed. KPMG look at someone's management style and how he or she gains the team's commitment to delivering the best result for clients. KPMG actively looks for evidence that the individual is developing and coaching staff to ensure that they are able to deliver on both short- and long-term objectives in a way that fosters team development and learning.

CASE STUDY

Within KPMG's performance management process, for example, people self-assess on achievement of targets, and also on how effectively they uphold the values of the firm. They will be asked to produce evidence of this. There is a well-embedded framework in the organization of giving feedback, and people have conversations at the end of any large project to discuss how the work went and any learning that emerges. People also e-mail each other for feedback, generally by asking, 'can you tell me what to stop, start and continue?' People take this evidence to their appraisal to reflect on with their performance manager who takes this into account, together with feedback the manager will have gathered. Overall performance ratings depend on the delivery of consistent results, as well as on demonstrating appropriate behaviours and upholding the firm's values.

Many appraisal processes will expect people to illustrate if they have upheld the firm's values, and this will contribute to the overall performance rating.

4. Competencies

Assessing people against competency profiles has long been a common part of appraisal systems. Often managers rate someone against a profile, individuals self-assess against the same profile, and the two then compare and contrast during the appraisal meeting. This is one of the practices that has brought appraisal into disrepute, as it is hard to know what value it brings. It is bureaucratic, unpopular and leads either to long, laborious appraisals or to the opposite: a quick rush through ticking all the boxes. Moreover, competency assessments often add to the conflict between line manager and appraisee over appraisal ratings. There is, of course, an irony here as the whole idea of competencies is to emphasize that *how* you achieve results is as important as *what* you achieve. It should follow, therefore, that if someone met their sales targets but failed to share information or support a colleague, and so did not uphold the teamwork competency, this should be reflected in their competency ratings, which should bring down their overall appraisal rating. Simple really! Except, of course, in reality it gives rise to difficult conversations and to conflict. Ironically, it is also common for competency assessments to be used to inflate someone's overall rating where they failed to achieve target. If you use this type of system, question what value it adds. I prefer to review performance against values, or to turn soft objectives into hard targets, as discussed above.

5. Conversations supported by data establish standards

The roundtable meetings that we have already discussed are effective ways of getting people to articulate standards of performance, and to create consistency around these. Take this example: one manager says that W is a high performer because he has called 100 investors, but another manager says, 'When I contacted the investors W suggested to me, I found that my proposal does not fit their strategy, and W had not had the "right" kind of conversation with them.' These contrasting views, firstly, serve to rebalance the performance assessment about W. Secondly, they help set a common standard. As discussed in the previous chapter, these conversations are most effective when they are facilitated and supported by data, such as people's internal CVs, performance records, aspirations, and indeed also management information such as sales data, which can be used for comparisons or for drawing conclusions. For example, those present might feel that D does not have the negotiating skills required for promotion to the next level. However, an examination of the projects that have been carried out over the past year might reveal that she was, through circumstance, engaged only in the smaller ones that did not give her the opportunity to display or master this capability. She might, therefore, be judged ready for promotion but with the requirement of extra support to develop this skill.

6. The importance of self-appraisal

I have introduced many appraisal programmes where individuals are completely in control of their own review, completing the documentation, giving a view of their performance and what they have achieved with evidence to support this. Their review conversation is based on this self-assessment with the reviewer or reviewers inputting from their own observation, or from the observations they have obtained from others. No system is perfect, and some people will have inflated views and others will downplay their achievements. The latter is easier to deal with, but I think problems with the former would have transpired anyway, irrespective of the appraisal process.

Individuals must make a point of collecting evidence about their performance throughout the year. In today's new world organization, it is unrealistic to expect managers to compile appraisal documentation, though I feel it never worked very well anyway.

7. Ratings

One argument against appraisal ratings is that they create a limited, bureaucratic approach and turn appraisal into a pay negotiation. Another is that there is an inherent problem in awarding performance ratings linked to objectives in that this is a short-term and, often, arbitrary approach linked to the financial or the 'pay' year. The year-end may not be the best time to assess whether an objective has been achieved. This is especially the case with people at the upper end of the organization's hierarchy, where impact must be long term.

However, ratings give an important macro-level view of performance and provide valuable management information. They are particularly suited to a shared management context, and where 'roundtables' are operated, in which case they can help create consistency around standards of performance.

An argument that is often levelled against performance ratings is that they allow managers to inflate ratings and award superior ratings to all. Forced ranking was developed to overcome this problem, as it requires a certain percentage (often 10 to 20 per cent) to be in the top rank and a similar percentage (often 10 per cent) of people to be in the bottom rank, from where they are usually shown the door. This is incompatible with my talent management approach, which is about raising performance levels generally and dealing with poor performance immediately and at source. Firstly, ranking is an easy way out of discussing and managing poor performance for managers who are able to say, 'I would have given you x but I couldn't because of forced ranking.' Secondly, it requires some people to be allocated to the bottom rank. Most managers dislike this, feeling that it does not help them manage staff as they wish. Moreover, steady and valuable contributors shy away from new or more challenging targets, as they fear suddenly finding themselves in that bottom tranche. If it is a secret process, this goes against the ethos of open and honest discussions about performance, which we encourage. Secrecy anyway, especially if records are kept, contravenes data protection legislation, which requires employees to be able to access information held about them. Finally, forced-ranking discussions can degenerate into battles among managers who manipulate the system to favour certain employees.

Those in favour of forced ranking generally argue that it allows more accurate cross-department comparisons and that it forces managers to think in greater depth about the quality of talent in their team than conventional performance appraisal systems typically require. They also argue that it forces managers to describe and verbalize their assessments about people and that this provides a good indicator of a critical aspect of the managers' leadership ability. I believe you can achieve all these benefits through 'roundtables' without using forced ranking.

8. Roundtables – on performance, potential and pay

As discussed previously, roundtables typically bring together managers in the unit to discuss appraisal ratings and pay awards so as to achieve consistency and cross-department comparisons. Sometimes these meetings are facilitated, either by the HR business partner, or especially in the case of more senior leaders by an external facilitator.

Senior managers are then required to review and discuss these proposals and justifications. This process helps identify problems, such as inconsistencies, favouritism or discrimination. The pay and ratings decisions are then openly discussed between manager and individual. This process is similar to the roundtables discussed in the previous chapter, which focus on potential and development.

A word of caution, however, is that managers sometimes treat roundtables as occasions to boost themselves and their functions by inflating their staff, and the results achieved. This can be avoided through careful preparation, producing evidence to back assessments, and through facilitation. Once embedded, they work well, as the Siemens example on page 167 shows.

CASE STUDY

At Siemens, so-called 'roundtables' are a well-embedded part of the annual performance management process and are highly effective. Typically, a peer group of managers, usually working in a management team, get together to finalize the performance reviews, development actions and compensation outcomes for all of their direct reports. This is a formal process that involves structured and facilitated conversation.

The process starts before the roundtable, when employees input their views about their performance and development into the HR appraisal system. Managers discuss these inputs with their people and also scale their performance. At the roundtable, managers discuss their people and the scores they have assigned to them. They discuss potential too and will identify people's particular strengths and talents, as well as flagging when it is critical that the person is retained or developed. Managers can extract data about their people from the data warehouse. Sometimes, these roundtables will consider a particular strategic issue, such as diversity or the lack of bench strength in the talent pipeline.

Roundtables are a way of moderating performance and potential reviews to ensure that people are being rewarded and measured consistently. They also link into the pay review, which is determined according to a combination of performance, affordability, and market benchmark data. After these meetings, individual managers hold a follow-up discussion with their people to let them know the outcome.

Siemens' Director of Human Resource Toby Peyton-Jones says that managers get very engaged and animated during these roundtable discussions, even though they involve a big time commitment, valuing the opportunity to discuss achievement and to identify development opportunities for people. Through this regular dialogue, which requires managers to provide evidence to support their assessments, managers develop a clear understanding of what good and outstanding performance look like.

9. 360-degree feedback

I discussed this extensively in Chapter 5, where I showed that especially because of problems of rater bias, I prefer not to use 360-degree feedback for assigning performance ratings, though it is useful for development purposes.

In conclusion, I have sought to give guidance on what works well in many situations. However, performance management needs to be tailored to each individual business. It is imperative to keep the system under review, and find out from people what helps them and what obstructs, and in particular to consider carefully whether it is helping management run the business.

Cultural messages

Performance appraisal and reward policies send out strong messages to people about what the organization values and what it sees as its priorities. The basis on which pay and bonus awards are allocated and on which people are promoted, especially to management roles, puts across vital messages about what is really important to the organization. Every element of your talent strategy must transmit consistent messages. Otherwise it is the messages of the promotion and reward practices that win through.

CASE STUDY

A professional services firm launched a culture change programme to improve the quality of people management. This was urgent as the firm's attrition rate was too high and they were losing critical people, which was damaging client relationships. In spite of concerted efforts and extensive training, nothing changed because pay and promotion were still based on fee income, and on client retention and satisfaction. When these criteria changed to include people management responsibilities, the new roles were taken seriously, with a corresponding decrease in attrition and improved client relationships.

If you wish the organization to value talent, then this must be rewarded and recognized through performance appraisal, pay and promotion, as well as more subtly by the behaviour of the people at the top. Similarly, it is vital to pay attention to how individual achievement is rewarded compared with team achievement. As technology makes it increasingly easier for us to interconnect, so it becomes more important for us to do so. In other words, collaboration and teamwork are becoming more central and must also be built into reward programmes where appropriate.

Reward

Earlier we looked at how to differentiate between levels of performance. The company's reward policy needs to support this, whether through the way it gives extrinsic, monetary rewards or intrinsically through a recognition programme.

Does pay motivate? This is a question that has been extensively researched and debated. One answer that always emerges is that when pay levels are perceived to be unfair they are hugely demotivating. This reaction seems to be deeply rooted in our animal nature: recent research showed that even dogs and monkeys, perceiving that others were rewarded more for performing the same tricks, would 'sulk' and become uncooperative. Perceived fairness, alongside trust, is at the core of a positive, engaging and high-performance-generating psychological contract in the workplace.[1] In light of continuing headlines about top-level salaries it is noteworthy that huge salary differentials weaken loyalty and erode the internal talent pool.[2] It is clear that perceived fairness of reward is essential to create the talent mind-set that we are aiming for.

To say that money does or does not actively motivate is rather too simplistic. One of the conclusions we can draw from the various studies is that the motivational mix varies for each person and is also likely to change over the course of their lives and careers. The lesson is that pay can be an effective motivator, but seldom on its own; managers still need to work on reinforcing motivators such as providing challenging and stretching work opportunities. On the other hand, when viewed as inadequate, unfair or insulting, pay can be a big demotivator regardless of any amount of praise or good management.

Non-financial recognition is an important part of the reward mix. This ranges from sending thank-you e-mails to running formal prize-winning schemes. From my experience, the most effective form of non-financial reward is where someone's contribution is widely recognized. This recognition must come from the person's manager, but from other directions also, such as senior management, or perhaps some form of public acknowledgement. For example, I gave a case study earlier in the book describing how we trained an internal cadre of coaches to support a new process we introduced. They received no extra money for this but absorbed it into their workload. Those whose managers recognized their effort and contribution were noticeably more motivated than those whose managers paid it scant regard.

Returning to the importance of differentiating levels of performance, high performers especially benefit from recognition on a wider platform. Consistency is important, however. I worked recently in an organization where the top team was constantly battling over whose business goals were the more important. The knock-on effect was that some high performance went unrecognized, while lesser contributions were publicly lauded. Needless to say, this caused considerable discontent.

The concept of financial rewards linked to performance arouses strong feelings among supporters and opponents. The most powerful argument advanced for contingent financial rewards is that it is only fair to recognize achievement with a share of what the individual has created – blurring the line between employee and owner. Many also see pay-for-performance schemes as preferable to the alternatives of service-related pay progression or spot rates.

CASE STUDY   A practical illustration of some problems

MNO is a small chain of shops whose managers, for historical reasons, have widely different rates of both basic pay and bonus. The longer-serving managers and those from the bigger, more profitable shops tend to earn more but there are exceptions: the long-serving manager of the most profitable shop is underpaid 'because he does not shout and kick up as much fuss'.

The board wants to revise the bonus scheme but faces a number of practical problems:

- *Do you reward performance or achievement?* Are the managers of those high-performing shops actually underperforming, perhaps benefiting from being in a good location that has nothing to do with them?

- *Should you reward those who cope with adversity?* A shop suffers a downturn when a competitor opens next door but the manager performs well and limits the damage: do you reward the performance or say, 'the shop is now losing money so we can't afford to pay more'?

- *Can you separate good performance from luck?* One highly profitable shop has benefited from a very favourable renegotiation of its rent and a very loyal client base but the shop manager has also established a very good team. How do you separate what has been achieved by the manager from luck that is outside her control?

- *Does rewarding individual unit performance discourage cooperation between units?* The high-performing manager may be reluctant to share stock or staff with a nearby underperforming shop because her bonus may suffer if her shop takings are affected.

I have used the word 'practical' twice because when you confront these real issues, theories fail to provide easy answers: that is because there are none. The solution is to identify what you are trying to achieve and to work imperfectly towards the least messy outcome.

Performance pay may well be a key objective and there is evidence that many employees agree that it is fair for those who contribute more to be paid more. This viewpoint is supported by CIPD survey findings regarding the use of performance-related reward, incentive and recognition schemes. 'The results for HR outcomes showed associations between increased usage of such schemes and a) better employee relations and b) reduced levels of expressed discontent with pay' (CIPD, 2012).

Pay equity

Adams's pay equity theory is helpful here (Adams, 1965). According to this, we arrive at our measure of fairness – equity – by comparing our balance of effort and reward, and other factors such as the perceived ratio of input to output, with that enjoyed by other people, whom we deem to be relevant reference points. Crucially, this means that equity does not depend on our input-to-output ratio alone – it depends on our comparison with others who comprise the marketplace as we see it. This helps to explain why people are so strongly affected by the situations (and views and gossip) of colleagues, friends etc in establishing their own personal sense of fairness or equity in their own work situations.

Adams's pay equity theory refers not only to how we perceive internal relativities but also to differences between individuals' remuneration packages and what they feel they could attain in the marketplace. If an organization's pay structure is far off the market position or if individuals with similar skills are being paid widely different salaries for undertaking the same job content then there is a problem, especially in cases where variances are exacerbated on the basis of gender, race or ethnicity. This part of the pay equity theory underlines the importance of open and clear communication of the basis on which pay awards are made. Communication should include market and job comparisons so that people can clearly see how they relate to others in the marketplace. This can be taken too far, however. One CEO recently claimed an excessive pay rise because there were others (one or two in far flung corners of the world?) who received that amount. Shareholders did not approve the increase.

The implications of pay equity theory for talent management are considerable. Pay for performance fits with one of our prime talent management notions, which is the importance of knowing who your high performers are and of giving them appropriate and balanced recognition. It can provide the incentive to differentiate performance levels. However, in our case for talent, we also emphasize that everyone matters, and Adams's equity theory reminds us that it is important to ensure that both recipient and colleagues perceive a differentiated pay award as fair.

The basis on which a contingent pay award is made needs to be clear, not only in the policy but in the way it is communicated by managers and supported by cultural values. This means being clear about the difference between a steady contributor and a high performer and ensuring that both feel differentials are fair and both feel their contribution is recognized.

Simply relying on financial measures is unlikely to provide a broad enough view of performance, and may also be counterproductive and drive the wrong behaviours. Take the sales team that measures performance according to client billings: this probably drives people to keep clients and client work to themselves, deters them from business development activities, probably deters them from spending time on developing their people, and is unlikely to encourage them to learn new things or develop new services or materials.

So if you are paying for performance in some way, there are many conundrums to address and balance out:

- How do you encourage individuals to achieve high performance, while also encouraging the sharing of ideas and teamwork?

- How do you encourage people to take short-term decisions with the long term in mind?

- How do you encourage autonomy and personal responsibility, while trying to break down functional or team 'silos' and create a more collegiate environment?

- How do you focus people on profitability, customers, research and development and so on, while at the same time ensuring that they adopt a talent mindset towards their employees and themselves, and also live up to your values and other key behavioural capabilities?

Additionally, there is a growing awareness of the need to take more account of the impact of your business and of your actions on the wider community and on the environment. These are key issues that are likely to become increasingly important to society.

There is no 'one-size-fits-all' pay scheme, but these are key questions to consider when determining your pay and performance management strategy. In all these cases, decisions on pay for performance require subjective as well as objective assessments about performance and results. Using subjective measures requires good communication and effective processes.

Processes for managers

As research demonstrates, managers are the critical linkage between reward principles and intentions on the one hand and the practical delivery and creation of a truly rewarding environment, conducive to high employee performance, on the other (Reilly and Brown, 2008).

In my experience, many organizations fail to involve managers in determining pay awards. Yet, pay is a major part of the individual's relationship with the organization. Leading organizations allocate a pool of funds to managers who are then held accountable for distributing them. They are also required to justify their decisions. It is hard to claim that managers are critical to driving high levels of employee engagement if they are excluded from pay discussions. Moreover, managers cannot truly take on a talent mindset if they do not fully appreciate how pay decisions affect different people and how they affect the motivational mix.

You may recall that in the case study about MVision, 'development advisers' contribute to pay discussions and are responsible for discussing them with their people. This gives the role clout, but it also creates greater transparency and understanding about pay decisions.

HR business partners should work closely with managers so that they understand the basis on which pay has been awarded and to support them in holding conversations about this with their staff. The manager's line manager also has a role here in providing support for what can be a difficult conversation.

Key points

- The management of people is often nowadays shared between project managers, people managers and HR.
- Focus performance appraisal on the future, not on the past: what behaviours do you want to encourage and what standards do you want to attain?
- Try to separate conversations about career and development from those about performance.

- Clearly articulated and thought-through performance standards drive successful business outcomes.
- Pay is not the only determinant but is an important element of the motivational mix and so managers must be involved in these discussions about their staff.
- Think carefully about what behaviours you want to drive – and balance opposing priorities – when thinking about performance-related pay.

Notes

1 Guest, D and Conway, N (2004) *Employee Well-being and the Psychological Contract*, Chartered Institute of Personnel and Development, London.
2 Reilly, P and Brown, D (2008) Employee engagement: what is the relationship with reward management? *World at Work Journal*, **17** (4).

Nearby management

N earby management', as we discussed in the last chapter, applies to everyone who has responsibility for managing others. In this chapter, I look further at what 'nearby managers' have to do. I consider the appropriate techniques, especially in the context of sharing management responsibilities with others (Figure 9.1). I describe some of the latest research and thinking about how our minds work and how this should affect the way we manage people to give of their best. I use these ideas to offer guidance on dealing with difficult management situations.

All managers are nearby managers to some

As discussed previously, with changing ways of working, the new management model often separates responsibility for managing the business results that someone is expected to achieve from the responsibility for assessing their performance and ensuring their development. The former responsibilities remain with the line manager, or project team leader, and the latter are assigned to a specially designated people manager. All these responsibilities fall within the definition of 'nearby management'. Within this new model, people may also have a coach, a mentor or a sponsor for specific reasons, such as coming to grips with a new role or for career development.

The trend for more than a decade has been to emphasize the importance of the nearby manager in getting the best out of people. HR has increasingly moved to being the enabler that provides the policies and practices, leaving the nearby manager to make use of them. In this scenario, on top of their responsibilities for their 'day job' such as dealing with clients and suppliers,

FIGURE 9.1 The four-point framework shows the steps to develop your talent and engagement strategy

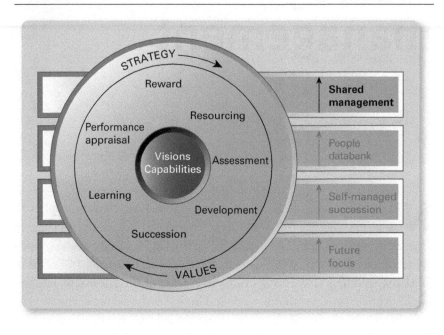

managing budgets and resources, and achieving business results, nearby managers are also expected to do everything concerned with managing their people: recruit, motivate, coach, support learning and development, handle performance appraisals, deal with disciplinary matters and poor performance, monitor absence and holidays. As we have discussed a great deal in this book, this is now an impossible way of working, as well as an impossible workload. Each of these people-management responsibilities requires particular expertise and knowledge. Additionally, managing poor performers requires different techniques from those needed for steady performers, and high performers demand yet different approaches. It is no wonder that research concludes that even in good times only a minority of employees are fully engaged at any one time. This old management model ultimately constrains the performance of your organization, as few people get enough attention.

This leads me to emphasize that senior management are also 'nearby managers'. This role is often neglected, perhaps because the necessity to actively manage direct reports gets lost in the transition to the top team. Their focus shifts to being strategic and outward looking and stepping back from the day-to-day. This is right, but should not be at the expense

FIGURE 9.2 Nearby management responsibilities

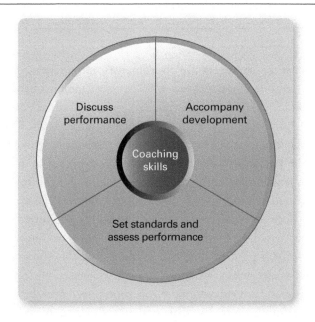

of managing direct reports, where I often see a failure on the part of CEOs and directors to have those all-important conversations about performance and careers. At this level especially, conversations often focus exclusively on 'hard' business objectives, and people at the top are often too 'hands off' in their role as nearby managers. As behaviours filter down, this is significant.

Three people-management responsibilities

The solution I set out in this chapter assigns three people-management responsibilities to nearby managers (Figure 9.2). This is always within the shared management structure, where a nearby manager may or may not also be responsible for someone's business results. The three responsibilities are to:

1 Accompany[1] the person's development. Ensure that they are given developmental work experience that aligns their aspirations with business needs.

2 Hold regular insightful and meaningful conversations with them to review performance, give feedback on performance, communicate pay and reward decisions, and discuss career options.

3 Set performance goals and standards so that the individual knows what is expected of them, has line of sight over their role and contribution to the organization, and knows how their performance will be measured.

In this role, nearby managers are coordinators and advisers. They are not administrators. There are others who handle administrative functions (absence, holidays, etc). They provide support and feedback to the people they 'manage', meeting on a regular, at least monthly basis. They keep in touch with the other managers involved with the person, who have responsibility for the business results the individual is expected to achieve. Their skills and understanding, and therefore preparation for the role, should be around how to manage steady performers – the majority. They must be able to recognize poor and high performance and will be supported in handling the issues that arise here by their HR advisers. They have full responsibility for the individual's performance appraisal, though this too is shared, and they input into pay reviews (Chapter 8). So the role has real clout. It must be seen as promotion, and success in the role should feed into the nearby manager's own performance review. This structure should continue to the highest levels in the organization. It is not just for junior people or new recruits.

This model gives individuals someone who is supporting and accompanying them, but it is a light-touch form of control. It is self-managed to a great extent, with individuals providing evidence of their performance, and raising the issues around which they particularly want feedback, or support. A spin-off benefit is that it generates additional conversations across the business and helps the formation of networks.

There are two parts to the nearby manager's role in accompanying development: one is to open developmental work-experience opportunities that match the person's aspirations. The other is to support them in coming to grips with these new opportunities, and getting the most from the learning.

Let us return to my comment that the people part of the manager's role has become too onerous. In this new model, the manager's default responsibility should be to differentiate between levels of performance, and then work in partnership with HR, who must support the nearby manager in helping high performers who are ready to move on. HR must also be there to support managers in handling poor performance. Although many businesses use the HR business partner model, where an HR manager builds relationships to support managers in a particular area of the business, few are sharing responsibilities in the way I suggest: they are continuing to expect nearby managers to be experts in handling all day-to-day people-management issues that arise, be coaches to their people, handle performance management and achieve their technical, business results too.

There is a big difference between fulfilling the three people responsibilities that I set out and being a coach. A coach provides a safe place for the coachee to discuss fears and concerns, try things out and make mistakes. This conflicts significantly with being a nearby manager who must assess performance, make judgements around suitability for different roles and assign pay rises. The inherent conflict in these two roles makes it unlikely that either will be performed particularly well. One of them has to go.

To satisfactorily carry out the three key responsibilities of the role, the nearby manager must, however, master a coaching style.

What coaching skills does the nearby manager require?

The underlying basic skills of a coaching style are those of 'active listening'. There are different definitions of active listening, but I describe it as a structured way of listening attentively, so as to bring to the surface, fully, the conscious message. It is a technique where the listener:

- *Pays attention* and shows they are doing so through their body language, which is positive, encouraging and supportive.

- *Asks 'open' questions* (beginning 'tell me about' or starting with who, what, where, why, when, how). It is difficult to respond to questions phrased this way with just a yes or no answer and so these questions encourage someone to think through their response. 'Probing' questions ask for more information to bring out more facts, but also to understand feelings, reactions and attitudes.

- *Suspends judgement.* Often we rush in quickly with our own views or judgements or we can't wait to talk about our own experiences. This prevents someone from opening up and exploring the issue. Instead, we must keep an open mind, not make assumptions, and keep questioning to encourage the other person to clarify their own thoughts and reach their own conclusions. It is particularly difficult to suspend judgement when we disagree with the opinions being expressed, or when we feel that we are being personally criticized, but these are times when it is even more important to do so.

- *Reflects back and clarifies.* Our personal filters sometimes distort what we hear. Reflect what has been said by paraphrasing, for example: 'What I am hearing is...' or 'It sounds as though you are saying...'. Ask questions to clarify points: 'What do you mean by...?' These techniques will ensure you are receiving the message as intended, but also help the other person clarify their own meaning.

- *Summarizes and plans.* At the end, make sure the learning points are clear, and ensure that the other person has a specific plan for how to apply this learning.

These skills are readily transferable to a range of other business situations, and should be in everyone's basic toolkit. In particular, use these skills to ask people about their work, and the pressures they are under. In this way you will build your understanding of functions that are outside of your area of expertise. I find that most people have been introduced to active listening skills at some stage in their careers, but have often let them slide, which is why I have included them here.

Let's now look more closely at the skills required to carry out the responsibilities of accompanying development, and giving feedback: responsibilities 1 and 2. (We considered goal setting and standards of performance in the last chapter.) It will be helpful to our consideration of these skills to relate some of the ideas to growing understanding of how the mind works.

Cognitive neuroscience

Cognitive neuroscience is the integration of psychology (the study of the human mind and behaviour) and neuroscience (the study of the anatomy and physiology of the brain). Over the past 30 years, this field has given rise to a new understanding of human nature and behaviour change. It has been made possible by new imaging technologies (such as functional magnetic resonance imaging (fMRI) and positron emission tomography (PET)), along with brain wave analysis technologies (such as quantitative electroencephalography), which have revealed neural connections in the human brain of which we were previously unaware. Advanced computer analysis of these connections has helped researchers develop an increasing understanding of how we perceive, think, feel and act. Although this field is still in its early stages, neuroscience research has developed my thinking, and supports many of the ideas I have derived from practice, which I know work.

Accompanying development

Most people, when asked, would say that we are 'conscious beings'. The reality is that our brains process millions of pieces of information per second at the non-conscious level, compared with the 10 or so pieces of information that we can hold in the conscious brain (pre-frontal cortex or 'PFC').

The human mind largely functions at the non-conscious level but, to do so, it has to be highly adept at transferring appropriate information between the conscious and the non-conscious. Once a neural pathway is 'written' at the non-conscious level, it works like the operating system of a computer, automating our responses and working away out of sight. It is important to understand this when seeking to support others in learning, adapting to change, and taking on new skills. Change is difficult because we need to overwrite the old neural pathways (habitual activities) with new ones and we have to do this by using the pre-frontal cortex, which has limited capacity and tires easily. This means that people should focus on making a few changes at a time until the new behaviour is itself a habit (operates at the non-conscious level). This helps us understand why change might be painful even when we can see its benefits. Happily, this explanation shows that it is possible for us to make a *conscious* choice to change behaviour, and it also shows how: through persistent use, and by pacing and phasing our learning. Practice makes perfect was once the rather tiresome mantra of parents to get children to learn their multiplication tables or practise the piano; now it's a clinically evidenced fact.

When accompanying someone it is frequently the case that the 'answer' is blindingly obvious to us. However, trying to tell them what to do or give them the answer does not work. As individuals, it is only when we find the answer for ourselves that we are energized and motivated to change. According to neuroscience expert David Rock (2011), this required energy is released through the generation of insight, an 'aha' moment, which comes when a complex set of new connections – or mental maps – is being created. 'These have the potential to enhance our mental resources and overcome the brain's resistance to change. But to embed this result, given the brain's limited working memory, we need to make a deliberate effort to "hardwire" that insight by paying it repeated attention' (Rock, 2009a). This means that nearby managers should focus on becoming skilled in generating insight in others and supporting their people in developing new habits. (Readers might refer to Rock's 'dance of insight' and 'create' models in *Quiet Leadership*, 2009c).

These neuroscience findings lend support to one of the central ideas of this book: the importance of a consistent approach to help people build understanding. The findings also offer clues to help us effectively accompany development, and manage change. Let's look at these clues.

Allow someone to arrive at their own solutions

Resist the temptation to impose an answer, or way of doing things. Instead use active listening to help the other person develop their thinking and identify their own solutions.

FIGURE 9.3 Projected learning cycle

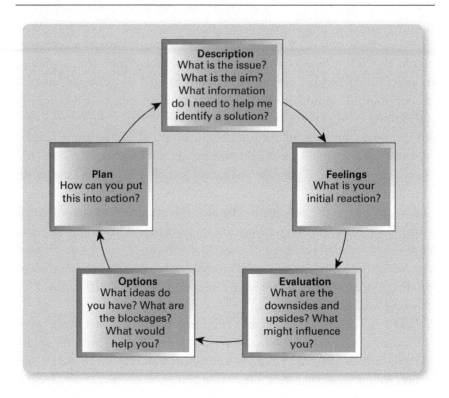

Using Kolb's theories of learning (Kolb and Fry, 1975), the learning cycle in Figure 9.3 offers a sequence and some questions to help you encourage someone to arrive at their own solution to a matter that is new to them.

Support learning through reflection, repetition, recognition

As we have seen, the brain takes on new learning by practice and repetition, so don't expect learning and change to happen instantly:

- Give the person time to reflect on the new behaviours, and how they are performing them, until they become habitual.
- Keep reminding them too by showing an interest, checking in on progress, and giving recognition for it also.
- Help them reflect back on what they have done so that they learn from the experience. As mentioned in Chapter 5, learning doesn't just

FIGURE 9.4 Reflective learning cycle

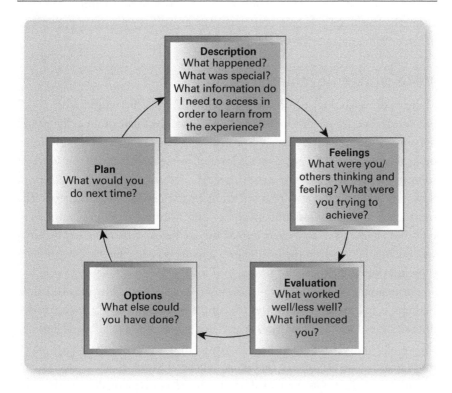

happen. We must make a conscious effort to learn from our experience. We will do this more effectively if we have someone to support us and facilitate the process.

This is an important part of the nearby manager's role, though peers can support one another in this way too. It can be an ideal role for internal coaches. The reflective learning cycle (Figure 9.4) offers a series of questions and a sequence you can follow to help someone reflect on what they have learned. It is the same as the projected cycle in Figure 9.3 but the questions encourage someone to look back on an experience, rather than project forward. This cycle is equally effective for your own self-reflection.

Reflective learning is also beneficial for use in a team, to reflect together on some aspect of work done collectively, and to seek continuous improvement. For example, interesting uses of reflective learning have been made in the medical profession, where the cycle has been used to help people audit and assess progress towards team targets, for instance towards hospital hygiene.

In this case, the reflective learning cycle was used in weekly team discussions and in formal diploma programmes, leading to significant improvements. Using the learning cycle on a team basis is a great way of inspiring people to achieve team goals, and work better together.

Make work enjoyable

Hungarian psychologist Mihalyi Csíkszentmihályi (Csíkszentmihályi, 2003) has researched into what makes us become so absorbed in an activity and deeply connected with it that we become oblivious to time and what is going on around us. If we can achieve this level of connectedness with our work, it follows that we will be more productive. He describes this as the concept of flow. His research suggests that we are happy when we are in control. 'The more a job inherently resembles a game – with variety, appropriate and flexible challenges, clear goals and immediate feedback – the more enjoyable it will be. By making even the boring into a game we can exercise control over our situation and experience flow...'.

For example: F has to compile weekly reconciliations. He finds this dull. Perhaps it will become more fun for him if he is challenged (or challenges himself) to reduce the error rate; or perhaps reduce the time it takes. Perhaps this can be linked to some form of reward. Finding ways to make such work more fun and absorbing can be highly beneficial for us all.

An important point we can draw from the concept of flow is the idea that people can be engaged, refreshed and excited through new goals and experiences they care about. This supports our ideas around the three-stage development plan, which emphasizes finding stretch and challenge for people in their current roles, and helping them work towards goals that suit their own aspirations.

Giving feedback

Giving feedback is one of the most difficult things to do. This is manifest by the many theories it has spawned, none of which make the task any easier. Neuroscience gives some interesting insights that might actually help. One of the most important findings in this respect is how the brain reacts to fear or threat.

How the brain reacts to fear or threat

In evolutionary terms our brains are designed to meet the needs of a hunter-gatherer. This means that we have a highly developed awareness of threat. The brain's response to this is an activation of the limbic system, which throws a chemical 'switch' to shut down, or at least inhibit, the conscious part of the brain (PFC). This allows the neural pathways that govern 'fight or flight' to kick in without interference from the 'thinking brain' – we don't have time to analyse the situation, we must react quickly to maximize the chances of avoiding a predator. In the 21st-century workplace we rely on the pre-frontal cortex to do our work, so a problem arises when we are put into even a mild threat state, because this tends to disable it and we become ineffective in our work.

This has profound implications for workplace culture. Many leaders and many organizations still believe in giving feedback in a way that is 'calling it as it is'. Moreover, they almost always only notice what is wrong. By doing this, leaders are triggering a limbic response, disempowering their people and exacerbating the very situation they were seeking to improve. As employees, we are so used to this behaviour that we compound the error in giving false feedback signals by 'sucking it up' and not showing that we are upset. At an extreme, this can create an unhelpful spiral of ever-decreasing performance.

This also impacts the way we design our organizations. Consider those organizations that encourage extreme competitiveness among their staff by sacking those they designate as their bottom 10 per cent of employees each year. In seeking to be the most innovative and flexible, the unintended consequence is to create an almost permanent threat state. This leads to individuals and teams being reluctant to share information or work collaboratively. Any gain in prestige someone else might achieve is effectively your loss – it is what is known as a zero-sum game – there is always a 90:10 split of people and for you to get out of the 10 per cent pool means that someone else must slide in to take your place. Some organizations that appear to employ these philosophies point to their business success as evidence that they work. Neuroscience leads us to ask how much more successful they might be were their people moved from a threat to a reward state.

Understanding what causes us to feel 'fear' or 'threat' can also help us to manage change. As Boyatzis (2011) points out, 'Research has suggested that negative emotions are stronger than positive emotions'. As a result, we would suspect that the contagion of negative emotions would ignite a stronger neural sequence than positive emotions. This may serve evolutionary functions but, paradoxically, it may limit learning. Arousal of strong negative emotions also stimulates the 'sympathetic nervous system', which inhibits access to existing neural circuits and invokes cognitive, emotional, and perceptual impairment (Sapolsky, 2004; Schulkin, 1999; Dickerson and Kemeny, 2004). Rock (2009b) suggests that this presents significant challenges to managers: 'People who feel betrayed or unrecognized at work – for example, when they are reprimanded, given an assignment that seems unworthy, or told to take a pay cut – experience it as a neural impulse, as powerful and painful as a blow to the head.' Clearly, such instances must make it harder for the person to move forward, and must lead to lack of engagement and commitment. 'They become purely transactional employees, reluctant to give more of themselves to the company, because the social context stands in their way.'

Certain situations are inherently prone to triggering threat states. Rock has identified that 'there are five domains of social experience that your brain treats the same as survival issues. These domains... [are] ... Status, Certainty, Autonomy, Relatedness and Fairness' (SCARF). Any perceived reduction in status etc will activate a limbic response. Performance appraisal is one example of a situation fraught with risk. It is performed by the boss, whose very position reduces my status; certainty is undermined because the outcome is unclear; the boss is in control (little autonomy); relatedness is diminished (hard to see the boss as a friend) and it is unlikely to feel fair. In a situation like this the individual will have a heightened sensitivity to threat. The leader can, however, dampen the limbic response by paying attention to the five areas, for example: enhance status by making it clear that they are an important member of the team; create certainty by being clear about the process and outcomes; strengthen autonomy by asking the individual to self-assess and describe what they are doing already to get better; emphasize relatedness by reminding them that as boss they too will be going through an appraisal; and emphasize the fair way in which the process is being conducted (Rock, 2009c).

Punishing or rewarding people's actions can similarly trigger such a response. Take the person who has sent a client a badly presented report. If you reprimand them for this, they will focus on the error and will experience feelings of threat which inhibit the conscious, analytical brain, preventing them from identifying how to achieve a better standard of presentation. By focusing them on the undesirable pattern you are also embedding the unhelpful neural pathway. If you reward someone else for producing reports to a high standard, either through public recognition or by giving them more interesting assignments, this will lead to further reduction in status and negative reaction from the first person, again inhibiting them from raising their standard of performance. A more positive feedback session where you focus the person on coming up with their own ideas for raising the standard of presentation of the report is more likely to result in learning (and learning across a broader field) and performance improvement.

Be solutions focused, and not problem focused. Build a mindset where everyone regularly identifies what could be even better. This removes the threat and instead gets people excited to self-assess and drive up standards and results. It becomes unnecessary to identify something that was 'wrong', or badly done. Adopting such an approach is a key way to help people thrive and raise their performance.

This does not mean that you cannot dismiss someone for poor performance; but it does mean that this step is only taken after a genuine effort to help them learn and improve.

How the mind reacts to positivity

A corollary of the avoidance of negative behaviour is to embrace the power of the positive approach. My approach to talent development has a strong connection with the field of positive psychology, which is about 'optimal human functioning' – studying and understanding people at their best. This is an important part of a talent mindset, which requires focusing on individuals' strengths and building their role around these. I recently met a professor from one of the leading medical schools in the United States who reminded me how, years ago, when he was a manager at a British medical school, he had sought my advice on how to deal with a member of his lab team who was not able to perform the role as required. Dismissing this person or moving him into a different role were not available options. My advice was to change the requirements of the role. Everyone has strengths and preferences. Find out what this person does best, and adapt the role to suit. This now high-ranking professor said that he has managed on this basis since and it has served him exceptionally well.

A focus on strengths and preferences benefits individual development but also encourages a creative, positive working environment and good teamwork. It removes the fear and the threat and frees people to focus on results and improvement.

Creating the conditions

We all benefit from feedback, and these ideas from neuroscience and positive psychology help us understand how to deliver this effectively. Firstly, we can see that we will gain more from a positive, solutions-oriented approach than from pointing out what someone has done badly. Secondly, we gain more from helping people build on strengths than from reinforcing weaknesses. However, there are many ramifications to giving feedback. These depend on the relationship between the feedback giver and receiver, the personalities of each, and the context in which they are operating. The purpose of the feedback is significant too. Is it to boost confidence, develop performance or achieve improvement? Is it about something the person is working on, or how the person is performing? Let me try to offer some guidance.

1. Firstly, we need to accept that we all benefit from feedback 'How am I doing?' This question is fundamental to the employee's level of engagement with the organization. We all want to know how our performance is viewed, how we are contributing, and what we might do next. We want to feel valued and our efforts to be recognized. We also want to improve and develop, and align our performance with the required standards. If we don't want these things, we probably don't care, and are actively disengaged. High-quality feedback that enables someone to learn or improve is a precious gift. It shows you have taken the time and invested the interest in them. It helps build trust, as well as engagement.

2. 5:1 ratio of positive to improvement feedback. Build your currency Regretfully, I no longer recall where I first learned of the 5:1 ratio, but the tip is to try to give five times as much good feedback (that is, recognition of good work and positive feedback that specifies what made it good) as feedback about what could be improved. This does not mean that during one performance appraisal conversation you seek to praise on five counts, or that you have to be literal about the concept. Rather you must create an ethos where feedback and recognition for good work exceed negative feedback by five counts to one. Such a balance is important, because if you only give praise and positive feedback, you lose credibility; people think you are insincere and they cease to value your opinion. The reverse is also true, and there is little chance of useful and constructive criticism being taken on board if the thrust is persistently and exclusively negative.

Managers often tell me that their staff ask to know what they don't do well, especially young and less experienced workers, because they think this is how they learn. But it misses the point that positive feedback helps us build on our strengths. We learn as much from it as from knowing what we could do better. Also, the fact that people might ask for negative feedback does not necessarily make it less threatening.

3. Recognize what people do well. Be specific We must, therefore, get into the habit of giving feedback that recognizes when someone does something well. As we have learned, people do not improve and develop through fear and threat, and this does not build relationships either. Unfortunately, it is often easier to spot what someone didn't do well than what was good. For years, when running training courses I introduced feedback skills following individual presentations people had made to the group. I asked delegates to give verbal positive feedback to one of the group, selecting always someone who had given a strong performance to be the subject of the feedback. Invariably, the feedback was negative and critical and ignored my explicit instructions to be positive. Why? Perhaps we have become conditioned to a critical approach: maybe our society values perceptiveness and clever criticism. Performance appraisal was, for years, thought of as the time to 'find out what is wrong with me'. Or perhaps we are embarrassed to give praise. This might be cultural (maybe it doesn't sit well with the British 'stiff upper lip'?), or to do with personality. If you have difficulty in giving positive feedback and praise, try to understand what your blockage is and overcome it.

A question I have asked often, 'How do you know if you are doing a good job?', is usually answered 'because nobody has told me I've done something wrong'. There are two problems with this: firstly, we do not always know what we do well, and having it pointed out to us can be valuable. It builds confidence, and when a manager gives this type of feedback, it reinforces the standards of performance expected. Take this example: J was appointed to the board six months ago, and has so far attended three board meetings. She always speaks out, questioning certain issues, challenging on others. The chair invites her to lunch to discuss how she's getting on. To J's surprise, the chair tells her that he and the CEO greatly value her contribution. They think she always get to the heart of an issue and identifies the most important point. Others just talk for the sake of it, or because it is their subject, but J is valued for her insight and her ability to prioritize. Before getting this feedback, J had worried that she spoke too much and came across as dogmatic. She had been thinking of toning down and speaking less. The feedback gave her confidence to keep developing this level of contribution. This was to the benefit of the business as well as to herself. The point here is that without this feedback J did not realize she had this strength, and the value of her contribution would probably have decreased.

Another point about positive feedback is that it also regulates behaviour. Most of us give ourselves feedback to a greater or lesser extent. We scrutinize what we do, and many of us are hard on ourselves. As in the example above, positive feedback frees us to recognize a particular strength, or a good result, and move on. There's also a sort of arrogance to relying solely on your own assessment of how you are doing. So a climate of feedback-giving keeps the culture in check too.

4. Giving feedback about what could be better Feedback mustn't only be positive. This doesn't mean we must look for fault. Rather it means that we must take notice, and then give feedback that is honest and sincere, and that will help the person develop. It is helpful to differentiate between feedback that aims to help someone do something better, and feedback about something they have done wrong, or poor performance, as these require different skills. With the former, a coaching style will help, but you might need to give input too: for example, if you are giving feedback to a journalist about an article, you might need to point out that the arguments were too weak, or the structure poor. I believe it is better to be direct and to the point in these cases. It will not be threatening if this is in the context of a strong relationship, where the other person feels valued, and you regularly give recognition to good work. The fact that you make an effort for them can be motivating. If in doubt, follow Rock's SCARF model, set out in the section above on 'how the brain reacts to fear or threat' (see page 186).

5. Handling performance shortfalls: be positive and solutions focused The argument to be direct and to the point applies also to giving feedback on a performance shortfall. Again this will be easier in the context of a relationship of mutual trust and respect. However, there are many permutations: often, people know if they have done something badly; in which case, you don't need to point it out as well, unless it warrants serious disciplinary action. What's happened cannot be undone. Focus on the future which can be changed, and use a coaching style and the projected learning cycle (Figure 9.3) to help the person plan how to improve, and to keep track of progress.

Sometimes, people do not recognize their performance shortfall. As we know from the neuroscience finding, receiving feedback is inherently threatening and people instinctively run away from it. As Rock points out, it threatens their need for 'status' and so knocks their self-esteem. Be sensitive to their feelings. Help repair self-esteem. The giver of feedback may be aware of this at an instinctive level and seek to avoid the discomfort of how they imagine the person they are dealing with may react. They do not want to have to experience the emotion the person may show or which they fear may be directed at them. But remember, not dealing with problems usually makes matters worse for everyone. The person's underperformance continues and reflects badly on their manager, while the delay may have cut out options for the underperformer:

- Ask the person to identify what is not working well, or what can be improved, and use a coaching style with them from that standpoint.
- If that fails, be direct, clear and specific about what is going wrong.
- Make it clear that you are being supportive.

- Emphasize that you wish to explore the way forward together, but give the person time to digest the feedback, and perhaps vent anger or upset before you put forward your ideas. Although it is better to let the other person work out their own solutions, in this case having some practical suggestions at the ready is probably wise.

- As you work through the way forward, identify the person's strengths and connect their strengths with the new actions.

- Make sure you are on hand to support the person in changing and adapting, and keep a high level of communication going with them for a while, to keep them focused and positive.

What about the person who cannot perform the role as required? I believe that this will become increasingly common as we require people to learn and adapt quickly to new challenges, and hard decisions will have to be taken. I hope the approaches in this book will help minimize the need for these hard decisions, but some are inevitable:

- In the first instance, do what you can to build roles around people's strengths, and what they can do and want to do.

- Everyone is important: always keep this in mind.

- Provide feedback and support to help people change and develop.

- If all this fails, then make sure you treat the person with the dignity they deserve. (See below.)

6. Build confidence in your judgement For feedback to have impact, it also needs to be perceived as reliable and trustworthy. In other words, build your reputation as someone whose feedback is valued and sought after. A coaching style will help you do this. Develop the habit of regularly asking people probing questions about their work and their activities. This will help you build your understanding of different disciplines, but will also help you build your own ability to evaluate and make judgements. It will also increase your visibility around the business. Be aware that people will probably discuss some of these conversations together, when you are not present. A non-partisan, objective approach will enhance your credibility with the team. Seek feedback from others about your own performance so that you role-model the idea of striving for continuous improvement.

7. Feelings Many people are reluctant to talk about feelings, either their own or other people's, and they often ask me if they can still be effective at giving feedback and at supporting learning. My answer is yes. The fact that you do not talk about feelings doesn't make you any less sensitive. Just speak about what feels right for you, and what you are comfortable with, but don't avoid discussing performance problems or offering support. If you are reasonably sensitive to others, this will come across in the practical support you give and in your non-verbal cues.

You don't have to be a super-hero to be a nearby manager. Just be yourself, be thoughtful about how you treat people, and about how you carry out the three responsibilities I have set out. Nonetheless, the pressures of our changing world are creating particular problems for nearby managers. These are not new, but are becoming more commonplace.

How can you motivate people to achieve change and growth, when you are making their colleagues redundant? Balancing acts are likely to become more common, where we are running down some activities while building up others, or losing some people while motivating others to achieve more. When tough decisions have to be taken, people need to feel confident that the right ones have been taken and that all concerned have been treated fairly. This requires trust, transparency and high levels of communication.

Robust redundancy and outplacement policies are also required, along with a great deal of emotional intelligence. Seek support also from your HR adviser. There are two basic rules of thumb here: one is that redundancy or dismissal should always be a last resort. We do not want to move back to the bad old days of 'hire and fire'. The second rule of thumb is to continue to value the person who leaves, whether they are leaving of their own accord or not, and support them as much as possible. Where leaving is forced:

- Work closely with employees and/or their representatives from the beginning of the process, which must be open and transparent. Be prepared to consider other options.

- Explain the redundancy process and practicalities.

- Handle matters with sensitivity and have advisers on hand to provide outplacement support. Train your HR people to provide this kind of support at all levels.

- Find out what leavers felt about the process, and handle matters sensitively.

- Social networks – often called alumni groups – for 'off-boarding' employees when they leave the organization, either voluntarily or otherwise, are beneficial. They provide a support network for leavers, and possibly a source of job referrals. They enable you to maintain connections with former employees, in anticipation of future openings.

- Be open and transparent with your team members, showing appreciation for past efforts of the people leaving, and making sure the leaver gets a good send-off.

Remember survivors' syndrome. Knowing that a colleague, or several, have been 'let go' demoralizes those remaining. This term may sound curious but there is a real 'grieving process' when colleagues leave, especially if you have been particularly good friends with them. Leave time for this, and don't be frightened to express your feelings and show that you too are 'grieving' in this way. As team leader, however, you must quickly refocus energy and maintain morale. This is a time when you need high levels of communication with the team collectively and individually.

This is also a time when it is important to keep reinforcing your vision and your strategic direction so that you energize people by giving them goals and inspiring confidence in the future. Pay attention to yourself too, as this will undoubtedly be painful for you. No one likes to be in this situation, so find someone to support you through what will be difficult for you too. Do not shut yourself away, or not face up to the conversations. This rarely helps anyone.

As we look to the combination of an uncertain economic future and rapid change, it is likely that periods of unemployment will be the norm for everyone. Previously, it was actors who had to be prepared for disappointment and rejection. They had to supplement low pay and periods of unemployment by taking different jobs. Now many people need to be prepared in this way.

Work is not just about money – a large part of our self-regard comes from our work. When that is lost, it affects our identity and sense of self and can give rise to many problems. It is partly a manager's understanding that redundancy is more than a financial blow that makes managers reluctant to be open about these things, either with the individual who must go or with colleagues who remain. Certainly, we will all benefit if we define ourselves by who we are as a person, and by our all-round talents and abilities, rather than through our work or our status.

The organization must assist the process by supporting and preparing the manager and by providing a reasonable package of help for leavers, and that this is perceived to be so by all concerned.

How do you energize people, especially when times are bad? This is a principal challenge facing managers after several years of downturn and a bleak economic outlook. Here are some tips:

1 Think about your own morale and well-being and make sure you are well supported. It is hard to energize others if you are feeling down.

This is especially important for the CEO, or whoever is perceived as the boss. Research shows that the CEO's (or boss's) mood is particularly contagious around the organization.

2 If we go back to neuroscience for some guidance, we find that the human brain is a social organ. 'Inspiring and supportive relationships are important – they help activate openness to new ideas and a more social orientation to others' (Boyatzis, 2011). Boyatzis suggests that insights such as these may move the thrust of a leader's actions away from 'results orientation' toward a 'relationship orientation'. This does not preclude the concern with results, but could show why being first and foremost concerned about one's relationships may then enable others to perform better and more innovatively – and lead to better results. Building on this, make the effort to create social occasions and establish social networks, including virtual networks, to include geographically dispersed employees.

3 Create a positive atmosphere and pay attention to people and their efforts. Reward kind actions. This corresponds to a social psychology construct known as reciprocity, which means that in response to friendly actions, people are frequently nicer and more cooperative than predicted by the self-interest model; conversely, in response to hostile actions they are frequently nastier and even brutal.

4 The 'shared values, visions and understanding' model requires high trust, high collaboration and high compassion, and encourages it also. Build trust by listening, learning, seeking out people's ideas and giving them feedback. Transparency is the basis of trust. Do what you say you will, and report back on it.

5 Many of the ideas in this book will energize people. For example:

- Give people tools to be self-managing.
- Ensure that people have a clear line of sight to the purpose, mission and goals of the organization through their day job.
- Give people chance to develop and grow in roles that have some 'stretch'.
- Create positive work environments so that people can feel part of a winning team.
- Ensure that people can gain appropriate reward and recognition, even if much of this is non-financial.
- Engage people with a higher purpose by getting your staff involved in good causes, which might motivate them more broadly at work.

This analysis of nearby management completes the four-point framework, as we have now been through the strategies, processes and mindsets needed to put strategic talent development in place. In the next chapter, I turn to faraway leaders and their overall strategic responsibility for this approach.

Key points

- All managers, however senior, are nearby managers to some.
- There are three key management responsibilities: accompany development, hold regular conversations to give feedback on performance and discuss careers, set performance goals and standards.
- A coaching style, using active listening as the key skill, is a powerful tool for accomplishing nearby management successfully.
- Cognitive neuroscience helps us understand how to make management and learning more effective:
  - Encourage concentration, repetition and reinforcement.
  - Help people learn through reflection.
  - Give positive and constructive feedback.
  - Be sensitive to people's feelings.
  - Create flow where people are engaged and excited in what they are doing by opening new and challenging experiences.
- Face hard decisions with firmness but compassion and dignity.
- Strategic talent development is a process that deals with issues such as engagement, goals and development, which help to energize everyone in hard times as well as good.

Note

1 I use the word 'accompany' rather than 'manage' or even 'ensure' because development should be self-managed but nonetheless enabled, guided and assisted by the manager. The word accompany seems to have the right emphasis and connotations to express this.

Faraway leadership

10

I n this chapter, I consider what faraway leaders must do to promote strategic talent development. I then put forward some ideas for helping current leaders adapt to the new world environment, and for developing emerging leaders.

Faraway management – in the C-Suite

Today's business leaders must seek and develop new business opportunities, protect and enhance brands, shift or create new organizational cultures to become more flexible and agile, and achieve results. This overall purpose contains four accountability areas that are directly connected to strategic talent development:

- Promote organizational culture.
- Create and implement strategy that leads to new business opportunities.
- Engage staff intellectually and emotionally with the aims and strategies of the enterprise.
- Develop talent to meet the capabilities required for a sustainable future.

While it is easy to list these roles, they have complicated interactions with each other and the management of people is both a specific role but also represents the entire process. Figure 10.1 tries to capture these ideas. It shows vision and values informing strategy creation, which, in turn, leads on to its implementation. It illustrates how communication to and from the 'team'

FIGURE 10.1 Faraway leadership responsibilities of the people at the top

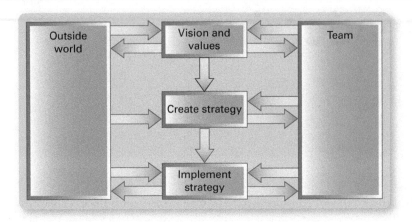

takes place during each process. It also shows this two-way communication with the outside world of investors, business partners and financiers, at the level of vision and values; but, while information from the outside world influences strategy, this is a one-way street. Finally, it shows a different form of communication through actions, as strategy is implemented.

Promote organizational culture

Leaders in the C-Suite have a profound impact on organizational culture, which propagates through their words, their deeds and their decisions. Organizational cultures constantly evolve and shift in response to the normal challenges and changes in personnel and events. But, sometimes, transformative culture change is required to reposition the business to meet strategic change, or indeed to embrace strategic talent development. It may be required to remedy dysfunction, which can creep into even the most cohesive of teams or the strongest cultures. We will discuss it further below.

We have already discussed culture change in Chapters 2 and 4, but it is worth reminding ourselves here that culture change requires an orchestrated approach that addresses the mechanics of change, and also the people aspects. It starts with your vision, which is the narrative of what the business is about; this vision inspires people and guides them along its broad direction. It enables the leader, but also others, to select goals and strategies that lead in the same direction. Of course, in tough times, you must also level with people about the current difficulties, but giving a clear sense of direction will engage them and secure their effort.

The awareness we have of culture and its strong impact on employee behaviour also gives leaders the opportunity to create a culture that supports strong moral and ethical behaviour.

Create and implement strategy

Senior leaders determine the overall strategic direction of the business, and the priorities for getting there. As discussed in Chapter 4, keeping the message simple – expressed in three priorities – gives people a good sense of direction and helps them know how to get a sensible outcome. The stress of hard work is lessened when it is in the context of a clear destination. This builds organizational resilience and capacity to deal with tough times.

In the new business environment this means seeking input from colleagues and subordinates; it means being able to create and spot change by making judgements between disparate views, and connections between superficially unrelated issues.

Despite widely varied opinions about the key characteristics required by leaders at the top of organizations, there is almost complete agreement by commentators that 'being forward-looking – envisioning exciting possibilities and enlisting others in a shared view of the future – is the attribute that most distinguishes leaders from non-leaders'. Kouzes and Posner surveyed tens of thousands of people and reported that: 'No other quality showed such a dramatic difference between leader and colleague' (Kouzes and Posner, 2009).

Wasserman's description of different levels of strategic thinking and development is helpful: 'Leaders on the front line must anticipate merely what comes after current projects wrap up. People at the next level of leadership should be looking several years into the future. And those... [at the top levels] ... must focus on a horizon some 10 years distant.' While we can debate the precise time focus, the important point is that the top leadership team must set a vision and develop strategies that extend years into the future. This is not to say that they are set in stone; strategic plans should adapt as the environment and markets change. Nonetheless, the broad thinking and direction must extend for a significant period beyond short-term planning cycles. This can often be a shock to newly appointed directors who, on the way up, have probably had only limited exposure to this high level of strategic thinking (Wasserman, 2009).

According to AG Lafley, Chairman and CEO of Procter & Gamble, 'the CEO has a very specific job that only he or she can do: link the external world with the internal organization'. He goes on to say that 'the CEO alone experiences the meaningful outside at an enterprise level and is responsible for understanding it, interpreting it, advocating it, and presenting it so that the company can respond in a way that enables sustainable sales, profit, and total shareholder return (TSR) growth' (Lafley, 2009).

This suggests that exposure to business strategy, and long-term thinking, should be given to people two rungs or so before they reach this level, as part of their development.

Strategy implementation

While everyone is clear that the top team have the prime responsibility for creating the business strategy, their role in implementing it is often hazy. I have known many instances where there is a clear disconnect between the people at the top and their direct reports. This arises because senior managers see their role as 'being strategic' and believe that 'being operational' is what their direct reports do. They fail to realize that unless they create a bridge between the two, it leaves a gap, with senior management not appreciating what is going on in the rest of the organization and with people below them feeling undirected, unsupported and unclear about what is expected of them. As well as leading to disaffection, this also means that the organization does not follow a clear strategic path but diffuses its effort. People at lower levels take the broad, and probably vague, 'strategy', and interpret the detail so that it may well diverge from what was originally intended. Often, the director moves in, late in the day, and others perceive this as moving the goalposts. This does not mean that people at the top should micro-manage. Far from it, but keeping too distant from strategy implementation – which often arises from keeping too distant from actually managing people – does not help create the 'shared vision' and 'shared understanding' required for the new leadership model. Good strategy implementation requires the right balance between being 'hands on' and 'hands off'.

One approach to achieving this balance is to 'lead with questions not answers'. As US business consultant, author and lecturer Jim Collins observes: 'Great leaders engage in dialogue and debate not coercion.' This argues for a coaching style and the 'shared values, visions and understanding' leadership model I set out in this book. It relates also to many of the ideas in the previous chapter, especially around reflective learning, and developing the habit of asking probing questions (Collins, 2001).

This example from Sergio Marchionne, CEO of Fiat, who is widely credited for having given Fiat a solid footing after near bankruptcy, is also insightful. Marchionne believes that it is important to get closely involved but he emphasizes that he is not prescriptive in his style: 'I immerse myself in the business not so that I can make decisions in my corner office but so that I can guide the folks on the ground to make the right decisions. I don't know what those will be going into a meeting, but I think my involvement makes it more likely that we will get the right ones coming out' (Marchionne, 2008). This approach is a far cry from prescriptive micromanagement, which demotivates staff and cuts off innovation, ideas and feedback from lower levels in the business.

The prime role of the leader is to ensure that their organization has an appropriate strategy and direction, though it is irrelevant whether leaders actually create it themselves. In fact, an attribute of strategic talent development is that strategic opportunities can be spotted, and created, by anyone, anywhere. Leaders are the enablers and communicators of vision, values and strategy, which leads on from the question of how they make it happen to the related one of how they make it change.

There is a marvellous quotation attributed to the economist John Maynard Keynes when he was challenged for having changed his position: 'When the facts change, I change my mind. What do you do?'

Facts do change; markets change; competitors come up with new ideas; technology changes. The need to adapt strategy to changing circumstances stresses the importance of effective communication through the management of people. Writers on strategy emphasize that the insights that lead to competitive advantage emerge not from ivory tower thinking but from a deep understanding of products, markets and companies' internal processes and capabilities. To achieve this, leaders need either to embody all these capabilities in themselves or else to enable their colleagues to input their expertise and insights into the development of new products, services and strategies, to make up for inevitable deficiencies.

This brings us back to the importance of leaders keeping involved in strategy implementation using debate and influence to create 'shared values, shared visions and understanding' but also to ensure strategy is thought through and driven through. To do this, they must constantly pose 'what-if' questions, play devil's advocate, test ideas and encourage their subordinates to do the same. This requires regular one-to-one meetings with their direct reports, as well as team meetings. In short, it requires good management, which, at the highest levels, strengthens implementation, motivation and strategic direction. Ian Livingston, CEO of BT plc, provides an apt illustration of this idea. Widely credited with slashing £3.5 billion in costs over five years and adding 17 million customers to get the company back in shape, Livingston said he will never abandon his 'more to do' approach to running the company. 'It used to be that people would love to tell you how well things were going. I said to my top team that their job is to tell me what needs to improve and my job is to tell them how well they've done, not the other way around' (Fildes, 2012).

Overall management of values, visions and strategy

I said at the outset of the chapter that these four leadership roles interact, so let us consider them as one integrated process, including the nearby management responsibilities discussed previously. Figure 10.1 illustrates how information and communication pass back and forth as the business leaders carry out their key roles. Quite separately from their role of recruiting, developing, motivating and deploying their staff, they are also communicating in ways set out in Table 10.1.

Think about the communication each leader has with the inside world and specifically with their team. This is both seeking and giving information, and giving instructions, but, while that is a separate role from, say, developing an individual, it is also indistinguishable from it. The conversation between leader and direct report that results in information passing each way also results in motivation and development of that individual and, through success in the latter process, improves the quality of the former. It is also how people achieve a common and 'shared' understanding. For example, the leader chooses to engage in a coaching style of behaviour with an individual in order to enable them to understand an issue for themselves and to be able to deal with similar situations on their own in future. Yet, during the same conversation the leader communicates an alteration in strategy and receives back an idea that will subsequently be agreed which will affect the implementation of strategy in the future. You cannot draw precise demarcation lines between the leadership roles and the process of leadership: they are intertwined. It is this process of constructive, open conversation that must be transmitted through the organization to generate a true performance management culture, where people get a

TABLE 10.1 Leadership roles: internal and external

Leadership roles	Inside world	Outside world
Values and vision	Communicating the company ethos and vision to their team and colleagues	Communicating the company ethos and vision to external stakeholders
	Receiving ideas, values and data that help to formulate and also feedback that helps to adjust vision and values, from their team and other colleagues	Receiving ideas, values and data that help to formulate and also feedback that helps to adjust vision and values, from external stakeholders
Creating strategy	Communicating the strategy to team and colleagues	Communicating strategy to external stakeholders such as investors and financiers
	Receiving ideas and data that help to formulate and also feedback on issues, problems and outcomes that helps to adjust strategy, from their team and other colleagues	Receiving ideas and data that help to formulate strategy and also feedback on issues, problems and outcomes that helps to adjust strategy, from external stakeholders
Implementing strategy	Directions to team	Actions to implement strategy
	Operational information and feedback on outcomes from team and colleagues	Outcomes and responses from the outside world

chance to input to and shape plans, and to understand how they contribute to achieving goals.

The interactions with the outside world in the realm of 'implementing strategy' comprise a rather different type of communication since they are primarily physical actions: things the company does and outcomes they observe.

The breakdown of collaboration

Effective leadership from the top is not only about fulfilling roles, but the senior management team sets the tone, often by how they behave together and how effectively they work as a team. The dysfunctional senior team is a common problem. To paraphrase Tolstoy, every dysfunctional team is dysfunctional in its own way; and yet… there are commonalities across many different situations. The key breakdown is often in the chief executive's role of managing direct reports: usually the rest of the top team. Often it results from the odd idea that once individuals reach the top of an organization they no longer need managing. Of course, this is quite untrue: the necessary style of management may be different but they are still a team and still need managing. I have known many cases where the CEO actively encouraged board rivalries, either in the mistaken belief that internal competition encourages performance or as a means of protecting his or her own position.

Dysfunctionality comes from directors competing for territory and priority, which leads to 'silo' working right through the organization, lack of coordination, wasted effort, low morale and an inability to reach agreement on policy or cooperation to implement it, with a consequent adverse effect on performance. They each compete for the chief executive's ear and try to avoid bad news. From my experience, as directors split into warring factions this can be reflected throughout the organization in the form of a subtle bullying culture, which leads to people's views, input and contribution often being ignored and definitely unrecognized. In terms of Figure 10.2, the information flows are disrupted and it is as if there are a series of vertical splits down the organization, as illustrated in Figure 10.3.

The different functions are not quite completely separate organizations, because they must communicate between and through each other. The marketing department still needs operations to do the manufacturing and still needs information from the sales department but, at each interface, there is a lack of coordination and information flow. As an example, in one organization the purchasing department placed orders for board and packaging four months ahead, yet the sales department forecasts of demand were done on a three-monthly cycle. The invariable result was a mismatch that led to either excessive stocks being held or an inability to supply customers. This was fundamentally a problem of the top team not being managed – nothing else can explain the buyers' failure to ask for four-month forecasts or the sales team's failure to ask why there was insufficient packaging.

FIGURE 10.2 The breakdown of collaboration

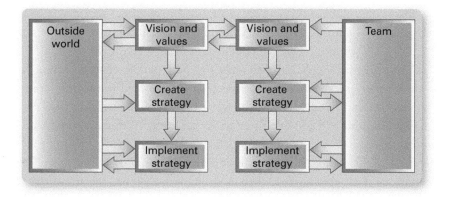

The encouragement of collaboration

While 'heroic' or 'charismatic' leadership models may no longer be appropriate, this in no way lessens the role of the CEO and the top team but it does emphasize the importance of teamwork at the top. In particular, it places the CEO as the main influencer, managing direct reports so as to drive employee engagement, building a culture of innovation and collaboration by creating a collegiate top team, mobilizing effort by promoting cultural values, and developing strategy and overseeing its implementation. These are key capabilities that need to start at CEO level.

A hugely impactful approach[1] is to pair members of the top team and make each responsible for reporting at board or committee meetings on the other's results. This brings people closer together, as they strive to please and support each other. It leads to more joint effort and fosters a greater understanding of each other's activities. It leads to a more seamless approach across functions as people identify how actions and decisions in one area impact on others. As people's results come under this different type of scrutiny, it also has the effect of raising the bar without creating a destructive competitiveness.

Leadership of innovation

Figure 10.2 and Table 10.1, by illustrating the interconnectedness of the roles and processes of the organization, also illustrate the importance of collaboration in so much of innovation: a process that, I continually stress, is needed everywhere in today's uncertain business world. What do we mean by innovation? How do people innovate and what encourages it?

Sometimes innovation is about a big transformational idea or a radical insight but much of the time it is about incremental improvements that make processes more efficient. Often it is somewhere between the two. Hofstede identifies cultural differences in how people champion innovation. In many Western cultures, especially the UK and the United States, he suggests that people need to be free of rules and constraints and need champions who will provide them with autonomy from rules, procedures and systems so that they can establish creative solutions to existing problems. While Hofstede's work is complex and contains many more permutations than can be described here, it does support the notion that, certainly in the UK and the United States, innovation is more likely to occur in organizational cultures that allow freedom, autonomy and flexibility (Hofstede, 2003).

Much of the time, innovation is about people sharing information and knowledge, building on each other's ideas and finding new ways of thinking about old problems. This requires people to work together cooperatively, being prepared to continually review and improve practices and processes. You can never remove competition completely from inside the organization, as people will always compete for jobs and resources, and some competition is healthy. However, as Lynda Gratton describes, 'innovative capacity comes from the intelligence, insights and wisdom of people working together. A combination of individual energy and relational energy generated between them.' Gratton's view is that successful organizations are places where people are excited about working together. 'Teams that create a Hot Spot in organizations are energized and buzzing with inspiration. They know that, working together, they will make a difference by achieving something brilliant, important and purposeful, with a strong impact on the bottom line' (Gratton, 2007).

Increasingly, forms of cooperation are becoming more diverse as businesses outsource or enter alliances, partnerships and joint ventures, so that many people in the organization have responsibilities and accountabilities across organizational boundaries. In such cases, you probably have no formal authority over people you depend upon to achieve your goals. Additionally, many people work in virtual teams or matrix structures which also require collaborative, rather than competitive, ways of working. As we set out in Chapter 2, values bind people, they create a corporate identity or brand and they help provide boundaries within which they operate. So in a sense, they enable the organization to loosen control and confine rules, systems and procedures to an essential minimum.

Dr Joe Raelin of the Boston Consortium for Higher Education proposes that modern leadership is concurrent – in any community, there can be more than one leader operating at the same time so that leaders willingly and naturally share power with others – and also collective (Raelin, 2006). The collective view suggests that leadership does not derive from individual influence as much as it does from the process of people working together for a common purpose. Although Raelin's ideas refer more to the concept of distributed leadership throughout the organization (Chapter 1), I believe that these ideas could be applied to leadership at the top. In this model, there will be a top team of equals, setting a model for collaborative working throughout the business. This model was adopted in ACE[2] (an international network of consultancy firms) about three years ago, and has worked successfully. The vision for the organization is to become a globally trusted and recognized brand. The co-leaders' objective is to steer the network towards this vision. The co-leaders recommend, but decisions are taken by the whole network. The model is similar to the partnership model of the big consultancies, or the Swiss Verein model of the big law firms. This example helps to show how a co-leadership model might work. Each of four co-leaders has specific roles assigned according to their strengths: strategic direction and new ideas; fostering team spirit and collaboration across the business; operations and monitoring KPIs; working through the detail of new ideas. This team is geographically dispersed but holds regular conference calls, and otherwise communicates regularly through e-mails, or shared documents. The entire network meets twice a year for at least two days at each session. The main ingredient to make this model work is a commitment for it to do so. Its elements include frequent communication, sharing and building on each other's ideas, consulting the whole network, valuing and recognizing each other's contributions and, not to be forgotten, self-regulation so that everyone devotes roughly equal amounts of time and effort. The main benefits include a shared workload, which enables more to be done and maintains the momentum of new initiatives. The diversity of backgrounds, ideas and experiences among the team, but also across the network, helps innovation and creates value. For such a model to work, the members of the organization must value consensus without driving the principle so far as to water everything down to a lowest common denominator; they must work to accommodate each other's needs but aim to arrive at the highest common denominator. This way of working requires constant effort to check values and behaviours and pull them back if they get out of kilter, but then this is the case with all ways of working.

Develop emerging talent

Attracting present and future leaders and ensuring a sufficient stream of people coming through is a major challenge for those in the C-Suite. Indeed, the 'war for talent' debate started from the research finding that there were insufficient leaders to go round.

Attracting talent and building future leaders isn't, as so many think, about management information, or control mechanisms (though these are required). It isn't something you can leave to HR and then blame on them if it goes wrong. This is something that the C-Suite team need to see as part of their responsibilities. In spite of the global recession, there is still a shortage of leaders worldwide. As Collins[3] so aptly puts it, 'First who then do' is of major importance, otherwise business leaders are going to find that they do not have the right people to take the business forward and bring new ideas to fruition. Taking an interest in the people coming through, taking a risk on them by giving them stretching opportunities for growth, involving them in top-level activities, and coaching and mentoring them should be major top-level responsibilities.

Marchionne illustrates this approach, seeing 'finding and engaging with new leaders' as a major aspect of his role, and he describes how he spends considerable time engaging with the people coming through the organization: 'I spend four to five months conducting performance reviews for the top 700 people. Of course I look at numbers in assessing performance, but I'm more interested in how well they lead people and lead change. I have long debates with people about whether or not they've displayed the right characteristics. My assessment is based overwhelmingly on this engagement. They know that I care about what happens to them.' Marchionne goes on to say that 'if the organization can feel that kind of connection with its leadership, you're going to get a pretty sound culture aligned around strongly held common values...', which also illustrates the point about communicating and managing (Marchionne, 2008).

Building the leadership pipeline is the most tangible of the leader's responsibilities for strategic talent development. This is wholly consistent with an inclusive approach, which emphasizes that everyone is important. Growing your own leaders is a necessity for the purposes of business continuity, but also to have the right people to enable the business to take advantage of growth opportunities. Moreover, evidence shows that promoting internal people to senior posts, instead of recruiting externally, has a positive overall impact on retention and motivation. Where your senior leaders do not readily embrace other aspects of strategic talent development, this can well be the hook to get them involved.

Measure leaders' performance

There is no one-size-fits-all solution, but this set of measurement criteria from Stephen Kaufman of the Harvard Business School is useful for focusing senior leaders' minds on what they need to do, and the skills they need to develop. Kaufman describes the evaluation process that Arrow Electronics uses to measure the performance of the chief executive:

- Leadership. How well does the CEO motivate and energize the organization and is the company's culture reinforcing its mission and values?
- Strategy. Is it working, is the company aligned behind it, and is it being effectively implemented?
- People management. Is the CEO putting the right people in the right jobs, and is there a stream of appropriate people for succession and to support growth goals?
- Operating metrics. Are sales, profits, productivity, asset utilization, quality, and customer satisfaction heading in the right direction?
- Relationships with external constituencies. How well does the CEO engage with the company's customers, suppliers, and other stakeholders?

Although this is stated rather differently from my diagram of leadership roles, it covers the same issues. What Kaufman (2008) calls leadership matches my vision and values; strategy amalgamates creation and implementation; people management is similar to mine, though possibly under-emphasizing the importance of being a nearby manager to one's team. I am also inclined to emphasize more strongly leadership accountability for attracting, developing, deploying and engaging talent; the operating metrics role relates to the implementation of strategy to the outside world and is represented by the arrows at the bottom left of my diagram; external constituencies are represented by my information flows between the organization and the outside world.

These measurement criteria are helpful, not only for measuring performance, but you can also use them to measure the capability gap for each individual leader to help them identify their development needs, and also to plan development for emerging leaders.

Leadership development

Organizational climate is influenced by leadership style – by the way leaders motivate direct reports, gather and use information, make decisions, manage change initiatives and handle crises. By understanding these styles and their impact, you can develop your own approach to leadership and become more effective. Leadership theory has evolved considerably since the early idea that effective leaders share a number of common personality 'traits'. The realization that there is no one correct, or best, type of leadership style led to theories that the best style is contingent on the situation. Contingency theories try to predict which style is best in which circumstance. The leadership style that relates most closely to the ideas and ethos of strategic talent development is known as 'transformational' leadership. Transformational leaders are inspiring because they seek and expect the best from everyone as well as from themselves. They show integrity and know how to develop a vision, and focus on the future. They motivate people to achieve this vision, and manage its delivery. They generate a collegiate atmosphere, which leads to high productivity and engagement from everyone. The weakness of this style is that it might not give sufficient recognition to the detail, or the transactional.

I have observed many disastrous situations brought about by poor leadership style, or lack of versatility. One example was the newly appointed director who spent all his time with the poor performer on his team, giving little attention to the others. They assumed the reverse of what was happening: that the person who in effect was a poor performer was favoured over them. The high performer on the team immediately found himself a new job outside the organization, and morale plummeted across the team. In another example, the board decided on a change of strategy to give greater prominence, and therefore resources, to the commercial department of an enterprise where the technical department was previously pre-eminent. Warfare broke out as the technical director put obstacles in the way of the commercial director. The CEO remained impassive through discussions when he should have been supporting the new strategy, and with it the commercial director, leaving the law of the jungle to prevail. In other circumstances, the CEO's open, participative style worked well, but in this case, he needed to show direction and use a more authoritative style. No one came out of this well, and the board removed all three. Both these examples illustrate the danger of a failure to adapt your leadership style.

So while the predominant style of strategic talent development is a transformational one, leaders need an understanding of different leadership theories, so as to use different styles to suit different circumstances. There is nothing magic, or natural, about being an effective leader. It just takes effort and persistence to learn certain ways of thinking and techniques that enable you to nuance and adapt your natural style and make the most of it. There are many appropriate and valid models to choose from. Be sure what you choose offers fluidity, and focuses on what resonates for you. I have chosen the following because they fit especially well with strategic talent development, and will help you adapt to the new world. Some of them are new but others have been around for a long time, but are well worth revisiting and refocusing on today's context.

Iperquest®

I have mentioned this elsewhere where I have stated the usefulness of this model and especially its accompanying profiling tool to creating an integrated self-managed suite of development tools for your business (see Chapter 5). It is possible to create a separate profile of capabilities for the leadership team, giving the advantage of differentiating the role, while also matching the firm's core model. It is a helpful diagnostic tool for a coaching programme. The model brings out our different thinking and decision-making styles, and shows how these styles impact, not only how we learn and how we process information, but also how we interact with, and learn from, other people. It tends to suit highly qualified people.

Extraordinary leadership

Jack Zenger (a leadership expert) and Joe Folkman (a statistician) have found a way to turn leadership from being a perceived 'soft' skill to a science. They conducted a piece of research performing 200,000 evaluations on 20,000 leaders. Using statistical correlation, they identified the 16 core competencies that drive financial performance and discovered that the top 10 per cent of leaders deliver *twice* as much profit, on average, as the middle 80 per cent. Their message is: 'good' is not enough, your organization needs you to be 'extraordinary'.

Zenger and Folkman also examined what causes leaders to fail. They showed that all leaders have a mix of positive and negative traits. A negative trait that undermines the overall positive perception of others is termed a 'fatal flaw'. This is either an area of weakness (below the 50th percentile) or an area of relative weakness where your organization needs you to be strong.

Zenger and Folkman have created a diagnostic tool and development process based on the research data that gives detailed practical guidance on how to become an extraordinary leader by building on your existing strengths and (if required) fixing fatal flaws.

This research-based, practical, down-to-earth approach to leadership is particularly well suited to 'data rational' organizations such as banks and financial services, accountants, oil and gas, mining and engineering (Zenger and Folkman, 2009).

Emotional intelligence, moral intelligence

While a high IQ can be an important asset for rising to the top, Goleman and others have shown that it is not adequate to predict executive competency and corporate success. Emotional intelligence (EQ) argues that to be successful requires the ability to understand and manage both your own emotions and those of the people around you. People with a high degree of emotional intelligence usually know what they're feeling, what this means, and how their emotions can affect other people. For leaders, having emotional intelligence is essential for success. There are five main elements of emotional intelligence:

1 self-awareness;

2 self-regulation;

3 motivation;

4 empathy;

5 social skills.

Managing each of these areas will make you more emotionally intelligent and, therefore, a more effective leader.

EQ rose to prominence with Daniel Goleman's book *Emotional Intelligence* (1996). Further weight has been given to his ideas from research carried out by the Carnegie Institute of Technology, which argues that 85 per cent of your financial success is due to skills in 'human engineering', your personality and your ability to communicate, negotiate and lead. Only 15 per cent is due to technical knowledge. Additionally, Nobel Prize-winning Israeli-American psychologist Daniel Kahneman found that people would rather do business with a person they like and trust, even if they are charging a higher price or offering lower quality (Kahneman, 2012).

Another idea that complements EQ and IQ is moral intelligence. It seems particularly appropriate to highlight this after a series of banking scandals has eroded trust in business leadership. These have also demonstrated the very real financial costs that can follow from unethical behaviour. That these issues are wider than just integrity is clear from the public outcry that followed revelations in 2012 that multinational businesses trading in the UK were avoiding UK corporation tax. A public perception that they had a moral duty to pay tax had financial consequences. One major corporation volunteered to pay tax and another that had moved its head office from the UK moved it back (Keld, 2012).

The above are alternative diagnostic and coaching tools. The following can be used in conjunction with either one.

Situational leadership

Hersey and Blanchard's situational leadership theory states that instead of using just one style, successful leaders should change their leadership styles based on the maturity of the people they're leading and the details of the task. Using this theory, leaders should be able to place more or less emphasis on the task, and more or less emphasis on the relationships with the people they're leading, depending on what's needed to get the job done successfully. It is useful for identifying different styles to use with individuals on the team (Hersey and Blanchard, 1977).

French and Raven's five forms of power

Leadership and power are closely linked, but leaders have power for different reasons. It might be because of position in the hierarchy (legitimate power), because you can give a pay rise, or assign work (reward power) or hire and fire (coercive power). More positively, you might have power arising from your perceived expertise in your field and solid judgement (expert power), or you have charisma, or command respect (referent power). This last carries a big responsibility. You don't have to do anything to earn it, but if someone lacks integrity they can use their referent power to hurt and gain personal advantage. Understanding these types of power can help you become an influential and positive leader, and it can also help you avoid being influenced by those who use less effective types of power. In the UK and the United States especially, reduced deference in society as a whole makes legitimate power less effective.

Five dysfunctions of a team

I referred earlier to dysfunctional teams, and how damaging these are to the rest of the organization. Even the best-led teams can become dysfunctional, and work by Patrick Lencioni looks at addressing key team-working problems.

The five dysfunctions are:

1 absence of trust;

2 fear of conflict;

3 lack of commitment;

4 avoidance of team accountability;

5 inattention to team objectives.

The chairman can use these as checkpoints for regular discussion with the CEO. Or the chairman, or an external facilitator, can usefully lead discussion around these five issues, perhaps during an away-day or board development session. It can be used whether one suspects there is a problem or just to confirm that the senior management team is being well managed and working well together (Lencioni, 2002).

Measuring C-Suite executives' impact on employee engagement

I was involved in running a 360-degree feedback programme for the directors of an organization. The project then involved drawing comparisons between the results of individuals and those from an employee engagement survey. Based on the Iperquest® model (Chapter 5), and including open questions around the theme 'what should I stop, start, continue?' (Chapter 8), it was striking for many directors to see the close correlations between their personal feedback and employee engagement results for their areas.

The choice of methods for helping executives in the C-Suite and other top management tiers develop their styles will be highly personal, but executive coaching is likely to be the first choice for many. One of the reasons for the explosion in the use of executive coaching in recent years has been to help people at the top who are leading significant organizational change. The old saying 'it is lonely at the top' is very true. The higher your position in the organization, the less likely you are to receive honest feedback, yet greater visibility is accompanied by higher levels of scrutiny because an executive's decisions become increasingly pivotal and mistakes prove more costly, the more senior you are within the organization. Good coaching fills the gap by providing frank, objective support and feedback. In the quest for innovation and creativity, a coach can give the business leader the opportunity to sound out and think through ideas without inadvertently creating disquiet among their team.

Just-in-time coaching

This (see Chapter 5) lends itself well to developing the contingent leadership styles recommended here, given that the coaching focuses on how to develop techniques and apply them to actual and current situations.

Development for emerging leaders

The thinking and ethos of strategic talent development requires there to be plenty of opportunity for learning and development provided for those aspiring to the top management tiers (Chapters 5 and 6).

Many of the ideas set out in self-managed succession (Chapter 5) can provide excellent development for emerging leaders. I would like to single out, however, the following approaches as being particularly appropriate to our fast-moving world.

Virtual simulation

Gaming can provide a powerful method for developing emerging leaders. For example, e-Simulator SUITE™ is a new, ground-breaking, innovative tool. It comprises online business simulations, at three management levels: junior, middle and top. It evaluates key competencies through a realistic, interactive virtual simulation. These 'three hours in the life of…' business-school-type cases result in focused development plans for level-appropriate leadership skills. This creative approach to leadership development is an enjoyable and challenging way to learn. It gives participants a taste of what it is like to operate at a higher level, while also giving them insights about themselves that form the basis of a coaching and development programme. It is a powerful tool for leadership and executive assessment and development, and is used for fast-track development, career transitions, and in executive coaching engagements.

One of the advantages of a simulation is that it brings individuals into contact with activities that they wouldn't normally encounter, and in a context where getting it wrong is not a disaster for the organization. It is especially helpful for developing the competencies or capabilities required for a role at the next level.

Real, client-focused experience

Young & Rubicam have also taken this idea of providing a development programme that gives people exposure to new experiences. In this case, they have developed their own in-house programme, which brings people together globally using a combination of virtual and classroom methods.

CASE STUDY

Young & Rubicam Group, headquartered in the United States, is part of WPP, which is the world leader in communications services. Y&R is a global, collaborative network comprising some of the most powerful brands in marketing communications, and operating in all the major economies around the world. Its areas of expertise include advertising, digital, media, public relations, social media, grassroots and direct marketing.

The Y&R mantra is 'Best Alone, Better Together'. 'Best Alone' recognizes that their individual brands are independent market leaders, and are iconic in their individual disciplines. They each operate in ways that allow them to maintain their competitive differentiation and individual brand identity. 'Better Together', of course, signifies the synergies and advantages that can be gained through collaboration and sharing. This two-pronged philosophy has inspired Rubicam University and 'SPECTRUM', two highly original developmental programmes.

In large agency holding companies, client teams cover a range of disciplines and companies. Individuals within the team can develop as subject matter experts, or rise within their individual companies. But while career progression, as a leader of the company's largest client relationships, may develop within a specific discipline, as you get to the top you must broaden out with at least a 'fluency' in other disciplines. This demands new skills that the Group had not previously developed, exposing succession planning vulnerabilities. Additionally, these broader skills are not widely available in external candidates and, even when someone is recruited externally, it takes considerable time to become oriented to leading multi-agency operations, let alone Y&R's culture and the unique nature of each client. The business imperative was to identify and develop the capabilities that were now required for such roles.

Rubicam University

Rubicam University is a one-week intensive programme that promotes the 'Better Together' concept by providing an opportunity for people to collaborate across disciplines and think in a multidisciplinary way. Its participants solve a complex challenge posed by a real client that requires an integrated solution. There is no cost to that client, though they make senior executives available to interact with the participants throughout the week. Y&R views it as an opportunity to demonstrate the power of the network to clients. Learning sessions focused on leadership, collaboration and communications are integrated throughout the course to build skills relevant to the challenge. The programme culminates in strategic recommendations from competing teams presented to the client on the final day. The best approaches are then synthesized and a core team goes on to develop the ideas further, using the resources of all the companies. Participants get to know each other and their disciplines well, and take the new understanding and the relationships back into their day-to-day responsibilities.

SPECTRUM

SPECTRUM addresses the question, 'What does it take to be a multidisciplinary client leader today?' Its success quickly led it to become a joint venture with parent WPP.

Key capabilities are captured in two frameworks. The first is 'The 10 Things Great Global Client Leaders Do'. Each of these has a descriptor, such as 'Have a world view' – which is then explained as 'Have an innate curiosity beyond marketing and communications. Understand the global and local dimensions of doing business. See beyond the brief. Really know the capabilities of Young & Rubicam Group and WPP.' Celia Berk, Y&R's Chief Talent Officer, has mapped out how to develop these ten attributes for three different competency levels: high potential, developing leaders, and today's global leaders, so that people can understand the requirements at each level, and plan their development accordingly.

The second framework is known as 'Super Skills', which are 'advancing the client's business agenda; inspiring teams to develop powerful ideas; delivering integrated solutions; opening new areas of growth'. These go beyond those that people might develop in the normal course of their work or within an individual company, and so to rise to this level takes extra development effort. SPECTRUM guides delegates on the development journey.

Cohorts are drawn mainly, but not exclusively, from teams working on the company's largest client relationships. Over 9–12 months, the programme:

- Starts with a webinar where delegates are introduced to each other, and to the concepts.

- Provides a social networking site where delegates can find materials and interact with each other.

- Features 360-degree feedback based on aspirational criteria. The feedback is debriefed individually and individuals draw up a 'Personal Leadership Plan'.

- Chooses a very senior executive sponsor for each participant.

- Allows delegates to follow through on their plan with their executive sponsor, and continue to interact and network with others from the cohort. They are encouraged to connect to the next cohort.

- Brings the cohort together physically once, for one week, about midway through the programme.

The involvement of executive sponsors is a particularly significant aspect of SPECTRUM. Berk found that identifying the right executives and matching them to participants is essentially a high-level recruitment exercise. Not all the relationships work well. Some sponsors are not able to make themselves as available as hoped, and sometimes the delegate does not take full advantage of the opportunity. But for many, the relationship is transformative as the sponsors open doors, make connections, broaden the participants' perspective, and help them operate with confidence with their most senior clients and colleagues.

Berk believes that the core benefit of the programme is the mindset change it achieves. Delegates think differently and are able to interact better as a peer at C-Suite level. This manifests itself in their relationships with their clients, and the solutions they provide for them. As with Rubicam University, another lasting benefit is the new relationships formed, which help graduates tap into expertise and resources around the world and across companies. An unexpected benefit has been the insights that the leaders of the client teams gain from getting to know each other, having sight lines into each other's teams, and learning how they are each structured and develop new capabilities.

While the focus of Rubicam University is real-world work done in an intensive setting, SPECTRUM combines the development of 'behavioural' and 'functional' capabilities over time. Many delegates cited improved listening skills and the ability to lead with virtual authority as important learning benefits. For both programmes, Berk views the first step of assembling a cohort as critical. It sends each person a message about how the organization views them and gives them a chance to see who is considered their peer group.

There are many interesting and unusual aspects to this case study. One of the most significant is that it is designed around actual client work, and therefore directly develops the service provided to the client, at the same time as helping participants develop their capabilities. It also helps people develop insight, understanding and capability that they would not have the opportunity for during their daily work. Additionally, it is future-oriented since it focuses on long-term business development.

The key points made in this chapter represent the overall hallmarks of strategic talent development: a focus on the future, outstanding career development opportunity for everyone, and excellent collaborative relationships across the organization.

Key points

- The leaders of a business are the chief influencers of strategic talent development in both word and deed.
- They must work through (perhaps with a coach) the leadership style(s) appropriate to them and the different situations they will face.

- How they promote vision and values, create and implement strategy, work together, and encourage collaboration and innovation connect directly to engagement and development.

- These will encourage a mindset that will help the business to:
  - retain flexibility in an uncertain and unpredictable world;
  - be ready to exploit the opportunities of change;
  - create business continuity and sustainable futures; and
  - achieve long-term success and competitive advantage.

- Most leaders today will benefit from development that will help them refocus their skills on the challenges of the new world.

Notes

1 With thanks to Andrew Dyckhoff.

2 Assessment Circle Europe: http://www.network-ace.com/

3 Jim Collins speaking at CIPD's Annual Conference and Exhibition, Manchester, 2009.

Strategic talent development checklist

The aim of strategic talent development is to secure long-term profitability by developing and engaging all your people in the goals and success of your business:

1. *Create shared visions and shared values.* The vision is the narrative of what the business is about: the story that inspires everyone and guides them along its broad direction. It enables the leader, but also others, to select goals and strategies that are aligned to the vision and values, which are consistent and all lead in the same direction.

2. *Set the strategic direction.* Create a shared understanding of your strategic goals. Align effort around these. Keep in touch with how the strategy is progressing, allowing people to input from the ground up.

3. *Generate conversations about the future.* Energize people around the future, encouraging them to be networking around the business and outside the business to identify trends and start working towards them.

4. *Articulate standards of performance and trust people to self-manage.* Be clear about the performance results expected. Set out the difference between good and outstanding performance. Recognize quickly when performance is below standard. Trust and enable people to self-manage and to self-appraise their performance.

5. *Provide outstanding development.* Provide stretching and challenging work. Recognize that most learning comes from developmental work experiences, and open such experiences for people. Open opportunity

that helps people meet their aspirations and move along their long-term career path. Link people's plans into your succession plans. These actions will create a learning environment.

6 *Be data driven.* Capture data about people to help you make better and faster decisions about people. Include data about behavioural capabilities and preferences, and especially about aspirations.

7 *Identify behaviours for success.* Articulate the behavioural capabilities that people must master to be successful in your organization and reference your assessment, development, and deployment processes around these.

8 *Establish shared people management structures.* Identify where linear, one-on-one line management no longer works. Create structures and processes so that people management becomes a shared process. Focus on regular conversations to provide feedback on performance and support for development. These are key factors in raising employee engagement.

9 *Provide opportunity to develop self-awareness.* Provide plentiful opportunity for people to raise their self-awareness. Self-awareness of the impact you have on others and on results, as well as how you manage your emotions and your feelings, is important to success and survival.

10 *Embed positive feedback in the culture.* Recognize success, identify what people do well, and tell them. Be sincere, and be specific. Identify problems and what isn't working, discussing these openly and frankly. Avoid blame, and take a solutions-focused approach. Be supportive and encouraging.

FURTHER READING

The following books, reports, surveys and articles have helped me in writing this book and I recommend them to anyone who wishes to further their understanding of this fascinating subject.

Please note that this is not an exhaustive list of all the references I have used in this book, which are set out at the end of the book.

Caplan, J (2003) *Coaching for the Future: How smart companies use coaching and mentoring*, CIPD, London

Cheung-Judge, M-Y and Holbeche, L (2011) *Organization Development: A practitioner's guide for OD and HR*, Kogan Page, London

Collins, JC (2001) *Good to Great: Why some companies make the leap... and others don't*, HarperCollins, London

Finch, BA (2011) *Financial Times Briefing on Corporate Governance*, Financial Times/Prentice Hall, Harlow

Garratt, R (2010) *The Fish Rots from the Head: The crisis in our boardrooms: Developing the crucial skills of the competent director*, Profile Books, London

Gratton, L (2011) *The Shift: The future of work is already here*, Collins, London

Gratton, L (2007) *Hot Spots: Why some companies buzz with energy and innovation – and others don't*, Pearson Education, Harlow

Hatum, A (2010) *Next Generation Talent Management*, Palgrave Macmillan, New York

Hofstede, G (2003) *Culture's Consequences: Comparing values, behaviors, institutions, and organizations across nations*, 2nd edn, Sage, Thousand Oaks, CA

Kahneman, D (2012) *Thinking, Fast and Slow*, Penguin, Harmondsworth

Kahneman, D and Tversky, A (2000) *Choices, Values, and Frames*, Cambridge University Press, Cambridge

Kotter, JP (2012) *Leading Change*, Harvard Business Review Press, Boston, MA

Mckee, A, Boyatzis, RE and Johnston, FE (2008) *Becoming a Resonant Leader: Develop your emotional intelligence*, Harvard Business School Press, Boston, MA

Neale, S, Spencer-Arnell, L and Wilson, E (2011) *Emotional Intelligence Coaching: Improving performance for leaders, coaches and the individual*, Kogan Page, London

Rock, D (2009) *Your Brain at Work: Strategies for overcoming distraction, regaining focus, and working smarter all day long*, HarperCollins, New York

Rock, D (2009) *Quiet Leadership: Six steps to transforming performance at work*, HarperCollins, New York

Schwartz, T, Gomes, J and McCarthy, C (2010) *The Way We're Working Isn't Working: The four forgotten needs that energize great performance*, Simon & Schuster, London

REFERENCES

Introduction

Cohn, J, Katzenbach, J and Vlak G (2008) Finding and grooming breakthrough innovators, *Harvard Business Review*, December, http://hbr.org/2008/12/finding-and-grooming-breakthrough-innovators/ar/1

Markoff, J (2011) Jacob Goldman, founder of Xerox Lab, dies at 90, *New York Times*, 21 December

PwC (2012) 15th Annual Global PwC CEO Survey: Delivering Results, Growth and Value in a Volatile World, PwC, London

The Economist (2012) The Nokia Effect, 25 August, p 59, http://www.economist.com/node/21560867

Chapter 1

Alimo-Metcalfe, B and Alban-Metcalfe, J (2009) Engaging Leadership, CIPD Insight Report, CIPD, London

Best Companies (2012) Wrexham, http://www.bestcompanies.co.uk/

CIPD (2009) Taking the Temperature of Coaching, Coaching survey, CIPD, London

Collins, JC (2001) *Good to Great: Why some companies make the leap... and others don't*, Random House, London

CRF Institute (2012) Top Employers 2012 – Leadership Development and Succession Management, International HR Best Practice Report, Elstree

Gladwell, M (2002) The Talent Myth: Are smart people overrated? Dept of Human Resources, 22 July, *The New Yorker*, http://www.newyorker.com/archive/2002/07/22/020722fa_fact; www.gladwell.com

Harter, JK *et al* (2006) *Gallup Q12 Meta Analysis*, Gallup Organization, Omaha

Herzberg, F (1987) One more time: how do you motivate employees? *Harvard Business Review*, **65** (5), 109–20

Hofstede, G (2003) *Culture's Consequences: Comparing values, behaviors, institutions, and organizations across nations*, 2nd edn, Sage, Thousand Oaks, CA

Lipman-Blumen, J (2004) *The Allure of Toxic Leaders: Why we follow destructive bosses and corrupt politicians – and how we can survive them*, Oxford University Press, New York

MacBeath, J (2005) Leadership as distributed: a matter of practice, *School Leadership and Management*, **25** (4), 349–66

Petrook, M (2009) Half of workers quit jobs due to bad management, *CMI website* [Online] www.managers.org.uk/news/half-workers-quit-jobs-due-bad-management

Purcell, J *et al* (2003) *Understanding the People and Performance Link: Unlocking the Black Box*, CIPD, London

Robinson, D, Perryman, S and Hayday, S (2004) *The Drivers of Employee Engagement*, Report 408, Institute for Employment Studies, London, April

Schein, EH (1999) *The Corporate Culture Survival Guide*, Jossey-Bass, San Francisco, CA

Tosi, HL, Misangyi, VF and Fanelli, A (2004) CEO charisma, compensation, and firm performance, *Leadership Quarterly*, **15** (3), June, 405–20

Towers Perrin (2005) Reconnecting with Employees: Quantifying the value of engaging your workforce, Towers Perrin, London

US Bureau of Labor Statistics (2012), Employee Tenure Summary, http://www.bls.gov/news.release/tenure.nr0.htm

Whicker, ML (1996) *Toxic Leaders: When organizations go bad*, Quorum Books, Westport, CT

Chapter 2

BBC (2012) Tony Hall appointed new BBC director general, 22 November, http://www.bbc.co.uk/news/uk-20441887

Bhide, A and Stevenson, HH (1990) Why be honest if honesty doesn't pay, *Harvard Business Review*, September

Caplan, J (2003) *Coaching for the Future: How smart companies use coaching and mentoring*, CIPD, London

Caplan, J (2011) *The Value of Talent: Promoting talent management across the organization*, Kogan Page, London

GE Annual Report 2000, http://www.ge.com/annual00/letter/index.html

Gratton, L (2011) *The Shift: The future of work is already here*, Collins, London

Guardian Media Group, www.gmgplc.co.uk

Handy, C (1995) *Gods of Management: The changing work of organizations*, Arrow, London

Harrison, R and Stokes, H (1992) *Diagnosing Organizational Culture*, Pfeiffer, San Francisco, CA

Macgregor, DA (1997) *Breaking the Phalanx*, Praeger, Westport, CT

Mayfield, C (2010) The private sector can learn from co-ops too, *The Times*, 3 March

National Defense University (nd) Strategic Leadership and Decision Making: Values and Ethics, Industrial College of the Armed Forces, National Defense University, Australia, http://www.au.af.mil/au/awc/awcgate/ndu/strat-ldr-dm/pt4ch15.html

Rokeach, M (1968a) *Beliefs, Attitudes and Values*, Jossey-Bass, San Francisco, CA

Rokeach, M (1968b) A theory of organization and change within value-attitude systems, *Journal of Social Issues*, **24** (January), 13–33

Standard Chartered Bank, http://www.standardchartered.com/en/about-us/our-brand-and-values/index.html

The Economist (2011) Special Report: The Future of Jobs, 10 September

The *Guardian* and the *Observer* (2008–09) Living Our Values: Sustainability Report, http://image.guardian.co.uk/sys-files/Guardian/documents/2009/07/22/Sustainabilityreport2009.pdf

Chapter 3

Gifford, J (nd) Command and control management: have we really moved on? http://jonathangifford.com/command-and-control-management/

IBM (2012) Leading Through Connections, IBM C-Suite report, Armonk, NY

Porter, M (2012) http://www.youtube.com/watch?v=ibrxIP0H84M; http://www.youtube.com/watch?v=NZt6kUKE-88

PwC (2012) 15th Annual Global PwC CEO Survey: Delivering Results, Growth and Value in a Volatile World, PwC, London

Chapter 4

CRF Institute (2012) Top Employers 2012 – Leadership Development and Succession Management, International HR Best Practice Report

guardian.co.uk (2011) Guardian News & Media to be a digital-first organisation, Series: Press releases 2011, Thursday 16 June 16.30

IBM (2012) Leading Through Connections, IBM C-Suite report, Armonk, NY

The Economist (2011) Special Report: The Future of Jobs, 10 September

Walsh, D (2011) Ferguson and me ... it was strictly business, *The Sunday Times*, 17 December

Chapter 5

Bresser, F (2008–09) Consulting Report: Executive Summary, *Global Coaching Survey 2008–2009*, http://www.frank-bresser-consulting.com/globalcoachingsurvey.html

Caplan, J (2003) *Coaching for the Future: How smart companies use coaching and mentoring*, CIPD, London

Eichinger, RW and Lombardo, MM (2004) Patterns of rater accuracy in 360-degree feedback, *Human Resource Planning*, **27** (4)

Gratton, L (2011) *The Shift: The future of work is already here*, Collins, London

Lombardo, MM and Eichinger, RW (2007) *The Career Architect Development Planner*, 3rd edn, Korn/Ferry International, Minneapolis, MN

Mount, MK, Judge, TA, Scullen, SE, Sytsma, MR and Hezlett, SA (1998) Trait, rater and level effects in 360-degree performance ratings, *Personnel Psychology*, **51** (3), 557–76

Paton, N (2006) Custom designed, HR Today, Saturday *Guardian*, 1 April

Sloman, M (2011) Do Trainers Need a New Model? www.martynsloman.co.uk/casestudies/newmodel.pdf

Sullivan, J (1998) HR Program Evaluation Template: 360-Degree Feedback. http://www.drjohnsullivan.com/articles/1998/net12.htm

The Scala Group and ACE Network (2005) International Barometer Survey, June

Vinson, M (1996) The pros and cons of 360-degree feedback: making it work, *Training and Development*, April, 11–12

Chapter 6

Cranfield (2003) Survey on Trends in International Working, Cranfield School of Management

CRF Institute (2012) Top Employers 2012 – Leadership Development and Succession Management, International HR Best Practice Report

Baumgarten, P, Desvaux, G and Devillard, S (2007) What Shapes Careers? A McKinsey Global Survey, https://www.mckinseyquarterly.com

Bureau of Labor Statistics (2012) *Frequently Asked Questions*, [Online] www.bls.gov/2012

Clutterbuck, D (2012) *The Talent Wave: Why succession planning fails and what to do about it*, Kogan Page, London

EU (2012) A Europe 2020 initiative: Women in Economic Decision-Making in the EU: Progress Report, European Commission – Directorate-General for Justice, Publications Office of the European Union, Luxembourg

Ibarra, H and Lineback, K (2005) What's your story? *Harvard Business Review*, January

Ibarra, H, Carter, N and Silva, C (2010) Why men still get more promotions than women, *Harvard Business Review*, September

Jacobs, K (2012) C-suite Culture Must Change if UK Women Are to Reach Their Full Potential, Claims SHL, 5 October, http://www.hrmagazine.co.uk/hro/news/1074894/c-suite-culture-change-uk-women-reach-potential-claims-shl

North, D and Delamare, T (May 2011) Talent, Careers and Organizations: Where next? Corporate Research Forum

PwC (2012) 15th Annual Global PwC CEO Survey: Delivering Results, Growth and Value in a Volatile World, PwC, London

Spencer Stuart (2012) Executive Search Consulting Firms, comment by Reinhold Thiele, leader of the European Industrial practice and a consultant in the Board Services practice at Spencer Stuart, Munich and Zurich

Vanderbroeck, P (2010) The traps that keep women from reaching the top and how to avoid them, *Journal of Management Development*, **29** (9), 764–70

Warren, AK (2009) *Cascading Gender Biases, Compounding Effects: An assessment of talent management systems*, Catalyst, New York

Westphal, J and Stern, I (2007) Flattery will get you everywhere (especially if you are a male Caucasian): how ingratiation, boardroom behavior and demographic minority status affect additional board appointments at US companies, *Academy of Management Journal*, **50** (2), 2678–888

Chapter 7

Cheese, P, Thomas, R and Craig E (2008) *The Talent-powered Organization*, Kogan Page, London

Hirsh, W (2000) *Succession Planning Demystified*, Report 372, Institute for Employment Studies, October

MacLeod, D and Clarke, N (2009) Engaging for Success: Enhancing performance through employee engagement, A report to government, London

Rucci, AJ, Kirn, SP and Quinn, RT (1998) The employee–customer profit chain at Sears, *Harvard Business Review*, January–February

Chapter 8

Achievers (2012) Achievers Intelligence: Insight Into Today's Workforce, http://www.achievers.com/sites/default/files/whitepaper-achievers-intelligence_0.pdf

Adams, JS (1965) Inequity in social exchange, *Advances in Experimental Social Psychology*, **62**, 335–43

CIPD (2012) Annual Survey Report: Learning, Training and Development Businesses Have Gaps in Performance Management Skills (in particular setting standards for performance and dealing with underperformance), CIPD, London

Guest, D and Conway, N (2004) Employee Well-being and the Psychological Contract, CIPD, London

Lawler, EE III (2012) Performance Appraisals Are Dead, Long Live Performance Management, http://www.forbes.com/sites/edwardlawler/2012/07/12/performance-appraisals-are-dead-long-live-performance-management/

Reilly, P and Brown, D (2008) Employee engagement: what is the relationship with reward management? *World at Work Journal*, **17** (4)

Chapter 9

Boyatzis, R (2011) Neuroscience and Leadership: The Promise of Insights, January/February, http://www.iveybusinessjournal.com/topics/leadership/neuroscience-and-leadership-the-promise-of-insights#.UPbLrehU2Uc

Csíkszentmihályi, M (2003) *Good Business: Leadership, flow, and the making of meaning*, Penguin, New York

Dickerson, SS and Kemeny, ME (2004) Acute stressors and cortisol responses: a theoretical integration and synthesis of laboratory research, *Psychological Bulletin*, **130** (3), 355–91

Kolb, DA and Fry, R (1975) Toward an applied theory of experiential learning, in C Cooper (ed) *Theories of Group Process*, John Wiley, London

Rock, D (2009a) *Your Brain at Work: Know your brain, transform your performance*, Harper Business, New York

Rock, D (2009b) Managing with the brain in mind, *Strategy + business*, issue 56, Autumn, Booz & Co

Rock, D (2009c) *Quiet Leadership: Six steps to transforming performance at work*, HarperCollins, New York

Rock, D (2011) The aha moment, *Training and Development*, ASTD, February

Sapolsky, RM (2004) *Why Zebras Don't Get Ulcers*, 3rd edn, HarperCollins, New York

Schulkin, J (1999) *Neuroendocrine Regulation of Behavior*, Cambridge University Press, New York

Chapter 10

Collins, JC (2001) *Good to Great: Why some companies make the leap... and others don't*, HarperCollins, London

Fildes, N (2012) After years nursing its injuries, a big player is fit and raring to go, *The Times*, London, 5 November

Goleman, D (1996) *Emotional Intelligence: Why it can matter more than IQ*, Bantam Books, London

Gratton, L (2007) *Hot Spots: Why some companies buzz with energy and innovation – and others don't*, Pearson Education, Harlow

Hersey, P and Blanchard, KH (1977) *Management of Organizational Behavior, 3rd Edition – Utilizing Human Resources*, Prentice Hall, Englefield Cliffs, NJ

Hofstede, G (2003) *Culture's Consequences: Comparing values, behaviors, institutions, and organizations across nations*, 2nd edn, Sage, Thousand Oaks, CA

Kahneman, D (2012) *Thinking, Fast and Slow*, Penguin, Harmondsworth

Kaufman, SP (2008) Evaluating the CEO First Person, *Harvard Business Review*, October

Keld, J (2012) Intelligence Is Overrated: What You Really Need to Succeed, http://www.forbes.com/sites/keldjensen/2012/04/12/intelligence-is-overrated-what-you-really-need-to-succeed/

Kouzes, JM and Posner, BZ (2009) To lead, create a shared vision, *Harvard Business Review*, January

Lafley, AG (2009) What only the CEO can do, *Harvard Business Review*, January

Lencioni, PM (2002) *The Five Dysfunctions of a Team: A leadership fable*, J-B Lencioni Series, Jossey-Bass, San Francisco, CA

Marchionne, S (2008) First person: Fiat's extreme makeover, *Harvard Business Review*, December

Raelin, J, (2006) Does action learning promote collaborative leadership? Northeastern University, Boston, MA, *Academy of Management Learning & Education*, 5 (2), 152–68

Wasserman, N (2009) Planning a start-up? Seize the day, *Harvard Business Review*, January

Zenger, J and Folkman, J (2009) Ten fatal flaws that derail leaders, *Harvard Business Review*, June, http://hbr.org/2009/06/ten-fatal-flaws-that-derail-leaders/sb1

APPENDIX: MIND THE GAP

Questions about the business environment

- What changes do you see on the horizon? (3? 5? 10 years?)
- Competitors, new products, new channels, new technologies, regulation etc?
- What threats do these pose to you?
- What opportunities do these pose?
- What value will be delivered to customers? How is this different from what happens now?
- What changes and capabilities are required? What is the gap between those that will be required and where we are now?
- Which are the most critical to strategy?
- Which processes are the most critical to strategy?
- How does this fit with our current strengths and weaknesses?

Questions specific to the business as a whole

- What is the business aiming to achieve?
- What will success look like?
- What might prevent this being achieved?
- What might help you achieve this?
- What is driving this change/idea?
- What might hinder it?

FIGURE A.1 Mind the gap

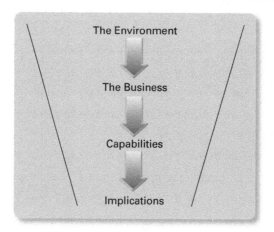

- What are your competitors doing?
- What are the variables?
- What are the current strengths of the business?
- What are the gaps?
- What are the milestones?
- What are the current operational income drivers? What's changing?
- What operational income drivers are projected over the next five years?
- What environmental challenges can we see?
- In the light of projected changes, what areas/activities will we keep/expand? What will we need to develop? Or lose?
- What data will confirm our observations?
- Which areas will require particular interventions?
- What are the key sustainability issues for our organization?
- How might these affect our business plans?
- What will we need to do differently as a result?
- What opportunities might this offer?

Questions specific to the business strategy

- On what strategic assumptions about the future does our strategy depend?
- Which of these assumptions is the most uncertain?
- What impact would it have on our strategy if these assumptions turn out differently?
- What are the 'what ifs?'
- What are the different assumptions among... (the top team)?
- What talent issues have the biggest impact on budget?
- Who are the most important new hires? Why?
- Where do we need to hire people who are significantly different in order to meet future business plans?
- In what jobs would turnover be a significant problem? Why?

Questions specific to line managers and/or to different business units

- What are our future business plans... Two years... Five years... Ten years?
- On what strategic assumptions are these plans based?
- What might help them be achieved?
- What are the obstacles?
- What demands will this place on people?
- What technical/behavioural capabilities will these require?
- Which are the strengths of the organization?
- Where are the gaps?
- What will people get excited about?
- What risks will be required?
- What does the new strategy require in terms of skills and capabilities in the short term?
- And in the long term?
- Where do these reside at present?

- What are the relatively stable and predictable requirements of this strategy?
- What are the unpredictable requirements of this strategy?
- Which decisions have long-term implications and what are they?

Capabilities required

- Which roles are critical to enabling us to achieve this strategy?
- What will people have to do differently and how will that be achieved?
- What capabilities will be required for this and objectives/ changes?
- Which are certain, which possible?
- What development will be required?
- What are the capability gaps? How are they changing?
- How can these be plugged?
- Which skills are in short supply?
- Where are the roles that need complex skills requiring long training periods?
- Which roles are critical to enabling us to achieve this strategy?
- Do we invest differentially in critical skills?
- Where does our strategy require talent and organization to be better than our competitors to work?
- Where should you pay more/spend more?
- What defines critical jobs?
- Which employees make the biggest difference?
- What makes this difference? (Performance, behavioural capabilities, knowledge, potential)
- What is the connection between performance differences and business outcomes?
- Where would more people/higher performance levels have the greatest effect?
- How will success depend on individual capability, opportunity or motivation?

Implications for achieving capabilities

- Do we need to recruit or are there individuals able to provide those capabilities?
- What development will they need?
- Will that take them where they want to go?
- Who will be developed to replace them?
- Who will succeed people who currently have key capabilities in two or three years?
- Who has scarce skills and to whom can they pass them and how?
- What are the key milestones in preserving and acquiring capabilities?

INDEX

NB: page numbers in *italic* indicate figures or tables